Jane's Dictionary of Military Terms

Jane's Dictionary of
MILITARY TERMS

Compiled by Brigadier P. H. C. Hayward

MACDONALD AND JANE'S · LONDON

First published in 1975 by
Macdonald & Jane's (Macdonald & Co (Publishers) Ltd)
Paulton House, 8 Shepherdess Walk,
London N1 7LW

Printed and bound in Great Britain by
Redwood Burn Limited, Trowbridge & Esher

ISBN 0 356 08261 X

Introduction

During the eighteenth and nineteenth centuries several military dictionaries were produced in England; but no one appears to have compiled one in the last seventy years or so. During this time conditions in the Armed Forces of the Crown have changed so completely that any nineteenth century work of this nature is only of interest in a purely historical context. Definitions of technical words and phrases in common use in those days will help to elucidate the narrative of battles fought before the first World War but have, in most cases, become obsolete today. Furthermore, a vast new technology has grown up which needs to be expressed in precise terms in order to make it comprehensible to the new generation which has to operate it.

Until recently the Army was only involved in hostilities on land. Any operation at sea, whether warlike or peaceful, was the prerogative of the Admiralty. Even in ports abroad like Port Said and Bombay, where the garrison was found by the Army, there was a naval officer ashore whose responsibilities started at the water's edge.

Although the initial impetus in military flying came from the Army, the Royal Flying Corps (RFC) did not survive the Trenchard innovations. The Royal Naval Air Service (RNAS) and the RFC were amalgamated to form the Royal Air Force. The situation *vis à vis* the three services today is quite different; the Royal Corps of Transport (RCT) mans and operates its own small fleet; the Army Air Corps (AAC) has its own aircraft. In the Ministry of Defence officers of the Royal Navy, Army and Royal Air Force work alongside each other and are integrated in some branches.

Before the First World War the Army lived an almost coenobitic life. As a rule the officers were drawn from one class of society. Son followed father in the same profession and frequently in the same Regiment. Most of their service was spent abroad, when communication with the United Kingdom presented far more difficulty and was attended with greater delay than at present. The Army was out of sight and largely out of mind to the bulk of the nation. A military dictionary would have been superfluous to the Service and of little interest to the general public, who only became conscious that they had an Army when some notable disaster edged its way into the newspapers.

August 1914 changed the picture completely. In a matter of months the whole nation was involved, predominantly in the Army. In the infantry, which bore the main brunt of the fighting, the prewar figure of less than one hundred and fifty regular battalions rose before the Armistice to nearly one thousand seven hundred Regular, Territorial and New Army battalions.

1

Similar expansion occurred in the Artillery, Engineers and Services. In a few months the language of the Army became the language of the nation. The colloquialisms of the barracks infiltrated themselves into every level of society from castle to cottage, for there was hardly a family in the United Kingdom which had not a close relative "over there".

At the end of the "war to end war" there was a rush to demobilise, and with it came reaction. The horror of the trenches was to be forgotten, swept under the carpet and not mentioned. They, the civilians turned soldier, had "done their bit", as indeed most nobly they had. Now they wanted to forget it all, to return to their homes and families, to get on with their civilian jobs and to enjoy the fruits of victory. The prewar regular Army had been decimated in the early battles. It built iteself anew on its old foundations with a cadre of survivors, but its ranks were largely filled by young men who wished to emulate the feats of their fathers − but had no opportunity to do so. There was little fighting in the 1920s once the Russian and Greeko-Turkish confrontations had been settled. Only on the North West Frontier of India and in such local disturbances as the Moplah rebellion could active service be experienced. The Army ceased to be news. It reverted to its prewar existence and only became of interest to the public on such occasions as the Amritzar "massacre".

Public apathy towards the Services was strengthened by what came to be known as the ten-year rule. This was a Cabinet statement conveyed to the Chiefs of Staff and renewed annually that there was no requirement to plan for a major war for the succeeding ten years. It affected every facet of Army life. Whilst Germany rearmed, at first clandestinely with Russian help, and later openly, the British Government denied the soldiers the means to bring the Army up to date in training and equipment. Despite the slump in the early 1930s recruiting was bad and units in England were seldom at much more than fifty per cent of their established strength. Most of their weapons and equipment were the same as those with which they had finished the First World War nearly twenty years previously. Only the first tentative steps had been taken towards mechanization; infantry battalions abroad still went on training exercises with animal transport: in Egypt in 1936 one unit left its barracks for the desert with 179 animals, chargers and light draught horses, mules, camels and donkeys! The Army once again withdrew into itself.

One peculiarity of the British soldier in the days of the Empire was his firm conviction that he was an accomplished linguist, and able to converse freely with a native of any country where he happened to be stationed. Within a few weeks of his arrival in India he would claim to be able to "boloh the bat" and he interlarded his conversation with vernacular words. Some of these have survived and can be found in any ordinary English dictionary. Their origin is forgotten: verandah, bungalow and khaki are examples. Other countries made a similar contribution. In Egypt an inefficient unit would be referred to as a yimkin mob. Surplus equipment was bukshi.

When the Second World War became imminent official purse strings were loosened. After years of neglect the equipment and weapons in general use in the Army, its swords and lances, its signalling equipment of flags, lamps and helio, its 13- and 18-pounder guns were clearly seen to be an anachronism. Fortunately, however, the Army, though denied the funds needed to re-equip itself for modern war, had not been idle. New mateial had been designed and in some cases issued to selected units for trial. As the nation changed from a peace to a war footing manufacture of the new equipment accelerated and brought new words and phrases into Army life. This was particularly noticeable in regard to transport. As the automobile replaced the horse a great number of new words entered the soldier's vocabulary. In many cases they were ones which were in common use in the motor car and allied technical trades, but others were specifically military, particularly in the case of armoured fighting vehicles for which there was no civilian counterpart.

As the Second World War progressed the Army took to the air. An overstrained and overstretched Air Force could not find the man power to implement its theory that all action above sea and land should be its own prerogative. The Army stepped in and the Parachute and the Glider Pilot Regiments were formed. The subsequent history of army-air relationship has not always been happy. To oversimplify the problem, it is based on two mutually contradictory theories. One is that control of air space is one indivisible responsibility: all matters air should therefore be controlled by one body. The other is that the air is a useful adjunct to all movement and hostilities but that the ultimate decision will be reached on land: ground forces must therefore be supplied with auxiliary equipment under its own control to make the best use of the air. The arguments on both sides are outside the scope of a work of this nature, but the compromise agreement at present in force, which gives to the Army a large stake in air matters, has resulted in a great number of specifically air words and expressions becoming common to both Services.

A similar compromise between the Royal Navy and the Army has resulted in the Army manning a small fleet and acquiring a number of naval technical terms.

During and immediately after the Second World War the whole nation was, for the second time in a generation, deeply involved in the Army. Until national service was brought to an end the youth of Great Britain was fed into the armed services for its two years training with very few exemptions. The Army was the largest consumer; and the chief sufferer. Regular officers and non-commissioned officers became trainers of soldiers and had little time to devote to their own techniques, but the Army and the public were once more speaking the same language.

When the decision was taken to revert to a full-time regular army, its equipment and weapons were again out of date. A vast new and complicated array of material was in the experimental stage but it would have been useless to make it available to men who had only two years service in which to learn all the techniques required of a trained soldier. It was not until the 1960s that a start was made to issue it to front line units. As technology advances so does weaponry: more and better material becomes available.

Another post-war development which affected the Service outlook and vocabulary was' the merging of the Admiralty, War Office and Air Ministry into one Ministry of Defence. The instigator of this change, Earl Mountbatten of Burma, probably visualised a decrease in the administrative staffs of the three Services as a result. In fact the opposite happened: there was an overall increase, particularly in the civilian element, and the resultant cross pollination of the Services has necessitated a greater amount of co-operation at the higher levels, and so an interchange of vocabulary.

This country's adherence to the North Atlantic Treaty Organization (NATO) and the close co-operation which has existed for many years with the United States has also brought with it a requirement for greater standardization of the exact meaning of words and phrases.

The problem facing the compiler of a military dictionary may be summarised as what to include and what to omit. How deeply should he delve into history and how comprehensively should he cover modern technical aspects? The musket of Peninsular days has disappeared with the prog and lush that sustained its owner. The Lancaster, a battle winner at Inkerman, has been replaced by nuclear artillery; a reference to the shave that rejoiced or depressed the visitor to Balaclava would be incomprehensible to the modern rumour monger. These and similar weapons and words which have not been used since the beginning of the century have been omitted. So have those words and phrases that are peculiar to the Royal Navy and Royal Air Force and which are not in general use by the Army element in those Services. They will be found in the Naval and Aerospace Dictionaries being published in conjunction with this work. Similarly, only the more common foreign weapons and words, chiefly those which have some connection with the British Army, have been included.

In compiling the Appendix on abbreviations and acronyms the same problems had to be faced as were encountered in the main body of the dictionary. A great number are in common use outside the Army, as for instance VHF (very high frequency). They do not need explanation to most users. But it is not only in the context of radio that military and civilian usage converge. The Army is a larger organization in financial terms than any of the huge commercial firms in the country. It has tentacles stretching out to every department of state and most industries. In selecting what to include and what to omit I have tried to cater for the general reader. The specialist will find his requirement in the appropriate technical handbook.

I have been helped by a great number of my friends in the Army in the preparation of this dictionary and to them all, too numerous to mention by name, I extend my most grateful thanks. The errors are my own.

4

Abatis (also Abattis). A form of defensive work formerly used in forest and jungle warfare made by binding together the trunks or branches of felled trees.

Abbot. A British self-propelled 105 mm gun mounted on a lightly armoured tracked vehicle.

Abeam. Bearing approximately 090° or 270° relative; at right angles to the longitudinal axis of a vehicle.

Abnormal load. A vehicle and load which together exceed the limitations on movement by road imposed by Statutory or other Regulations for which special authority has to be obtained.

Abort.
1. Failure to accomplish a mission for any reason other than enemy action. It may occur at any point from initiation of operation to destination.
2. Discontinue aircraft take-off run or launch.

Abrasions. In photography, scratches or marks produced mechanically on emulsion surfaces or film base.

Absolute altimeter. Radio or similar apparatus that is designed to indicate the true vertical height of an aircraft above the terrain.

Absolute altitude. The height of an aircraft directly above the surface or terrain over which it is flying. See also **Altitude.**

Absorbed dose. The amount of energy imparted by nuclear (or ionizing) radiation to unit mass of absorbing material. The unit is the rad. (qv)

Acceleration error. An error caused by the deflection of the vertical reference due to any change in the velocity of the aircraft.

Acceptable alternate product. One which may be used in place of another

for extended periods without technical advice. See also **Emergency substitute; NATO unified product; Standardized product.**

Acceptance trials. Trials carried out by nominated representatives of the eventual military users of the weapon or equipment to determine if the specified performance and characteristics have been met.

Accommodation.
1. The ability of the human eye to adjust itself to give sharp images of objects at different distances.
2. In stereoscopy, the ability of the human eyes to bring two images into superimposition for stereoscopic viewing.

Accompanied. Baggage. That portion of a passenger's baggage within the author-ised scale which actually accompanies the passenger on a journey. ***Personnel.** An officer or soldier travelling with his family. ***Posting.** An assignment to a unit or employment where facilities exist or can be provided for the family of an officer or soldier.

Accompanying. Cargo. All classes of cargo carried by units into the objective area. ***Supplies.** All classes of supplies carried by units into the objective area.

Accountable item. An item of *matériel* for which a formal record of holdings is maintained and for which documentary evidence, as provided in regulations, is required to support any changes in the quantity or condition of holdings.

Accounting unit (*matériel*). A unit which is required to maintain auditable records in respect of materiel.

Accuracy of fire. The measurement of the precision of fire expressed as the distance of the mean point of impact from the centre of the target.

Acknowledgement (Ack.). A message from the addressee informing the originator that his communication has been received and understood.

Aclinic line. *See* **Magnetic equator.**

Acquittance roll. The document which records the pay of soldiers.

Action information centre. *See* **Combat information centre.**

Activate. To put into existence by official order a unit, post, camp, station, base or shore activity which has previously been constituted and designated by name or number, or both, so that it can be organized to function in its assigned capacity.

Activation detector. A material used to determine neutron flux or density by virtue of the radioactivity induced in it as a result of neutron capture.

Active. Air defence. Direct defensive action taken to destroy or reduce the effectiveness of an enemy air attack. It includes such measures as the use of aircraft, anti-aircraft guns, electronic countermeasures and surface-to-air guided missiles. ***Defence.** The employment of limited offensive action and counter-attacks to deny a contested area or position to the enemy. *See also* **Passive defence. *Electronic countermeasures.** The impairment of enemy electronic detection, control or communications devices/systems through deliberate jamming or deception. *See also* **Electronic countermeasures; Electronic deception; Electronic jamming. *Homing guidance.** A system of homing guidance wherein both the source for illuminating the target, and the receiver for detecting the energy reflected from the target as the result of illuminating the target, are carried within the missile. ***Material.** Material, such as plutonium and certain isotopes of uranium, which is capable of supporting a fission chain reaction.

Actual ground zero. The point on the surface of the earth below, at, or above

the centre of a nuclear burst. *See also* **Desired ground zero; Ground zero.**

Actuator. A mechanism that furnishes the force required to displace an aircraft, a control surface or other flight control element.

Acute dose. Total dose received at one time over a period so short that biological recovery cannot occur.

Adjustment of fire. Process used in artillery and naval gunfire to obtain correct bearing, range and height of burst (if time fuses are used) when engaging a target by observed fire. *See also* **Spot.**

Adjutant. A Commanding Officer's principal staff officer.

Adjutant General (AG**).** The member of the Army Board responsible for personnel.

Administration.
1. The management and execution of all military matters not included in tactics and strategy; primarily in the fields of logistics and personnel management.
2. Internal management of units.

Administrative Area Control Centre (AACC). When a DMA (*qv*) or BMA (*qv*) is formed an *ad hoc* Headquarters is formed for the co-ordination of administration and defence: known as an *.

Administrative chain of command. The normal chain of command as determined by the administrative organisation. *See also* **Chain of command.**

Administrative control. Direction or exercise of authority over subordinate or other organizations in respect of administrative matters such as personnel management, supply, services, and other matters not included in the operational missions of the subordinate or other organizations. *See also* **Operational command; Operational control.**

Administrative lead time. The interval, expressed in months, between the date a requirement for an item of *materiel* is determined by the authority responsible for overall provisioning and an order is placed for purchase, manufacture or repair.

Administrative loading. A loading system which gives primary consideration to achieving maximum utilization of troops and cargo space without regard to tactical considerations. Equipment and supplies must be unloaded and sorted before they can be used.

Administrative movement. A movement in which troops and vehicles are arranged to expedite their movement and conserve time and energy when no enemy interference, except by air, is anticipated.

Administrative order. An order covering traffic, supply, maintenance, evacuation, personnel and other administrative details.

Administrative units. Service units which supply the wants of the combat units, drawn from the RCT, RAMC, RAOC, REME, RMP, RAPC, RAVC, RAEC, RADC, RPC, ACC and QARANC. (*See* Appendix No. 3.)

Advance. A forward movement. ***Force** (amphibious). A temporary organization within the amphibious task force which precedes the main body to the objective area. Its function is to participate in preparing the objective for the main assault by conducting such operations as reconnaissance, seizure of supporting positions, minesweeping, preliminary bombardment, underwater demolitions, and air support. ***** in Contact. A forward movement when contact has already been made with the enemy. ***to Contact.** A forward movement to gain or regain contact with the enemy after it has been lost or before it has been attained. ***Warning.** Warning of the probability of enemy air attack which originates from sources other than early warning radar.

Advanced. A unit or installation located in front of the main body. ***Base.** A base located in or near a theatre of operations whose primary mission is to support military operations. ***Dressing Station** (ADS). One or two are formed by each Field Ambulance (*qv*) where casualties are classified in priorities for treatment or evacuation. Each is equipped to deal with 150 casualties at a time. *** Guard.** The leading element of an advancing force. The primary mission is to ensure the uninterrupted advance of the main body. It has the following functions:
1. To find and exploit gaps in the enemy's defensive system.
2. To prevent the main body of the advancing force running blindly into enemy opposition.
3. To clear away minor opposition or, if major opposition is met, to cover the deployment of the main body.
*Landing field. An airfield, usually having minimum facilities, in or near an objective area. *See also* **Airfield.**

Advisory area (air traffic). A designated area within a flight information region where air traffic advisory service is available.

A echelon. The vehicles and stores of a unit required for hour to hour replenishment of F echelon (qv) under unit control.

Aerial photograph. *See* **Air photograph.**

Aerodrome. *See* **Airfield.**

Aerodynamic missile. A missile which uses aerodynamic forces to maintain its flight path, generally employing propulsion guidance. *See also* **Ballistic missile; Guided missile.**

Aeromedical evacuation. The movement of patients to and between medical treatment facilities by air transportation. ***Control centre.** The control facility established by the commander of an air transport division, air force, or air command. It operates in conjunction

with the command movement control centre and co-ordinates overall medical requirements with airlift capability. It also assigns medical missions to the appropriate aeromedical evacuation elements in the system and monitors patient movement activities. *Co-ordinating Officer. An officer of an originating, intransit, or destination medical facility/establishment who co-ordinates the aeromedical evacuation activities of the facility/establishment. *Operations officer. An officer of the airlift force or command who is responsible for activities relating to planning and directing aeromedical evacuation operations, maintaining liaison with medical airlift activities concerned, operating a Control Centre, and otherwise co-ordinating aircraft and patient movements. *System. A system which provides:
1. control of patient movement by air transport.
2. specialized medical attendants and equipment for in-flight medical care;
3. facilities on, or in the vicinity of, air strips and air bases, for the limited medical care of intransit patients entering or leaving the system;
4. communication with destination and *en route* medical facilities concerning patient airlift movements.
* Staging unit. A medical unit operating transient patient beds located on or in the vicinity of an emplaning or deplaning air base or air strip that provides reception, administration, processing, ground transportation, feeding and limited medical care for patients entering or leaving an aero-medical evacuation system.

Aeronautical chart. A representation of a portion of the earth, its culture and relief, specifically designed to meet the requirements of air navigation.

Aeronautical information overprint. Additional information which is printed or stamped on a map or chart for the specific purpose of air navigation.

Aeronautical information section. A ground organization established to provide aeronautical information.

Aeronautical topographic chart. A representation of features of the surface of the earth, designed primarily as an aid to visual or radar navigation, which shows selected terrain, cultural or hydrographic features and supplementary aeronautical information.

Aerospace. Of, or pertaining to, the earth's envelope of atmosphere and the space above it; two separate entities considered as a single realm for activity in launching, guidance and control of vehicles which will travel in both entities.

Afterburning.
1. The characteristic of some rocket motors to burn irregularly for some time after the main burning and thrust has ceased.
2. The process of fuel injection and combustion in the exhaust jet of a turbojet engine (aft or to the rear of the turbine).

After-flight inspection. General ex-amination after flight for obvious defects, correction of defects reported by air-craft crews, replenishment of consumable or expendable stores, and securing air-craft. Also known as 'Post flight inspection'.

Age of moon. The elapsed time, usually expressed in days, since the last new moon.

Agent. In intelligence usage, one who is authorised or instructed to obtain or to assist in obtaining information for intelligence or counterintelligence purposes.

Agonic line. A line drawn on a map or chart joining points of zero magnetic declination for a specified epoch.

Agreed point. A predetermined point on the ground, identifiable from the air, and used when aircraft assist in fire adjustment.

Aide de Camp (ADC). A commissioned officer in personal attendance on a General Officer commanding troops. ***General to the Queen,** an honour awarded to selected General Officers. **Honorary * to the Queen,** an honour awarded to a senior officer WRAC. **Personal * to the Queen,** an appointment held by certain officers who are Her Majesty's close relations.

Aigulette. The corded ornamentation worn over the shoulder by aides de camp and certain other officers and soldiers assigned to duties around the Sovereign.

Air base (photogrammetry).
1. The line joining two air stations or the length of that line.
2. The distance, at the scale of the stereoscopic model, between adjacent perspective centres as reconstructed in the plotting instrument.
See also **Air station** (photogrammetry).

Airborne.
1. Applied to personnel, equipment, etc., transported by air; eg airborne infantry.
2. Applied to *matériel*, being, or designed to be, transported by aircraft, as distinguished from weapons and equipment installed in and remaining a part of the aircraft.
3. Applied to an aircraft, from the instant it becomes entirely sustained by air until it ceases to be so sustained. A lighter-than-air aircraft is not considered to be airborne when it is attached to the ground, except that moored balloons are airborne whenever sent aloft.
See also **Air-transportable units. *Alert.** A state of aircraft readiness wherein combat-equipped aircraft are airborne and ready for immediate action. *See also* **Fighter cover. *Assault.** *See* Assault. ***Early warning and control.** Air surveillance and control provided by early warning aircraft which are equipped with search and height-finding radar and communications equipment for controlling weapons. *See also* **Air pickets.**

*Forces liasion officer. An officer who is the representative of the airborne units and who works with the air force on airfields being used for airborne operations. ***Forces.** Forces composed primarily of ground and air units organized, equipped and trained for airborne operations. ***Operation.** An operation involving the movment of combat forces with or without their logistic support into an objective area by air. ***Radio relay.** A technique employing aircraft fitted with radio relay stations for the purpose of increasing the range, flexibility or physical security of communications systems.

Airburst. An explosion of a bomb or projectile above the surface as distinguished from an explosion on contact with the surface or after penetration. *See also* **Types of burst.**

Air cargoes schedules. Schedules designed specifically for the routine movement of cargo by air.

Air cartographic camera. A camera having the accuracy and other characteristics essential for air survey or cartographic photography (*qv*).

Air cartographic photography. The taking and processing of air photographs for mapping and charting purposes.

Air contact officer. An officer or NCO who has been trained to operate ground to air radio and to indicate ground targets to a pilot.

Air control. *See* **Air traffic control centre; Airway; Control and reporting centre; Control area; Control zone; Controlled airspace; Tactical air control centre; Terminal control area; Transport control centre (air transport). *Centre.** The joint operations agency established on land in limited war to control and co-ordinate all means of air defence and all aircraft movements in the objective area. ***Team.** A team especially organized to direct close air support strikes in the vicinity of forward ground elements by visual or other means.

Air controller. An individual especially trained for and assigned the duty of the control (by use of radio, radar or other means) of such aircraft as may be allotted to him for operations within his area. *See also* **Tactical air controller.**

Air corridors. Restricted air routes of travel specified for use by friendly aircraft and established for the purpose of preventing friendly aircraft from being fired on by friendly forces.

Aircraft. Includes all types of aeroplane, seaplane and helicopter. ***Climb corridor.** Positive controlled airspaces of defined vertical and horizontal dimensions extending from an airfield. ***Dispersal area.** An area on a military installation designed primarily for the dispersal of parked aircraft, whereby such aircraft will be less vulnerable in the event of an enemy air raid. ***Flat pallet.** A stressed pallet capable of supporting and restraining a specifically rated load. It is specifically designed for tie-down in an aircraft. *See also* **Palletized unit load. *Guide.** *See* * **Marshaller.** * **Handover.** The process of transferring control of an aircraft from one controlling authority to another. * **Inspection.** The process of systematically examining, checking and testing aircraft structural members, components and systems, to detect actual or potential unserviceable conditions. * **Loading table.** A data sheet used by the force unit commander containing information as to the load that actually goes into each aircraft. * **Marshaller.** A person trained to direct by visual or other means the movement of aircraft on the ground, into and out of landing, parking or hovering points. Also known as '***Guide**'. ***Marshalling area.** An area in which aircraft may form up before take-off or assemble after landing. * **Mission equipment.** Equipment that must be fitted to an aircraft to enable it to fulfil a particular mission or task. ***Modifica-**

tion. A change in the physical characteristics of aircraft, accomplished either by a change in production specifications or by alteration of items already produced. ***Picketing.** Securing aircraft when parked in the open to restrain movement due to the weather or condition of the parking area. ***Repair.** The process of restoring aircraft or aircraft materials after damage, or wear, to a serviceable condition. ***Replenishing.** The refilling of aircraft with consumables such as fuel, oil and compressed gases to pre-determined levels, pressures, quantities or weights. Rearming is excluded. ***Role equipment.** *See* * **Mission equipment.** * **Scrambling** Directing the immediate take-off of aircraft from a ground alert condition of readiness. * **Tie down.** *See* * **Picketing.** ***Vectoring.** The directional control of in-flight aircraft through transmission of azimuth headings.

Air defence. All measures designed to nullify or reduce the effectiveness of the attack of aircraft or guided missiles in flight. *See also* **Active air defence; Passive air defence.** ***Action area.** An area and the airspace above it within which friendly aircraft or surface-to-air weapons are normally given precedence in operations except under specified conditions. ***Area.** A specifically defined airspace for which defence must be planned and provided. ***Commander.** The officer in charge of all the AA defence allotted to him. ***Control centre.** The principal information, communications and operations centre from which all aircraft, anti-aircraft operations, air defence artillery, guided missiles and air warning functions of a specified area of air defence responsibility are supervised and co-ordinated. *See also* **Combat information centre.** ***Defended point.** *See* 'Vulnerable point (air defence)'. ***Early warning.** Early notification of approach of enemy airborne weapons or weapons carriers obtained by electronic or visual means. * **Identification zone.** Airspace of defined dimensions within which the ready identification, location and control of aircraft is required. ***Operations area.** A geographical area defining the boundaries within which procedures are established to minimize interference between air defence and other operations and which may include designation of one or more of the following: *Action area; *Area; *Identification zone; Firepower umbrella. ***Region.** A geographical subdivision of an air defence area. ***Sector.** A geographical subdivision of an air defence region.

Air despatch squadron. A Royal Corps of Transport squadron which is trained in preparing stores for despatch by air, in loading aircraft, and in the ejection of cargo from aircraft in flight.

Air despatcher (cargo). A person trained in the ejection of cargo from aircraft in flight.

Airdrop. Delivery of personnel or cargo from aircraft in flight. *See also* **Air movement; Free drop; High velocity drop; Low velocity drop. *Platform.** A base on which vehicles, cargo or equipment are loaded and lashed for airdrop or low altitude extraction.

Air evacuation. Evacuation by aircraft of personnel and cargo.

Airfield. An area prepared for the accommodation (including any buildings, installations and equipment), landing and take-off of aircraft. *See also* **Alternative *; Main *; Redeployment *. * Traffic.** All traffic on the manoeuvring area of an aerodrome and all aircraft flying in the vicinity of an aerodrome.

Airframe. The structure of an aircraft without engines or power plants.

Air freighting. The non-tactical movement of cargo by air.

Air ground operation system. An Army/ Air Force system providing the ground commander with the means for receiving, processing, and forwarding the requests of subordinate ground commanders for air support missions and for the rapid dissemination of information and intelligence.

Airhead.
1. A designated area in a hostile or threatened territory which, when seized and held, ensures the continuous air landing of troops and *matériel* and provides the manoeuvre space necessary for projected operations. Normally it is the area seized in the assault phase of an airborne operation.
2. A designated location in an area of operations used as a base for supply and evacuation by air. *See also* **Beachead; Bridgehead; *Maintenance area/Forward maintenance area.** (AMA/FMA) The maintenance area located adjacent to the Airhead being used by the Medium Range Transport aircraft. When the RMA (qv) is established the AMA will become known as the FMA.

Air interception. To effect visual or radar contact by a friendly aircraft with another aircraft.

Air interdiction. Air operations conducted to destroy, neutralize, or delay the enemy's military potential before it can be brought to bear effectively against friendly forces at such distance from them that detailed integration of each air mission with the fire and movement of friendly forces is not required. *See also* **Interdict.**

Air landed. Moved by air and disembarked, or unloaded, after the aircraft has landed. *See also* **Air Movement.**

Air liaison officer. A tactical air force or naval aviation officer attached to a ground unit or formation as air adviser.

Airlift.
1. The total weight of personnel and/or cargo that is, or can be, carried by air, or that is offered for carriage by air.
2. To transport passengers and cargo by use of aircraft.

3. The carriage of personnel and/or cargo by air.
See also Payload. ***Capability.** The total capacity expressed in terms of number of passengers and/or weight/cubic displacement of cargo that can be carried at any one time to a given destination by the available air transport service. *See also* **Allowable cabin load (air); Allowable. cargo load (air); Payload; Planned load (aircraft).** ***Requirement.** The total number of passengers and/or weight/ cubic displacement of cargo required to be carried by air for a specific task.

Air logistic support. Support by air-landing or airdrop including air supply, movement of personnel, evacuation of casualties and prisoners of war and recovery of equipment and vehicles.

Air maintenance. *See* **Air logistic support.**

Air mission. *See* **Mission.** ***Intelligence report.** A detailed report of the results of an air mission, including a complete intelligence account of the mission.

Airmobile operations. Operations in which combat forces and their equipment move about the battlefield in air vehicles under the control of a ground force commander to engage in ground combat.

Air movement. Air transport of units, personnel, supplies and equipment including airdrops and air-landings. *See also* **Airdrop; Free drop; High velocity drop; Low velocity drop.** ***Officer.** An officer trained for duties in air movement or Air traffic section. ***Table.** A table prepared by a ground force commander in co-ordination with an air force commander. This form, issued as an annex to the operation order:
1. indicates the allocation of aircraft space to elements of the ground units to be airlifted.
2. designates the number and type of aircraft in each serial.
3. specifies the departure area, time of loading and take-off.

*Traffic section. A section located on those airfields which serve transport aircraft. It is responsible for the loading and unloading of aircraft, and for the handling of passengers, mail and materials.

Air observation post. *See* **Observation post.**

Air observer. An individual whose primary mission is to observe or take photographs from an aircraft in order to adjust artillery fire or obtain military information.

Air passenger movement. The movement by air of military personnel and their dependents, service sponsored personnel and their dependents.

Air passenger schedules. Schedules designed specifically for the movement by air of personnel and their dependents to meet routine requirements.

Air photograph. Any photograph taken from the air.

Air photographic reconnaissance. The obtaining of information by air photography, divided into three types:
1. strategic photographic reconnaissance.
2. tactical photographic reconnaissance.
3. survey cartographic photography — air photography taken for survey/carto- graphic purposes and to survey/carto- graphic standards of accuracy. It may be strategic or tactical.

Air pickets. Airborne early warning aircraft disposed around a position, area, or formation primarily to detect, report, and track approaching enemy aircraft or missiles and to control inter- cepts. *See also* **Airborne early warning and control.**

Air plot.
1. A continuous plot used in air navi- gation of a graphic representation of true headings steered and air distances flown.

2. A continuous plot of the position of an airborne object represented graphically to show true headings steered and air distances flown.

Airport. An aerodrome at which facilities available to the public are provided for the shelter, servicing, or repair of aircraft, and for receiving or despatching passengers or freight.

Air portable. Denotes equipment which can be carried in an aircraft with not more than such minor dismantling and reassembling as would be within the capabilities of user units. This term must be qualified to show the extent of air portability.

Air position. The calculated position of an aircraft assuming no wind effect.

Air priorities committee. A committee set up to determine the priorities of passengers and cargo. *See also* **Air transport allocations board.**

Air reconnaissance. The acquisition of intelligence information employing aerial vehicles in visual observation or the use of sensory devices.

Air route. The navigable airspace between two points, identified to the extent necessary for the application of flight rules.

Air space warning area. *See* **Danger area.**

Airspeed. The speed of an aircraft relative to its surrounding air mass.

Air staging post.
1. The unit whose function is the handling, reception, servicing and despatch of aircraft and control of their loads.
2. An airfield en route which is used for refuelling, servicing, etc.

Air staging unit. A unit situated at an airfield and concerned with the reception, handling, servicing and preparation for departure of aircraft and control of personnel and cargo.

Air station (photogrammetry). The point in space occupied by the camera lens at the moment of exposure. *See also* **Air base** (photogrammetry).

Air strip. An unimproved surface which has been adapted for take-off or landing of aircraft, usually having minimum facilities. *See also* **Airfield.**

Air superiority. That degree of dominance in the air battle of one force over another which permits the conduct of operations by the former and its related land, sea and air forces at a given time and place without prohibitive interference by the opposing force.

Air supply. The delivery of cargo by airdrop or air-landing.

Air support. All forms of support given by air forces on land or sea. *See also* **Call mission; Close*; Immediate*; Indirect*; Preplanned*; Tactical*. *Operations centre.** The joint staff agency in the field responsible for tasking the strike and reconnaissance effort allotted to it by the Joint Operations Centre.

Air supremacy. That degree of air superiority wherein the opposing air force is incapable of effective interference.

Air surveillance. The systematic observation of air space by electronic, visual or other means, primarily for the purpose of identifying and determining the movements of aircraft and missiles, friendly and enemy, in the air space under observation. *See also* **Surveillance.** ***Plotting board.** A gridded, small scale, air defence map of an appropriate area. It is maintained at the air control centre. On it are posted current locations, number, and altitudes of all friendly or enemy aircraft within current range of radar or ground observer facilities.

Air survey camera. *See* **Air cartographic camera.**

Air survey photography. *See* **Air cartographic photography.**

Air to Surface Missile (ASM). A missile system mounted on an aircraft, including helicopter, designed to engage ground targets.

Air Traffic Control (ATC). The system controlling aircraft in flight. *Centre. A unit combining the functions of an area control centre and a flight information centre. *See also* **Area control centre; Flight information region.** *Clearance. Authorization by an air traffic control authority for an aircraft to proceed under specified conditions. *Service. A service provided for the purpose of:
1. preventing collisions between aircraft and between aircraft and obstructions;
2. expediting and maintaining an orderly flow of traffic.

Air transportable units. Those units, other than airborne, whose equipment is adapted for air movement. *See also* **Airborne; Airborne operation.**

Air transport allocations board. The joint agency responsible within the theatre for the establishment of airlift priorities and for space allocation of available aircraft capabilities allotted to the theatre. *See also* **Air priorities committee.**

Air transported troops. Forces which are moved by air.

Air transport liaison officer. An officer attached for air transport liaison duties to a headquarters or unit.

Air transport liaison section (army). A sub-unit of the movement control organization deployed to airfields and responsible for the control of service movement at the airfield in connection with air movement operations and exercises.

Air transport movement control centre (ATMCC). The joint agency responsible within the theatre for all air movement

and control of air transport allotted to the theatre. It is also responsible for co-ordinating with external authorities movements into and out of the theatre of externally controlled air transport forces.

Air transport operations. *See* **Strategic air transport operations; Tactical air transport operations.**

Air transport operations centre (ATOC). The joint air transport agency in the field which is responsible for co-ordinating air transport requirements in the area of operations and for tasking air transport resources allotted by theatre headquarters. It co-ordinates plans for air movement into and out of the area.

Air trooping. The non-tactical air movement of personnel. *See also* **Air movement.**

Airway. A control area or portion thereof established in the form of a corridor marked with radio navigational aids.

Air waybill. A document listing items for conveyance by air.

Alert.
1. Readiness for action, defence or protection.
2. A warning signal of a real or threatened danger, such as an air attack.
3. The period of time during which troops stand by in response to an alarm.
4. To forewarn; to prepare for action. *See also* **Airborne alert.**

Alerting service. A service provided to notify appropriate organizations regarding aircraft in need of search and rescue aid, and to assist such organizations as required.

Alighting area. A specified surface, reserved for vehicles that depend upon water surfaces for their landing.

Alignment.
1. The bearing of two or more conspicuous objects (such as lights, beacons, etc.) as

seen by an observer.
2. Representation of a road, railway, etc., on a map or chart in relation to surrounding topographical detail.

Allied Command Europe (ACE). The Headquarters which commands the three main area commands in Europe: **AFNORTH** *qv*, **AFCENT** *qv*, and **AFSOUTH** *qv*.

Allied Command Europe Mobile Force (Land). Consists of units from Belgium, Canada, Germany, Italy, Luxembourg, UK and USA, the largest contingent being British. The permanent field headquarters is at Heidelberg.

Allied Forces Central Europe (AFCENT). Consists of two Army Groups, **NORTHAG** (*qv*) and **CENTAG** (*qv*). It is charged with the defence of Germany from the North Sea to the Swiss border. It is part of **ACE** (*qv*).

Allied Forces Northern Europe (AFNORTH). Comprise some German and most of the Danish and Norwegian Armed forces. It is responsible for the defence of Scandinavia and the Baltic. It is part of **ACE** (qv).

Allied Forces Southern Europe (AFSOUTH). Is responsible for the defence of Italy, Greece and Turkey with land forces provided by the countries concerned. It is also responsible for the safety of the Mediterranean area.

Allied Headquarters. *See* Allied staff.

Allied staff. A staff or headquarters composed of two or more allied nations working together.

Allocation (nuclear). The specific numbers and types of nuclear weapons allocated to a commander for a stated time period as a planning factor only.

Allowable cabin load (air). The amount of cargo and passengers, determined by weight, cubic displacement and distance to be flown, which may be transported by specified aircraft. *See also* **Load** (air).

Allowable cargo load (air). The amount of cargo, determined by weight, cubic displacement and distance to be flown, which may be transported by specific aircraft. *See also* **Load** (air).

Alongside date. The date on which a consignment is to be available at the point of loading.

Alternate aerodrome. An aerodrome specified in the flight plan to which a flight may proceed when a landing at the intended destination becomes inadvisable.

Alternate escort operating base. A base providing the facilities and activities required for the support of escort units for short periods of time.

Alternative airfield. An airfield with minimum essential facilities for use as an emergency landing ground, or when main or redeployment airfields are out of action or as required for tactical flexibility. *See also* **Airfield.**

Alternative tank position. A position adjacent to the primary one, still covering the task of the primary one, to which the tank may jockey as required.

Altitude. The vertical distance of a level, a point or an object considered as a point, measured from mean sea level. *See also* **Absolute*; Critical*; Drop*; Elevation; Height; Minimum safe *; Pressure*; Transition*. * Acclimatization,** A slow physiological adaptation from prolonged exposure to significantly reduced atmospheric pressure. ***Datum.** The arbitrary level from which vertical . displacement is measured. The datum for height measurement is the terrain directly below the aircraft or some specified datum; for pressure altitude, the level at which the atmospheric pressure is 29.92 inches of mercury (1013.2 m.bs); and for true altitude, mean sea level. ***Delay.** Synchronization delay introduced between the time of transmission of the radar pulse and the start of the trace on the indicator, for the purpose of eliminating the altitude hole on the planned position indicator-type display. *Hold. In a flight control system, a control mode in which the barometric altitude existing at time of engagement is maintained automatically. *Hole. The blank area at the origin of a radial display, on a radar tube presentation, the centre of the periphery of which represents the point on the ground immediately below the aircraft. In side looking airborne radar, this is known as the altitude slot. *Sickness. The syndrome of depression, anorexia, nausea, vomiting and collapse, due to decreased atmospheric pressure, occurring in an individual exposed to an altitude beyond that to which acclimatization has occurred.

Ammo. Slang for ammunition. (*qv*).

Ammunition. A contrivance charged with explosives, propellants, pyrotechnics, initiating composition, or nuclear, biological, or chemical material for use in connection with defence or offence, including demolitions. Certain ammunition can be used for training, ceremonial or non-operational purposes. *See also* Chemical *; Fixed *; Semifixed *; Separate loading *. * Point (AP). A designated area where ammunition is kept loaded on vehicles for the replenishment of the fighting units.

Ammunition and toxic material open space. Area especially prepared for storage of explosive ammunition and toxic materials. For reporting purposes, it does not include the surrounding area restricted for storage because of safety distance factors. It includes barricades and improvised coverings.

Amphibious. As an adjective used to qualify a noun or phrase and denoting a capability of use on sea or land. *Command ship. A naval ship from which a commander exercises control in amphibious operations. *Control group. Personnel, ships and craft designated to control the waterborne ship-to-shore movement in an amphibious operation. *Demonstration. A lesser type of amphibious operation; conducted for the purpose of deceiving the enemy by a show of force with the expectation of deluding the enemy into a course of action unfavourable to him. *Force. A naval force and landing force, together with supporting forces that are trained, organized and equipped for amphibious operations. *Group. A command within the amphibious force, consisting of the commander and his staff, designed to exercise operational command of assigned units in executing all phases of a division-size amphibious operation. *Lift. The total capacity of assault shipping utilized in an amphibious operation, expressed in terms of personnel, vehicles, and measurement or weight tons of supplies. *Observation regiment/battery/troop. A Royal Artillery unit which provides:
1. teams ashore to direct the fire of naval guns on targets in support of the army.
2. a liaison party in each bombarding party.
*Operation. An attack launched from the sea by naval and landing forces, embarked in ships or craft involving a landing on a hostile shore. *Raid. A limited type of amphibious operation; a landing from the sea on a hostile shore involving swift incursion into, or a temporary occupancy of, an objective, followed by a planned withdrawal. *Squadron. A tactical and administrative organization composed of amphibious assault shipping to transport troops and their equipment for an amphibious assault operation. *Vehicle. A wheeled or tracked vehicle capable of operating on both land and water. *See also* Landing craft; Vehicle. *Vehicle launching area. An area, in the vicinity of and to seaward of the line of departure, to which landing ships proceed and launch amphibious vehicles.

Amplifying report. *See* Contact report.

Analysis staff. *See* Central analysis team.

Anchor cable (air transport). A cable in an aircraft to which the parachute strops are permanently attached. The D-ring of a parachute static line is clipped into a metal attachment on the end of a strop and secured by a safety pin device.

Anchor line extension kits. A device fitted to an aircraft equipped with removable clamshell doors to enable paratroopers to exit from the rear.

Ancillary armament. Secondary weapons, eg machine guns on a battle tank.

Anfo. (slang). Home made explosive used in Northern Ireland.

Angle. The point at which two lines meet. *of convergence. The angle subtended by the eyebase of an observer at the point of focus. Also known as Angular parallex; Parallactic angle. *of depression.
1. the angle in a vertical plane between the horizontal and a descending line.
2. in air photography, the angle between the axis of an obliquely mounted air camera and the horizontal. *See also* Tilt. * of safety. The minimum permissible angular clearance, at the gun, of the path of a projectile above the friendly troops. It is the angle of clearance corrected to ensure the safety of the troops. *of view.
1. the angle between two rays passing through the perspective centre (rear nodal point of camera lens to two opposite corners of the format).
2. in photogrammetry, twice the angle whose tangent is one-half the length of the diagonal of the format divided by the calibrated focal length.

Angular parallax. *See* Angle of convergence.

Annex. A supplement amplifying a report, paper or letter, may itself be amplified by an appendix, thus reversing normal civilian practice.

Annotated print. A photograph on which interpretation details are indicated by words or symbols.

Annotation. A marking placed on imagery or drawings for explanatory purposes or to indicate items or areas of special importance.

Anteroom. The lounge or drawing room of a service mess; so called because its original use was to serve as a meeting place for members before going into dinner.

Anti airborne minefield (land mine warfare). A minefield laid primarily for protection against airborne attack. *See also* Minefield (land mine warfare).

Anti-aircraft operations centre. The tactical headquarters of an anti-aircraft commander. The agency provided to collect and evaluate information and disseminate intelligence for the anti-aircraft defence, and through which operational control over subordinate units is exercised.

Anti amphibious minefield (land mine warfare). A minefield laid primarily for protection against amphibious attack. *See also* Minefield (land mine warfare).

Anti-ballistic missile system. A weapon system designed to locate, intercept and destroy enemy ballistic missiles (*qv*). Sensors and data processing units guide the missile to its target.

Anticrop agent. A living organism or chemical used to cause disease or damage to selected food or industrial crops.

Anticrop operations. The employment of anti-crop agents in military operations to destroy the enemy's source of selected food or industrial crops.

Anti-G suit. A device worn by aircrew to counteract the effects on the human body of positive acceleration.

Antilift device (land mine warfare). A device arranged to detonate the mine to which it is attached, or to detonate another mine or charge nearby, if the mine is disturbed.

Antimaterial agent. A living organism or chemical used to cause deterioration of, or damage to, selected materials.

Antimateriel operations. The employment of antimateriel weapons or agents in military operations.

Anti-personnel mine (land mine warfare). A mine designed to cause casualties to personnel. *See also* **Mine** (land mine warfare).

Anti-personnel minefield (land mine warfare). A minefield laid primarily for protection against infantry attack. *See also* **Minefield** (land mine warfare).

Antiradiation missile. A missile which homes passively on a radiation source.

Anti-tank Guided Weapon Systems (ATGW). A missile system of comparatively short range and high lethality designed for use against armour by infantry or artillery units.

Anti-tank Laser Assisted System (ATLAS). An Anglo-Belgian anti-tank weapon project in course of development.

Anti-tank mine (land mine warfare). A mine designed to immobilize or destroy a tank. *See also* **Mine** (land mine warfare).

Anti-tank weapon ranges.
1. Long Range. An anti-tank weapon with an effective maximum range of more than 2,000 metres.
2. Medium Range. An anti-tank weapon with an effective maximum range of more than 1,000 but less than 2,000 metres.
3. Short Range. An anti-tank weapon with an effective maximum range of less than 1,000 metres.

Antivigneting filter. A filter bearing a deposit which is graduated in density to correct for the uneven illumination given by certain lenses, particularly wide-angle types.

Aperture. The opening in a lens diaphragm through which light passes.

Apogée. The point at which a missile trajectory or a satellite orbit is farthest from the centre of the gravitational field of the controlling body or bodies.

Apparent horizon. The visible line of demarcation between land/sea and sky.

Appendix. *See* **Annex.**

Applicability. An indication of equipment to which an item of *matériel* may be fitted or applied.

Appliqué armour. Extra armour attached to the basic plates of AFVs.

Appreciation of the situation. A flexible form of logical thought, either verbal or written, which evaluates the factors affecting a tactical situation and leads to the formulation of a plan of action. NATO equivalent: **Estimate of the situation** (*qv*).

Approach. The continuously changing position of an aircraft in space directed toward effecting a landing on a predetermined area. *Control. A function of air traffic control to control IFR flights arriving at, departing from, and operating in the vicinity of airfields by means of direct communication with persons in command of the aircraft. *Lanes. Extensions of the boat lanes from the line of departure toward the transport area. They may be terminated by marker ships, boats or buoys. *Schedule. The schedule which indicates, for each scheduled wave, the time of departure from the rendezvous area, from the line of departure, and from other control points and the time of arrival at the beach. *Sequence. The order in which aircraft are to approach a given point. *Time. The time at which an aircraft commences its final approach preparatory to landing.

Apron (airfield). A paved surface or prepared area where aircraft stand for purposes of loading or unloading passengers or cargo, refuelling, parking or servicing.

Area.
1. A subdivision of a District (*qv*) which is usually commanded by a Brigadier.
2. Any defined and delimited tract of land. ***Bombing.** Bombing of a target which is in effect a general area rather than a small or pin-point target.
*Command. A command which is composed of those organized elements of one or more of the armed services, designated to operate in a specific geographical area, which are placed under a single commander; eg Commander of a Unified Command, Area Commander. *See also* **Command. *Control centre.** A unit established to provide air traffic control service to controlled flights in control areas under its jurisdiction. *See also* **Air traffic control centre.**
*Damage control. Measures taken before, during or after hostile actions or natural or man-made disasters, to reduce the probability of damage and minimize its effects. *See also* **Damage control; Rear security. *of influence.** The portion of the assigned zone and the area of operations wherein a commander is directly capable of influencing the progress or outcome of operations by manoeuvres of his ground-gaining elements or by delivery of firepower with the fire support systems normally under his control or command. It is a geographical area, the size of which depends upon the mission, organization and equipment of the force involved.
*of interest. That area of concern to the commander, including the area of influence, areas adjacent thereto, and extending into enemy territory to the objectives of current or planned operations. This area also includes areas occupied by enemy forces who could jeopardize the accomplishment of the

mission. ***of military significant fallout.** The area in which radioactive fallout affects the ability of military units to carry out their normal mission. ***of operations.** That portion of an area of war necessary for military operations, either offensive or defensive, pursuant to an assigned mission, and for the administration incident to such military operations. ***of responsibility.** A defined area of land in which responsibility is specifically assigned to the commander of the area for the development and maintenance of installations, control of movement and the conduct of tactical operations involving troops under his control along with parallel authority to exercise these functions. ***Target.** A target consisting of an area or zone rather than a single point.

Arisings. The assemblies, sub-assemblies, detail parts or scrap recovered as a result of the breaking down of an item of *matériel*.

Armbrust (German). A manportable, shoulder-fired infantry anti-tank weapon.

Armed forces. The military forces of a nation or a group of nations. *See also* **Force(s).**

Armed mine. A mine ready for actuation. *See also* **Mine.**

Armed reconnaissance. An air mission flown with the primary purpose of locating and attacking targets of opportunity *i.e.*, enemy *matériel*, personnel, and facilities, in assigned general areas or along assigned ground communications routes, and not for the purpose of attacking specific briefed targets.

Arming. As applied to explosives, the changing from a safe condition to a state of readiness for initiation.

Armistice. An agreement to cease hostilities which may be of indefinite duration as a prelude to peace negotiations or for a stated period and purpose, *eg* burial of dead.

Armour Piercing (AP). Used of rounds fired by rifles or guns which can penetrate armour by the force of their kinetic energy. *Discarding Sabot (APDS).** A highly effective armour piercing round.

Armoured car (AC). A wheeled armoured fighting vehicle employed in the role of light cavalry.

Armoured Command Vehicle (ACV). A vehicle primarily designed as one from which a commander can control his forces.

Armoured Fighting Vehicle (AFV). Includes both tanks and armoured cars (*qv*).

Armoured Forces. A formation which contains a preponderance of armour, *eg* tanks, armoured cars and SP guns. Usually supported by infantry in APCs (*qv*).

Armoured Personnel Carrier (APC). An armoured vehicle with cross country capability for transport of troops within the battle area.

Armoured Recovery Vehicle (ARV). Is one fitted with tackle to receover disabled AFVs and trucks from the battle area.

Army.
1. The land forces of the crown including regular and TAVR (*qv*).
2. A tactical formation of two or more Army Corps (*qv*) usually commanded by a Lieutenant General. *Act. *See under* Manual of Military Law.* *Air transport organization.** The organization which, when circumstances demand, may be set up by the army to carry out, in co-operation with the air forces the ground administrative duties and air despatching in connection with operations which are allotted transport support by the air forces. *Cadet Force (ACF). *See under* Force.* *Corps.** An organization larger than a division and smaller than a field army usually consisting of two or more divisions together

with supporting arms and services. *Fire Service (AFS).** Units of the Ordnance Corps equipped and trained to prevent and extinguish fires on WD land. *Forces.** The arms of a nation.
*Group.** Several field armies under a designated commander. *Photographic interpretation section (APIS).** A small unit specially trained for this purpose.
*Service area.** The territory between the corps rear boundary and the combat zone rear boundary. Most of the administrative establishments and service troops are usually located in this area.
*Youth Team (AYT).** A team of five soldiers commanded by an Officer or WO who assist groups of young people in character building activities, both indoor and outdoor, inform them about life in the Army and encourage people of the right calibre to join.

Arrest. An officer or soldier is placed under arrest if he is suspected of having committed a crime and remains so until released or tried. If the suspected crime is a serious one he is confined to his quarters or the guard room and suspended from all duties (under close arrest). Otherwise he is merely forbidden to leave barracks except on duty (open arrest).

Arsenal. A depot or store for weapons; now obsolescent but subsists in Woolwich once the main arsenal of England.

Articulated vehicle. *See* **Semi-trailer.**

Artificial daylight. Illumination of an intensity greater than the light of a full moon on a clear night. (The optimum illumination is the equivalent of daylight.) *See also* **Battlefield illumination.**

Artificial horizon. A device that indicates attitude with respect to the true horizon. A substitute for a natural horizon, determined by a liquid level, bubble pendulum, or gyroscope.

Artificial moonlight. Illumination of an intensity between that of starlight and that of a full moon on a clear night. *See also* **Battlefield illumination.**

Artillery (Arty). A generic term which previously denoted tube weapons which fired shells as opposed to bullets and were too heavy to be operated by a single soldier. With the advent of mortars and missiles it can be taken to embrace all the primary weapons of a country's Artillery Corps. ***Control Console (ACC).** The primary man-machine interface at the Fire Direction Control which provides a true, real-time general purpose entry/query capability for a large data base. ***Meteorological System (AMETS).** A mobile self-contained upper air system which supplies meteorological information to troops on the ground. ***Preparation.** Artillery fire delivered before an attack to disrupt communications and disorganise the enemy's defence. **Royal Regiment of Artillery** comprises all gunner regiments, and includes Royal Field Artillery (RFA), Royal Horse Artillery (RHA) (See Appendix 3.) Anti-aircraft Artillery Regiments, etc. The difference between them is now less distinct than before mechanization. **Corps/Divisional Artillery.** Units specifically allotted to certain formations.

Aspect change. The different appearance of a reflecting object viewed by radar from varying directions. It is caused by the change in the effective reflecting area of the target.

Assault.
1. The climax of an attack; closing with the enemy in hand-to-hand fighting.
2. In an amphibious operation, the period of time from the crossing of the line of departure by the first scheduled wave to the seizure of the initial objectives.
3. To make a short, violent, but well-ordered attack against a local objective, such as a gun emplacement, a fort or a machine-gun nest.
4. A phase of an airborne operation beginning with delivery by air of the first lift into the objective area and

extending through attack on objectives and consolidation of the airhead.
***Aircraft.** Powered aircraft, including helicopters, which move assault troops and cargo into an objective area and which provide for their re-supply.
***Echelon (air transport).** The element of a force which is scheduled for initial assault on the objective area. ***Scale.** *See* **Scale (logistic).** ***Shipping.** Shipping assigned to the amphibious task force and utilized for transporting assault troops, vehicles, equipment and supplies to the objective area. ***Wave.** *See* **Wave.**

Assembly area.
1. An area in which a command is assembled preparatory to further action.
2. In a supply installation, the gross area used for collection and combining components into complete units, kits, or assemblies.

Assign.
1. The placement of units or personnel in an organization where such placement is relatively permanent and/or where such organization controls and administers the units or personnel for the primary function, or greater portion of the functions, of the unit or personnel.
2. The detailing of individuals to specific duties or functions where such duties or functions are primary and/or relatively permanent. *See also* **Attach.**

Assigned forces. Forces in being which have been placed under the operational command or operational control of a NATO commander.

Assistant Adjutant and Quartermaster General (AA & QMG). In small formations where there is no justification for a Grade 1 staff officer (GSO 1) for both A & Q work, both branches are controlled by the AA & QMG. He is the senior administrative staff officer in a division.

Assistant Provost Marshal (APM). A senior officer of military police.

A Staff. That section of the staff which deals with matters within the jurisdiction of the Adjutant General. They include discipline, welfare, postings, promotion, discharge and certain aspects of individual training.

Astro altitude. The arc of the vertical circle measured from the celestial horizon to the body.

Astro compass. An instrument used primarily to obtain true heading by reference to celestial bodies.

Astronomical twilight. *See* **Twilight.**

Astro-tracker. A navigation equipment which automatically acquires and continuously tracks a celestial body in azimuth and altitude.

Atmosphere. The air surrounding the earth. *See also* **Ionosphere; stratosphere; tropopause; troposphere.**

Atomic demolition munition. A nuclear device designed or adapted for use as a demolition munition.

Atomic weapon. *See* **Nuclear weapon.**

Attach.
1. The placement of units or personnel in an organization where such placement is relatively temporary. Subject to limitations imposed in the attachment order, the commander of the formation, unit, or organization receiving the attachment will exercise the same degree of command and control thereover as he does over the units and persons organic to his command. However, the responsibility for transfer and promotion of personnel will normally be retained by the parent formation, unit, or organization.
2. The detailing of individuals to specific functions where such functions are secondary or relatively temporary, *ie* attach for quarters and rations, attach for flying duty. *See also* **Assign.**

Attack. Any offensive move against the enemy. ***Aircraft.** A fighter-bomber or bomber aircraft capable of delivering conventional (non-nuclear) weapons.

***Group.** A subordinate task organization of the Naval Forces of an amphibious task force. It is composed of assault shipping and supporting naval units designated to transport, protect, land and initially support a landing group. ***Position.** *See* **Forming up place.**

Attention. Soldiers are called to attention before any other drill move may be ordered.

Attenuation. Decrease in intensity of a signal, beam, or wave as a result of absorption of energy and of scattering out of the path of a detector, but not including the reduction due to geometric spreading, *ie* the inverse square of distance effect. ***Factor.** The ratio of the incident radiation dose or dose rate to the radiation dose or dose rate transmitted through a shielding material. This is the recriprocal of the transmission factor.

Attitude. The position of a body as determined by the inclination of the axes to some frame of reference. If not otherwise specified, this frame of reference is fixed to the earth.

Attrition. The reduction of the effectiveness of a force caused by loss of personnel and *matériel*. ***Rate.** A factor, normally expressed as a percentage, reflecting the degree of losses of personnel or *matériel* due to various causes within a specified period of time. **War of*.** A prolonged conflict in which the object is to wear down and destroy enemy personnel and *matériel*.

Audit cross check. Verification of a transaction or item in one account by reference to an independent record or account maintained elsewhere.

Audit observation. A formal request for an explanation of apparent shortcomings revealed during the course of internal audit.

Authentication.
1. Evidence by proper signature or seal

that a document is genuine and official.
2. A security measure designed to
protect a communication system against
fraudulent transmissions.

Authenticator. A letter, numeral, or
groups of letters or numerals, or both,
attesting to the authenticity of a message
or transmission.

Authentic document. A document bearing a signature or seal attesting that it is
genuine and official. If it is an enemy
document, it may have been prepared
for purposes of deception and the
accuracy of such a document, even
though authenticated, must be confirmed by other information, *eg*
conditions of capture.

Automat Kalashnikov (AK). Standard
Russian rifle firing 7.62 mm round
which is not interchangeable with the
NATO 7.62 mm round.

Automatic approach and landing. A
control mode in which the aircraft's
speed and flight path are automatically
controlled for approach, flare-out and
landing.

**Automatic Command to Line of Sight
(ACLOS).** In Guided Weapon Systems
the operator engages a target and then
needs to take no further action because
a target and missile tracker with a computer measure errors in flight path and
apply adjustment through a command
link and control system. E.g, **Rapier.** (qv)

Automatic flight control system. A
system which includes all equipment to
control automatically the flight of an
aircraft or missile to a path or attitude
described by references internal or
external to the aircraft or missile.

**Automatic Intruder Detector Alarm
(AIDA).** A surveillance system suitable
for use in areas of high seismic activity.

Automatic levelling. A flight control
system feature which returns an aircraft
to level flight attitude in roll and pitch.

Automatic pilot. That part of an automatic flight control system which
provides attitude stabilization with
respect to internal references.

Automatic re-supply. The replenishment
of a unit's stock of *matériel* by a supply
authority, without demand by the unit,
when the unit's stock level falls to a
pre-determined level.

Automatic search jammer. An intercept
receiver and jamming transmitter system
which searches for and automatically
jams signals which have specific
radiation characteristics.

Automatic throttle. A flight control
system feature which actuates an aircraft
throttle system based on its own computation and feed-back from appropriate
data sources.

Automatic trim. A flight control system
feature which adjusts the trim of an
aircraft in flight.

Autonomous operation. One mode of
operation of a unit in which the unit
commander assumes full responsibility
for control of weapons and engagement
of hostile targets. This mode may be
either directed by higher authority or
result from a loss of all means of communication.

Auxiliary contours. Additional contours
used to portray unique ground forms
not adequately portrayed by the
selected contour interval.

Available supply rate (ammunition).
The rate of consumption of ammunition
that can be allocated, considering the
supplies and facilities available, for a
given period. For ammunition items
fired from weapons, this rate is expressed
in rounds per weapon per day. For other
items, such as anti-tank mines, hand
grenades, demolition explosives, etc.,
the rate is expressed in terms of units of
measure for specified items, *eg* per day,
per week. (Each unit of measure,
kilos, pounds or tons, metric, short,
long is specified.)

Average heading. The average heading maintained for a given period. It should be the same value as desired heading if the actual drift was as predicted.

Average speed. The average distance travelled per hour calculated over the whole journey excluding specifically ordered halts.

Aviation medicine. The special field of medicine which is related to the biological and psychological problems of flight.

Avionics.
1. The technology of the use of electronics in all its forms in airborne and aerospace vehicles.
2. Airborne equipment produced by the use of such technology.

Axial mining (land mine warfare). Continuous or intermittent nuisance mining in great depth along the axis of enemy advance.

Axial route. A route running through the rear area and into the forward area. *See also* **Route.**

Axis.
(1. ground). The general line astride which a unit or formation moves.
(2. air). In an automatic flight control system, that section of the system which controls an aircraft in one plane.
* **of advance.** A line of advance assigned for purposes of control; often a road or a group of roads or a designated series of locations extending in the direction of the enemy.

Azimuth. An imaginary arc descending from the heavens to the horizon. When used in gunnery a change in azimuth denotes a traversing move of the gun barrel, as opposed to a vertical one which changes the elevation. * **Angle.** An angle measured clockwise in the horizontal plane between a reference direction and any other line. * **Resolution.** The ability of radar equipment to separate two reflectors at similar ranges but different

bearings from a vehicle. Normally the minimum separation distance between the reflectors is quoted and expressed as the angle subtended by the reflectors at the vehicle.

Backdoor. Gaining a commission in the army by any means other than passing through the Royal Military Academy at Sandhurst is known as backdoor entry.

Background count. The evidence or effect on a detector of radiation, other than that which it is desired to detect, caused by any agency. In connection with health protection, the background count usually includes radiations produced by naturally occurring radioactivity and cosmic rays. * **Radiation.** Nuclear (or ionizing) radiations arising from within the body and from the surroundings to which individuals are always exposed.

Backloading. The rearward move of equipment casualties and materials within a theatre.

Back-Up Interceptor Control (BUIC) (US). A computer and communication system used by the American and Canadian air defence organization.

Back-scattering. Radio wave propagation in which the direction of the incident and scattered waves, resolved along a reference direction (usually horizontal), are oppositely directed. A signal of this kind is often referred to as 'back-scatter'.

Backsight. Either a U or aperture sight mounted above the rear end of the barrel of a small arm. Usually adjustable for range. *See also* **Foresight.**

Back-up. Sometimes used to indicate printing on the reverse of a map sheet, *eg* to supplement marginal information.

Badge. Cap badge, collar badge, worn on uniform where indicated to denote corps or regiment. Formation badge worn on sleeve to denote corps, division, etc. Good conduct badge awarded after a number of years of crime free service. Skill at arms badge denotes proficiency at weapon training. Tradesman's badge denotes proficiency at trade training.

Baggage Master. The officer in charge of the movement of all arms, stores and equipment not carried on the man during a peace move of a unit.

Balanced collective forces. The requirement for 'balance' in any military force stems from the consideration that all elements of a force should be complementary to each other. A force should function as a combined arms team, and the term 'balance' implies that the ratio of the various elements of this team is such that the force is best constituted to execute its assigned mission effectively. Applied multinationally, the term may be defined as a force comprised of one or more services furnished by more than one nation, the total strength and composition of which is such as is best to fulfil the specific mission for which it is designed.

Balance station zero. *See* **Reference datum.**

Balisage. The marking of a route by a system of dim beacon lights enabling vehicles to be driven at near day-time speed, under blackout conditions.

Ballistic. As n. pl s, the study of the flight of projectiles. * **Missile.** Any missile which does not rely upon aerodynamic surfaces to produce lift and consequently follows a ballistic trajectory when thrust is terminated. *See also* **Aerodynamic missile; Guided missile.** * **Missile Early Warning System (BMEWS).** The US radar and telecommunication system designed to detect missiles aimed by the USSR at the USA by the Arctic route. * **Trajectory.** The trajectory traced after the propulsive force is terminated and the body is acted upon only by gravity and aerodynamic drag. * **Wind.** That

constant wind which would have the same effect upon the trajectory of a bomb or projectile as the wind encountered in flight.

Bandolier. A belt to which a number of cartridge cases are attached and worn over the shoulder by some mounted regiments. Now purely ceremonial.

Bantam. An Anti-tank Guided Weapon System (ATGW) in use in Sweden and Switzerland.

Bar Mine. A tough plastic mine effective against armour.

Barometric tendency. The change in barometric pressure during the three hours before the observation.

Barracks. Permanent buildings erected to house troops.

Barrage. A curtain of heavy fire brought down to seal off an enemy position. **Creeping** *, one which moves forward in front of advancing infantry. * **Fire.** Fire which is designed to fill a volume of space or area rather than aimed specifically at a given target. *See also* **Fire.** * **Jamming.** Simultaneous electronic jamming over a broad band of frequencies. *See also* **Jamming.** * **Rocket.** A combined blast and fragmentation weapon designed for firing from ship to shore in amphibious attack.

Barrel. The tube along which the bullet or shell moves after the trigger mechanism has been operated.

Barricade. An obstacle to movement constructed from any material ready to hand. Usually used in street fighting.

Barrier. A co-ordinated series of obstacles designed or employed to canalize, direct, restrict, delay or stop the movement of an opposing force, and to impose additional losses in personnel, time and equipment on the opposing force. * **Minefield** (land mine warfare). A minefield laid to block enemy attack formations in selected areas, especially to the flanks, and to deflect his approach into selected battle areas. *See also* **Minefield** (land mine warfare).

Bar scale. *See* **Graphic Scale;** *also* **Scale.**

Base.
1. A locality from which operations are projected or supported.
2. An area or locality containing installations which provide logistic or other support. *See also* **Establishment.**
* Ammunition Depot (BAD). The unit in the Base Area which holds, issues and replenishes stocks of all ammunition required in the forward areas. *** Area.** The area, virtually free from guerrilla interference, that has a defensive perimeter, and from which offensive operations may be mounted and supported.
* Command. An area containing a base or group of such bases organized under one commander. *See also* **Command.**
* Development. The improvement or expansion of the resources and facilities of an area or a location to support military operations. *** Ejection shell.** A type of shell which ejects its load from its base. *** Fuse.** Fuse located in the base of a projectile or bomb. *See also* **Fuse.**
* Line.
1. (surveying) A surveyed line established with more than usual care, to which surveys are referred for co-ordination and correlation.
2. (photogrammetry) The line between the principal points of two consecutive vertical air photographs. It is usually measured on one photograph after the principal point of the other has been transferred.
3. The line established for offensive action by a force with no established interior lines of communication.
* Map. A map chart showing certain basic information, used as a base upon which additional data of specialized nature are compiled or overprinted. Also a map containing all the information from which maps showing specialized information can be prepared. *See also* **Chart base. *Map symbol.** A symbol used on a base map or chart as opposed to one used on an overprint to the base map or chart. *** Symbol.** *See* **Base map symbol.**
* Surge. A cloud which rolls out from the bottom of the column produced by a subsurface burst of a nuclear weapon. For underwater bursts the surge is, in effect, a cloud of liquid droplets which has the property of flowing almost as if it were homogeneous fluid. For subsurface land bursts the surge is made up of small solid particles but still behaves like fluid.

Basic cover (photogrammetry). Air coverage of any installation or area of a permanent nature with which later cover can be compared to discover any changes that have taken place.

Basic intelligence. General reference material for use in planning, concerning other countries, which pertains to capabilities, resources or potential theatres of operations. *See also* **Intelligence.**

Basic load (ammunition). That quantity of non-nuclear ammunition which is authorized and required by each nation to be on hand within a unit or formation at all times. It is expressed in rounds, units or units of weight as appropriate.

Basic undertakings. The essential things, expressed in broad terms, that must be done in order to implement the commander's concept successfully. These may include military, diplomatic, economic, psychological and other measures. *See also* **Strategic concept.**

Basket. The hand guard of a sword or claymore.

Bathymetric contour. *See* **Depth contour.**

Batman. Originally civilian hired servants in charge of baggage horses. Now used to denote an officer's soldier servant.

Baton. A truncheon conferred on Field Marshals as a symbol of authority.

Battalion. Normally denotes the basic infantry unit, commanded by a Lieutenant Colonel and consisting of approximately 700 to 900 all ranks. It contains three or four rifle companies and a company of light supporting weapons. There are variations in composition and level of command according to role both in UK and in other countries.

Battery. Tactical and administrative artillery unit or subunit corresponding to a company or similar unit in other branches of the Army. *** Display Unit (BDU).** An equipment located at the firing batteries which displays and provides hard copy print out of fire orders, etc. It works on existing artillery communication nets.

Battlefield illumination. The lighting of the zone of action of ground combat and combat support troops by artificial means other than invisible rays. *See also* **Artificial daylight; Artificial moonlight.**

Battlefield surveillance. The continuous (all weather, day and night) systematic watch over the battle area to provide timely information for combat intelligence. *See also* **Surveillance.**

Battle honour. A unit, regiment or battalion taking part in a major succesful action is awarded the name of that action as a battle honour, *eg* Waterloo, and is entitled to have it inscribed on its colours, or in the case of Rifle Regiments, who have no colours, on its accoutrements.

Battle position. A position sited tactically from which to engage the enemy with direct fire weapons.

Bayonet. The short thrusting sword affixed to the end of a rifle for use in close quarter combat. Rifle Regiments refer to them as swords.

Bazooka. A slang term for any anti-tank rocket launcher. *** plates.** Armour plate suspended at a distance from the sides of a tank hull or its turret.

Beach Armoured Recovery Vehicle (BARV). Mounted on a Centurion chassis, can recover drowned vehicles whilst operating in over 9 feet of water.

Beach capacity. An estimate, expressed in terms of measurement tons, or weight tons, of cargo that may be unloaded over a designated strip of shore per day. *See also* **Port capacity.**

Beach commander. Normally a Royal Marine Officer responsible to the naval assault group commander and who commands the beach organization during an amphibious operation.

Beach group. *See* **Shore party.**

Beachhead. A designated area on a hostile shore which, when seized and held, ensures the continous landing of troops, equipment and supplies, and provides manoeuvre space requisite for subsequent projected operations ashore. It is the physical objective of an amphibious operation. *See also* **Airhead; Bridgehead.**

Beachmaster. The naval or Royal Marine Officer responsible for controlling the beaching of craft and amphibians on one beach. He commands the naval beach unit.

Beach organization. A joint naval/army unit consisting of a naval beach unit and army beach troop which controls the landing and movement of men, vehicles and stores across one or more beaches in the early stages of an amphibious landing.

Beach reserves. In an amphibious operation, an accumulation of supplies of all classes established in dumps in beachhead areas.

Beach width. The horizontal dimensions of the beach measured at right angles to the shoreline from the line of extreme low water inland to the landward limit of the beach.

Beacon. *See* **Crash locater beacon; Fan marker beacon; Localizer; Meaconing; Radio beacon; 'Z' marker beacon.**

Beam rider. A missile guided by radar or radio beam.

Beam riding. In guided weapon systems a beam riding guidance element determines the flight path of the missile position in relation to the beam axis.

Beam width. The angle between the directions, on either side of the axis, at which the intensity of the emission power drops to one-half the value it has on the axis.

Bearing. The horizontal angle at a given point measured clockwise from a specific reference datum to a second point.

Bearskin. The ceremonial headdress of the Footguards.

B echelon. The vehicles and men of a unit not required at short notice in battle; *ie* those not included in F and A echelons.

Before-flight inspection. Pre-flight check to ensure general aircraft safety and that disposable loads, *eg* fuel and armament equipment, etc., are correctly adjusted for the particular operation or sortie. Also known as 'pre-flight inspection'.

Bent. The notch in the bolt which engages the sear in a small arm.

Berm. The level piece of earth between a parapet and the scarp of a trench.

Beyond economic repair (BER). An equipment so damaged that is must be scrapped.

Beyond local repair (BLR). An equipment so damaged that it cannot be repaired in the workshops to which it has been sent and must be re-assigned.

Bilateral infrastructure. Infrastructure which concerns only two NATO members and is financed by mutual agreement between them (*eg* facilities required for the use of forces of one NATO member in the territory of another). *See also* **Infrastructure.**

Billet. Temporary accommodation.

Bill of lading. A document signed by a shipping company or the Master of a ship which provides *prima facie* evidence of the receipt of the goods described therein and is also conclusive evidence of the order and condition of the goods at the time of loading. It is also a document of title to the goods and it contains, or is evidence of the existence of, a contract of Carriage or Affreightment.

Bi-margin format. The format of a map or chart on which the cartographic detail is extended to two edges of the sheet, normally North and East, thus leaving two margins only.

Binding. The fastening or securing of items to a movable platform called a pallet. *See also* **Palletized unit load.**

Bins. External boxes for carrying tools and loose equipment attached to the sides of AFVs.

Biographical intelligence. That component of intelligence which deals with individual foreign personalities of actual or potential importance.

Biological agent. A micro-organism which causes disease in man, plants or animals or causes the deterioration of *matériel*. *See also* **Chemical agent.**

Biological half-time. *See* **Half-life.**

Biological Operations. Employment of biological agents to produce casualties in man or animals and damage to plants and *matériels,* or defence against such

Biological Warfare. The use of germs to spread disease whether fired from a gun, dropped from an aircraft or transmitted in any other way to an enemy country or army. Outlawed by the Geneva Convention of 1925.

Biological weapon. An item which projects, disperses, or disseminates a biological agent including arthropod vectors.

Biscuit. A military mattress consisting of two squares of coir-filled canvas placed on top of a soldier's bed. Now replaced by a more conventional mattress.

Bivouac. n. A temporary encampment where tents are not supplied. v. To form such an encampment.

Blank. Of ammunition. A cartridge manufactured without a bullet so that it makes a noise on discharge but does not project a missile. However, the wadding which keeps the powder in place can cause injury up to a few yards range.

Blast. The brief and rapid movement of air vapour or fluid away from a centre of outward pressure, as in an explosion or in the combustion of rocket fuel; the pressure accompanying this movement. This term is commonly used for 'explosion', but the two terms may be distinguished. * **Wave.** A sharply defined wave of increased pressure rapidly propagated through a surrounding medium from a centre of detonation or similar disturbance. *See also* **Shock wave.**

Bleeding edge. That edge of a map or chart on which cartographic detail is extended to the edge of the sheet.

Blind. n. A projectile which fails to explode on impact. * **Bombing zone.** A restricted area (air, land, or sea) established for the purpose of permitting air operations, unrestricted by the operations or possible attack of friendly forces. * **Message.** R/T and W/T messages sent over air without first establishing contact with intended recipient.

Blip. The display of a received pulse on a cathode-ray tube.

Blister fitting. *See* **Semiflush fitting.**

Blitz (slang). Concentrate maximum effort on, *eg* weapon training. * **Krieg** (German) lightning war, a rapid advance where security is sacrificed for speed.

Blocked-in stowage. The stowage in a vessel of any goods in such a manner that they are completely surrounded by other cargo (or by the vessel's structure and other cargo) so as to be made completely inaccessible until they arrive at the intended destination.

Blocking and chocking. The use of wedges or chocks to prevent the inadvertent shifting of cargo in transit.

Block stowage. A system of stowing in a vessel whereby specified items are stowed together for any reason. * **Loading.** A method of loading whereby all cargo for a specific destination is stowed together. The purpose is to facilitate rapid off-loading at the destination, with the least possible disturbance of cargo intended for other points. *See also* **Loading.**

Block time. The period from the moment the chocks are withdrawn and brakes released, or moorings dropped, to the return to rest or take-up of moorings after the flight.

Block timing. The fixed timings between which a road or portion of a road is allotted to a particular serial formation or unit. *See also* **Block time.**

Bloodhound. A British surface to air land-based guided weapon system.

Blowback.
1. Escape, to the rear and under pressure, of gases formed during the firing of a weapon. Blowback may be caused by a defective breech mechanism, a ruptured cartridge case or a faulty primer.
2. Type of weapon operation in which the force of expanding gases acting to the rear against the face of the bolt furnishes all the energy required to initiate the complete cycle of operation.

A weapon which employs this method of operation is characterized by the absence of any breech-lock or bolt-lock mechanism.

Blowpipe. A one-man, supersonic Surface to Air Guided Weapon system (SAGW) in use with the British Army.

Blue forces. Denotes those forces used in a friendly role during exercises.

Blue key. A blue image on any medium which is not reproduced when the superimposed work is reproduced, used as a guide for scribing or drawing.

Boat lanes. Lanes for amphibious assault landing craft, which extend seaward from the landing beaches to the line of departure. The width of the boat lanes is determined by the length of the corresponding beach.

Boattail. The conical section of a ballistic body that progressively decreases in diameter toward the tail to reduce overall aerodynamic drag.

Boatwave. *See* **Wave.**

Body.
1. In small arms the part of the weapon between the barrel and the butt.
2. Of a map or chart. That area of a map or chart contained within the neatline.

Bogie. A wheel forming part of a tank's suspension. Usually one of several within an assembly.

Bolt. The part of a small arm which holds the round in the chamber. After firing it moves to the rear, usually now automatically, and then returns to the forward position pressing a new round into the chamber during its forward movement.

Bomb. An explosive device, similar to a shell or grenade fired from a mortar or dropped from an aircraft.

Bombardier (bdr.). A rank in the Royal Artillery equivalent to Corporal in other arms.

Bombing angle. The angle between the vertical and a line joining the aircraft to what would be the point of impact of a bomb released from it at that instant.

Bomb report (BOMBREP). Similar to a Shelling report (*qv*) but with reference to hostile bombing.

Bombline. *See* **Fire support co-ordination line.**

Bonded storage. A type of storage where goods subject to clearance by Customs and Excise are held.

Booby trap (mine warfare). An explosive charge which is exploded when an unsuspecting person disturbs an apparently harmless object or performs a presumably safe act.

Booster.
1. A high explosive element sufficiently sensitive as to be actuated by small explosive elements in a fuse or primer and powerful enough to cause detonation of the main explosive filling.
2. An auxiliary or initial propulsion system which travels with a missile or aircraft and which may or may not separate from the parent craft when its impulse has been delivered. A booster system may contain, or consist of, one or more units.

Border. In cartography, the area of a map or chart lying between the neatline and the surrounding framework. * **Mark.** A cartographic technique used when it is required to extend a portion of the cartographic detail of a map or chart beyond the sheetlines into the margin.

Border crosser. An individual, living close to a frontier, who normally has to cross the frontier frequently for legitimate purposes.

Bore-safe fuse. Type of fuse having an interrupter in the explosive train that prevents a projectile from exploding until after it has cleared the muzzle of a weapon. *See also* **Fuse.**

Borescope. A slim optical instrument for viewing the insides of gun barrels, pipes and similar hollow equipment.

Bound.
1. Single movement, usually from cover to cover, made by troops often under artillery fire or small-arms fire.
2. A tactical feature which can be held if necessary.

Boundary.
1. The limits of an area within which a formation or unit may operate without reference to higher authority *eg* divisional boundary would be natural features separating the areas of operation of two contiguous divisions and invariably given as inclusive to one of them.

2. * (*de facto*). An international or administrative boundary whose existence and legality is not recognized but which is a practical division between separate national and provincial administering authorities.
3. * (*de jure*). An international or administrative boundary whose existence and legality is recognized.
4. * **Disclaimer.** A statement on a map or chart that the status and/or alignment of international or administrative boundaries are not necessarily recognized by the government of the publishing nation.

Box magazine. The rectangular metal container which holds rounds before the activation of the bolt of a small arm.

Bracketing. A method of adjusting artillery fire in which a bracket is established by obtaining an over and a short along the spotting line, and then successively splitting the bracket in half until a target hit or desired bracket is obtained.

Breaching. The employment of any available means to secure a passage through an enemy minefield or fortification. *See also* **Deliberate breaching** (land mine warfare); **Hasty breaching** (land mine warfare).

Breakaway. The onset of a condition in which the shock front moves away from the exterior of the expanding fireball produced by the explosion of a nuclear weapon.

Break-up. In detection, the separation of one solid return into a number of individual returns which correspond to the various objects or structure groupings. This separation is contingent upon a number of factors including range, beam width, gain setting, object size and distance between objects.

Breech. The part of a weapon behind the barrel into which the shell or cartridge is inserted. **Breech loading weapon,** as opposed to muzzle loading where the projectile is inserted from the end of the barrel.

Bren. A light machine-gun now obsolete in UK but still in use in some armies abroad.

Brevet. As a reward for distinguished service an officer may be awarded brevet rank above that for which he is paid. This confers seniority in the Army but not within his regiment.

Brevity code. A code which provides no security but which has as its sole purpose the shortening of messages rather than the concealment of their content.

Bridge broken. The bridge is temporarily closed to allow river traffic to use the waterway.

Bridge closed. The bridge is not in a condition to be used by road traffic. (This definition should never be qualified, *eg* a bridge should never be described as 'Bridge closed to all traffic above class 30'.)

Bridgehead. An area of ground held or to be gained on the enemy's side of an obstacle. *See also* **Airhead; Beachhead.** * **Line.** The limit of the objective area in the development of the bridgehead. *See also* **Objective area.**

Bridge open. The bridge is in a condition to be used by any road traffic. (This definition may need to be qualified in some cases in order to restrict the use of the bridge to the particular type of traffic, *eg* 'Bridge open to class 30 traffic'.)

Briefing. The act of giving in advance specific instructions or information.

Brigade. A tactical formation comprising three or more battalions/ armoured regiments with ancillary arms. * **Administrative Area (BAA).** An administrative area may be formed if a brigade is operating away from its parent division. It then functions in the same way as a DAA (*qv*). * **Major.** The senior staff officer in a Brigade.

Brigadier. The rank of an officer between those of Colonel and Major General. He may command a brigade or be employed on the Staff.

Brinell. An index of metal hardness.

Bring on charge. Enter an item as a receipt on an accounting record.

British Army Review, The (BAR). A periodical devoted to defence matters mostly from an army viewpoint issued by the Training Directorate of the British Ministry of Defence. The House Journal of the British Army.

Broadcast control. *See* **Broadcast controlled air interception.**

Broadcast-controlled air interception. An interception in which the interceptor is given a continuous broadcast of information concerning an enemy raid and effects interception without further control. *See also* **Air interception; Close-controlled air interception.**

Broken-back War. The situation when control/direction of a country's war effort has been destroyed and resistance is continued by isolated groups operating as guerrillas.

Broken stowage. Space wasted in a vessel by goods of irregular shape, or by the irregularity of cargo spaces in relation to the goods stowed. The term is applied to space wasted by special lashing, shoring or dunnage, or by the need to give ready access during the voyage to any particular piece of cargo.

Browning.
1. The name of the American arms designer after whom a number of his products were called. The British Cavalry used the Browning machine-gun instead of the infantry Bren.
2. A rust prevention process applied to the metal work of rifles.

Brushfire operations. Improvised conflict on a small scale.

Buffer. A spring at the end of the body of a weapon which absorbs surplus energy from the discharge.

Buffer distance (nuclear).
1. The horizontal distance which, when added to the radius of safety will give the desired assurance that the specified degree of risk will not be exceeded. The buffer distance is normally expressed quantitatively in multiples of the delivery error.
2. The vertical distance which is added to the fallout safe-height of burst in order to determine a desired height of burst which will provide the desired assurance that fallout will not occur. It is normally expressed quantitatively in multiples of the vertical error.

Bugler. A private soldier in the bugle band of light infantry and rifle regiments.

Build-up. The process of attaining prescribed strength of units and prescribed levels of vehicles, equipment, stores and supplies. Also may be applied to the means of accomplishing this process. * **Control** (amphibious). The organization set up in the area of the landing, immediately after an amphibious assault to control the build-up of personnel, vehicles and stores.

Bulk breaking point (BBP). The area where supplies are converted from commodity to unit loads. * **petroleum products.** Liquid petroleum products which are normally transported by pipeline, rail tank car, road tank truck, road tank trailer, barge, harbour or coastal tanker and ocean-going tanker and stored in a tank or container having a full capacity greater than 45 Imperial gallons (55 United States gallons).

Burial. *See* **Emergency burial; Group burial; Trench burial.**

Burnout. The point in time or in the missile trajectory when combustion of fuels in the rocket engine is terminated by other than programmed cut-off. * **velocity.** The velocity attained by a missile at the point of burnout.

Busby. The ceremonial headdress of Hussar Regiments and the Royal Artillery.

Bushmaster. A powered-axle trailer primarily for use with a Landrover.

Bussing. A German wheeled armoured car.

Butt.
1. On a small arm the end piece behind the body which rests against the firer's shoulder.
2. The part of a firing range where the targets are exposed.

Button on. Armament or equipment which is fitted to a vehicle after it has been issued to troops is said to be buttoned on, *eg* machine-guns fitted to helicopters.

Cabin. In an aircraft, all compartments used for the carriage of passengers or cargo.

Cable drag drop. Ultra low level airdrop technique using the drag of an arrester cable ground installation to extract and halt airdrop loads.

Cactus. A Surface to Air Guided Weapon System (SAGW) in use in France, South Africa and Lebanon.

Cadre. A small body of troops assembled for instructional purposes. Reduced to cadre denotes a unit reduced to a small number of key personnel.

Calibrated airspeed. Indicated airspeed corrected for instrument and installation errors. Also known as 'rectified airspeed'. *See also* **Airspeed.**

Calibrated altitude. Indicated altitude corrected for instrument and installation errors.

Calibrated focal length. An adjusted value of the equivalent focal length, so computed as to equalize the positive and negative values of distortion over the entire field used in a camera. *See also* **Focal length.**

Calibre. Internal diameter of a gun barrel.

Call for fire. A request for fire containing data necessary for obtaining the required fire on a target.

Call mission. A type of air support mission which is not requested sufficiently in advance of the desired time of execution to permit detailed planning and briefing of pilots prior to take-off. Aircraft scheduled for this type of mission are on air, ground or carrier alert, and are armed with a prescribed load.

Call sign. Any combination of characters or pronounceable words, which identifies a communication facility, a command, an authority, an activity, or an unit; used primarily for establishing and maintaining communications. *See also* **Collective call sign; Indefinite call sign; International call sign; Net call sign; Tactical call sign; Visual call sign; Voice call sign.**

Camberley. A small town in Surrey where the Army Staff College is situated. To go to Camberley denotes that an officer is posted to the student or instructor staff of the college. *See also under* **Staff.**

Camera axis. An imaginary line through the optical centre of the lens perpendicular to the negative photo plane. * **Direction.** Direction on the horizontal plane of the optical axis of the camera at the time of exposure. This direction is defined by its azimuth expressed in degrees in relation to True/Magnetic North.

Camera calibration. The determination of the calibrated focal length, the location of the principal point with respect to the fiducial marks and the lens distortion effective in the focal plane of the camera referred to the particular calibrated focal length.

Camera magazine. A removable part of a camera in which the unexposed and exposed portions of film are contained.

Camera nadir. *See* **Photo nadir.**

Camera station (photogrammetry). *See* **Air base** (photogrammetry); **Air station** (photogrammetry).

Camera window. A window in the camera compartment through which photographs are taken.

Camouflage. The use of concealment and disguise to minimize the possibility of detection and/or identification.*See also* **Concealment; Cover.** * **Net.** A flexible covering of open mesh which can be placed over or around a vehicle, weapon or other equipment to conceal

its presence. It is frequently adorned with colour patches (*qv*) to make it blend with its surroundings.

Camouflet. The resulting cavity in a deep underground burst when there is no rupture of the surface.

Campaign plan. A plan for a series of related military operations aimed to accomplish a common objective, normally within a given time and space.

Cannibalize. To remove serviceable parts from one item of equipment in order to install them on another item of equipment.

Cap. In a cartridge the case holding the detonating charge which ignites the propellant.

Captain. In the army the rank between Lieutenant and Major.

Captive firing. A firing test of short duration, conducted with the missile propulsion system operating while secured to a test stand.

Cardinal point effect. The increased intensity of a line or group of returns on the radarscope occurring when the radar beam is perpendicular to the rectangular surface of a line or group of similarly aligned features in the ground pattern.

Cardinal points. The directions: NORTH, SOUTH, EAST and WEST.

Career officer. (US) Equivalent to regular officer.

Cargo. *See* **Dangerous *; Essential *; Immediately vital *; Non-vital *; Valuable *. * Sling.** A strap, chain, or other material used to hold securely cargo items which are to be hoisted, lowered, or suspended.

Carl Gustav. A recoilless anti-tank weapon developed in Sweden. In use in the British Army.

Carpet bombing. The progressive distribution of a mass bomb load upon an area defined by designated boundaries, in such manner as to inflict damage to all portions thereof.

Carriage. *See* **Gun carriage.**

Carrier borne ground liaison officer (CBGLO). A specially trained Army or Royal Marine officer attached to an aircraft carrier who is responsible for army/naval air liaison. * **Section** (CBGLsect.). A variable number of Army or Royal Marine officers and other ranks together with a vehicle and trailer embarked in aircraft carriers to assist with army/naval air liaison.

Cashier (an officer). v. To dismiss him from the Service by sentence of a General Court Martial. An officer so punished cannot be re-employed in the armed forces.

Cassette. In photography, a reloadable container for either unexposed or exposed sensitized materials which may be removed from the camera or dark-room equipment under lightened conditions.

Casualty. Denotes any change in the status of a soldier *eg* posted from his unit. Battle casualty denotes killed, wounded or POW. * **Clearing station** (CCS). A medical unit designed to hold 200 and upwards battle casualties and provide early essential surgery; there are normally three in each Corps area. It receives battle casualties from Advanced Dressing Stations and evacuates them to General Hospitals. Not itself mobile it can form a number of Field Dressing Stations (FDS) (*qv*) which are mobile. * **Collecting post** (CCP). A forward point where casualties enter the medical evacuation organization. * **Staging unit.** *See* **Aeromedical staging unit.**

Catalogue. An authorized list of items of *matériel* identified by names and/or numbers and arranged in a systematic order for ease of reference.

Catapult. A structure which provides an auxiliary source of thrust to a missile or aircraft; must combine the functions of directing and accelerating the missile during its travel on the catapult; serves the same functions for a missile as does a gun tube for a shell.

Caution area. *See* **Danger area.**

Cavalry. The arm of the Service originally mounted on horses, but now converted to armour and forming part of the Royal Armoured Corps. Only the Household Cavalry maintain a mounted element.

Cease fire. The order to suspend hostilities.

Celestial equator. The great circle formed by the intersection of the place of the earth's equator with the celestial sphere.

Celestial horizon. The great circle on the celestial sphere whose plane passes through the centre of the earth and is parallel to the sensible horizon.

Celestial poles. The points where the earth's axis, if produced, would intersect the celestial sphere.

Celestial sphere. An imaginary sphere of infinite radius concentric with the earth, on which all celestial bodies except the earth are imagined to be projected.

Central analysis team. A team composed of representatives from two or more senior NATO Commanders, responsible jointly to their superiors for the detailed analysis and reporting of a large scale NATO exercise.

Central Army Group (CENTAG). The more southerly of the two commands comprising AFCENT (*qv*). Consists of German and American forces.

Central Planning Team. A team composed of representatives of two or more senior

NATO Commanders, responsible jointly to their superiors for the production of the General Instructions for an exercise in accordance with the agreed concept. Regional planning groups may be set up prior to the formulation of the Central planning team in order to provide the Team with information about certain phases of the exercise.

Central Treaty Organization (CENTO). A defence pact signed in 1955 by UK, Iraq, Pakistan, Persia and Turkey from which Iraq and Pakistan have now withdrawn. It is the Near East's equivalent to NATO but is not so highly organized.

Centralized control. In air defence, the control mode whereby a higher echelon makes direct target assignments to fire units. *See also* **Decentralized control.**

Centre of burst. *See* **Mean point of impact.**

Centre of gravity limits. The limits within which an aircraft's centre of gravity must lie to ensure safe flight. The centre of gravity of the loading aircraft must be within these limits at take-off, in the air, and on landing. In some cases, take-off and landing limits may also be specified.

Centurion. A British battle tank being replaced by Chieftain.

Certificate of design. The document signed by the Design Authority to certify that the *matériel* to which it relates complies with the requirements of the approved specification, except as otherwise stated.

Chaff. Radar confusion reflectors, which consist of thin, narrow metallic strips of various lengths and frequency responses, used to reflect echoes for confusion purposes. *See also* **Rope; Window.**

Chain of command. The succession of commanding officers from a superior to

a subordinate through which command is exercised. Also called 'command channel'. *See also* **Administrative chain of command; Operational chain of command.**

Chalk commander (air). The commander of all troops airtransported under one chalk number (*qv*).

Chalk number. The number given to a complete load and to the air transport carrier.

Chalk troops. The aircraft load of troops defined by a particular chalk number. *See also* **Chalk commander; chalk number.**

Challenge. Any process carried out by one unit or person with the object of ascertaining the friendly or hostile character or identity of another. *See also* **Countersign; Password; Reply.**

Chamber. In a small arm the rear part of the barrel which holds the cartridge before it is fired.

Change lever. In a small arm the lever which controls the type of fire; *eg* single shot or bursts.

Change of operational control. The date and time (Greenwich Mean Time/Greenwich Civil Time) at which the responsibility for operational control of a force or unit passes from one operational control authority to another.

Chaparral. A US surface-to-air mobile guided missile system.

Chaplain to the Forces (CF). A minister of religion serving in or attached to the Royal Army Chaplains Department. (Senior Chaplain to the Forces (SCF).)

Char. (slang from Urdu). A cup of tea.

Charge.
1. The powder which, on ignition, propels the bullet or shell.
2. The act of closing with the enemy.
3. The specification of a crime.

Charged demolition target. A target on which all charges have been placed and which is in one of the states of readiness *ie* safe or armed.

Charging point. A connection on an aircraft, or aircraft component, through which the aircraft or aircraft component can be replenished with a specific commodity, *eg* oxygen, air or hydraulic fluid, etc.

Charlie (US slang). A member of the Viet Cong.

Chart base. A chart used as a primary source for compilation or as a framework on which new detail is printed. Also known as 'topographic base'. *See also* **Base map.**

Chart index. *See* **Map index.**

Chart series. *See* **Map; map series.**

Chart sheet. *See* **Map; map sheet.**

Checkout. A sequence of functional, operational, and calibrational tests to determine the condition and status of a weapon system or element thereof.

Check point.
1. A predetermined point on the surface of the earth used as a means of controlling movement, a registration target for fire adjustment, or a reference for location.
2. Centre of impact; a burst centre.
3. Geographical location on land or water above which the position of an aircraft in flight may be determined by observation or by electrical means.
4. A place where military police check vehicular or pedestrian traffic in order to enforce control measures and other laws, orders and regulations, *eg* Checkpoint 'Charlie' on the road to Berlin.

Chemical agent. A chemical compound which, when suitably disseminated, produces incapacitating lethal or damaging effects on man, animals, plants or materials. *See also* **Biological agent.**

Chemical ammunition. A type of ammunition, the filler of which is primarily a chemical agent.

Chemical, biological and radiological operations. A collective term used only when referring to combined chemical, biological and radiological operations.

Chemical defence. The methods, plans and procedures involved in establishing and executing defensive measures against attack by chemical agents.

Chemical mine. A mine containing a chemical agent designed to kill or disable personnel or to contaminate *matériel* or terrain.

Chemical operations. Employment of chemical agents (excluding riot agents) to:
1. kill, or incapacitate for a significant period of time, man or animals.
2. deny or hinder the use of space, facilities, or *matériel*.

Chemical warfare. *See* **Chemical operations.**

Chevron. The distinguishing mark on the sleeves of non-commissioned officers.

Cheyenne. A US combat helicopter with integral, as opposed to button on (*qv*), armament.

Chieftain. The main British battle tank since 1965.

Chief of Staff. The senior staff officer of a formation who co-ordinates the Commander's plan with the branches and services.

Choke point. (US). An artificially created bottleneck where essential supplies such as food and fuel can be controlled by government and denied to insurgents.

Chop. *See* **Change of operational control.**

Chopper. Slang for helicopter (*qv*).

Chronic dose. Radiation dose absorbed in circumstances such that biological recovery may have been possible. It is arbitrarily accepted that a chronic dose can only mean absorption occurring after 24 hours following the burst.

Chuffing. The characteristic of some rockets to burn intermittently and with an irregular noise.

Circular error probable. An indicator of the accuracy of a missile/projectile, used as a factor in determining probable damage to a target. It is the radius of a circle within which half of the missiles/projectiles are expected to fall. *See also* **Delivery error; Deviation; Dispersion error; Horizontal error.**

Civil affairs. Questions relating to relations in wartime between the commander of an armed force and the civilian populations and governments in areas where the force is employed, and which are settled on the basis of a mutual agreement, official or otherwise.

Civil defence. Mobilization, organization, and direction of the civil population, designed to minimize by passive measures the effects of enemy action against all aspects of civil life.

Civil disturbance. Group acts of violence and disorder prejudicial to public law and order.

Civilian preparedness for war. All measures and means taken in peace-time, by national and allied agencies, to enable a nation to survive an enemy attack and to contribute more effectively to the common war effort.

Civil military operation. All actions and measures undertaken between NATO commanders and national authorities, military or civil, in peace or war, which concern the relationship between allied armed forces and the government, civil population, or agencies in the areas where such armed forces are stationed, supported or employed.

Civil military relations (in non-NATO countries). All activities undertaken by NATO commanders in war directly concerned with the relationship between allied armed forces and the government, civil population, or agencies of non-NATO countries where such armed forces are stationed, supported or employed.

Civil twilight. *See* **Twilight.**

Clandestine operations. Activities to accomplish intelligence, counter-intelligence, subversion and other similar activities sponsored or conducted in such a way as to assure secrecy or concealment.

Clansman. An integrated system of radio equipment designed for operation in combat zones anywhere in the world.

Classification of bridges and vehicles. Standard procedure for the parallel classification of bridges (or rafts, including their landing stages) and vehicles based on a range of vehicle types. The classification is applied by the allocation of class numbers to be marked on each vehicle and each bridge or raft.

Classified item. An item of equipment, which has been accorded a security classification of 'Restricted' or above.

Classified matter. Official information or matter in any form or of any nature which requires protection in the interests of national security. *See also* **Unclassified matter.**

Claymore.
1. A type of sword carried by officers in Scottish Regiments.
2. A type of mine.

Cleansing station. *See* **Decontamination station.**

Clean. In bomb disposal/counter insurgency operations an area is said to be clean when it has been searched by the bomb disposal organisation and pronounced free from explosive devices. * **Weapon.** A nuclear weapon in which measures have been taken to reduce the amount of residual radio-activity relative to a 'normal' weapon of the same energy yield.

Cleared route. A route from which the enemy must be cleared by the unit or formation responsible.

Clearway. In air traffic control, a defined rectangular area at the end of a strip or channel in the direction of take-off selected or prepared as a suitable area over which an aircraft may make its initial climb to a specified height.

Clerk of the Cheque. *See* Queen's Bodyguard of the Yeoman of the Guard and Gentlemen-at-Arms.

Clerk of the Cheque. *See* Queen's Bodyguard of the Yeoman of the Guard.

Climb. In a flight control system, a control mode in which aircraft climb is automatically controlled to a pre-determined programme. * **Corridor.** *See* **Clearway.**

Close air support. Air action against hostile targets which are in close proximity to friendly forces and which require detailed integration of each air mission with the fire and movement of those forces. *See also* **Air support.**

Close control. *See* Close controlled air interception.

Close controlled air interception. An interception in which the interceptor is continuously controlled to a position from which the target is within visual range or radar contact. *See also* **Air interception; Broadcast-controlled air interception.**

Closed area. A designated area in or over which passage of any kind is prohibited.

Close reconnaissance. Reconnaissance initiated by a battle group or a brigade commander on specific tasks within his area of influence.

Close support. The action of the supporting force against targets or objectives which are sufficiently near the supported force to require detailed integration or co-ordination of the supporting action with the fire, movement or other actions of the supported force. *See also* * **Supporting fire.**

Close supporting fire. Fire placed on enemy troops, weapons, or positions which, because of their proximity present the most immediate and serious threat to the supported unit. *See also* **Support.**

Cloud amount. *Also* Cloud cover. * **Cover.** The proportion of sky obscured by cloud, expressed as a fraction of sky covered.

Cluster.

1. Fireworks signal in which a group of stars burns at the same time.

2. Group of bombs released together. A cluster usually consists of fragmentation or incendiary bombs.

3. Component of a pattern-laid mine-field. It may be anti-tank, anti-personnel or mixed. It consists of one to five mines and no more than one anti-tank mine.

4. Two or more engines coupled together so as to function as one power unit.

5. Two or more parachutes for dropping light or heavy loads.

Clutter. *See* Radar clutter.

Coastal refraction. The change of the

direction of travel of a radio ground wave as it passes from land to sea or from sea to land. Also known as 'land effect' and 'shore line effect'.

Cobra 2000.
1. An Anti-tank Guided Weapon System (ATGW) in use in Germany, Italy, Denmark, Pakistan and Turkey.
2. *See* **Huey Cobra.**

Cock. A weapon is said to be cocked when it is ready to fire.

Cocking handle. The part of the bolt which the firer pulls to the rear to prepare a small arm for firing.

Cocooning. The spraying or coating of an aircraft or equipment with a substance, *eg* a plastic to form a cocoon-like seal against the effects of the atmosphere.

Code word. A word which conveys a meaning other than its conventional one, prearranged by the correspondents. Its aim is to increase security.

Collate. The grouping together of related items to provide a record of events and facilitate further processing.

Collection. *See* **Intelligence cycle.**
* **Agency.** Any individual or specialized organization used in collecting and/or processing intelligence information.

Collective call sign. Any call sign which represents two or more facilities, commands, authorities or units. The collective call sign for any of these includes the commander thereof and all subordinate commanders therein. *See also* **Call sign.**

Collective training. Exercises involving the use of more than one arm of the Service designed to practise co-operation within the formation.

Collimating marks. Index marks, rigidly connected with the camera body,

which form images on the negative. These images are used to determine the position of the optical centre or principal point of the imagery. Also known as 'fiducial marks'.

Collision course interception. Any course whereby the interception is accomplished by the constant heading of both aircraft.

Colonel. The rank between Lieutenant Colonel and Brigadier.

Colour patches. Pieces of material of varying shades, sizes and colours which are added to camouflage nets (*qv*) to blend with the surrounding terrain.

Colours. The standard, flag or guidon of a unit which symbolizes loyalty to the Sovereign (Queen's Colour) and the Regiment (Regimental Colour) and is saluted at all times when uncased, *ie* displayed on parade.

Colour separation. Separation of the colours of a map or chart by photographic or drafting processes for subsequent reproduction.

Column cover. Cover of a column by aircraft in radio contact therewith, providing for its protection by reconnaissance and/or attack of air or ground targets which threaten the column.

Column formation. A formation in which elements are placed one behind the other.

Column gap. The space between two consecutive elements proceeding in the same direction on the same route. It can be calculated in units of length or in units of time measured from the rear of one element to the front of the following element.

Combat air patrol. An aircraft patrol provided over an objective area, over the force protected, over the critical area of a combat zone, or over an air defence area, for the purpose of intercepting and destroying hostile aircraft before they reach their target. *See also* **Patrol.**

Combat control team. A team of specially trained air force personnel who can air-drop into forward areas, to advise on all aspects of landing area requirements, and to provide local air control.

Combat effectiveness. Used to assess an army unit or formation in terms of its training, both individual and collective, strength and equipment.

Combat film. A film exposed to record combat.

Combat information centre. The agency in a ship or aircraft manned and equipped to collect, display, evaluate, and disseminate tactical information for the use of the embarked flag officer, commanding officer, and certain control agencies. Certain control, assistance and co-ordinated functions may be delegated by command to the combat information centre. *See also* **Air defence control centre.**

Combat intelligence. That knowledge of the enemy, weather, and geographical features required by a commander in the planning and conduct of tactical operations. *See also* **Intelligence.**

Combat load. The total war-like stores carried by an aircraft.

Combat loading. The arrangement of personnel and the stowage of equipment and supplies in a manner designed to conform to the anticipated tactical operation of the organization embarked. Each individual item is stowed so that it can be unloaded at the required time. *See also* **Loading.**

Combat patrol. Tactical unit sent out from the main body to engage in independent fighting; detachment assigned to protect the front, flank or rear of the main body, by fighting if necessary. *See also* **Airborne alert;**
Combat air patrol; Patrol; Reconnaissance patrol (ground).

Combat readiness. An army unit or formation to be in state of combat readiness must:
1. be at such a manpower strength and scale of transport and equipment that it can fight immediately without delay imposed by mobilization;
2. be within 15% of its authorized strength;
3. be independent of the call up of reservists;
4. be able to fight when required within a laid down maximum period.

Combat ready-readiness.
1. Applied to organizations or equipment, means availability for combat operations.
2. Applied to personnel, means qualified to carry out combat operations in the unit to which they are assigned.

Combat supplies (C Sups). Articles supplied by the RAOC which are required daily to enable troops to fight *ie* ammunition, explosives, rations and POL. *See also* **Stores.**

Combat Supplies Platoon. A unit of the RAOC which supplies the daily wants of combat units.

Combat survival. Those measures to be taken by service personnel when involuntarily separated from friendly forces in combat, including procedures relating to individual survival, evasion, escape, and conduct after capture.

Combat troops. Those army units or organizations whose primary mission is destruction of enemy forces and installations. Also called 'Teeth arms'.

Combat zone.
1. That area required by combat forces for the conduct of operations.
2. The territory forward of the Army rear area boundary. *See also* **Communications zone.**

Combined. Between two or more forces or agencies of two or more allies. When all allies or services are not involved, the participating nations and services shall be identified. *See also* **Joint. * Common user items.** Items of an interchangeable nature which are in common use by two or more nations. *** Force.** A military force composed of elements of two or more allied nations. *See also* **Forces. * Operation.** An operation conducted by forces of two or more allied nations acting together for the accomplishment of a single mission. *** Staff.** A staff composed of personnel of two or more allied nations. *See also* **Integrated staff; Joint staff; Parallel staff.**

Combuster. A name generally assigned to the combination of flame holder or stabilizer, ignitor, combustion chamber and injection system of a ramjet or gas turbine.

Command.
1. The authority vested in an individual of the armed forces for the direction, co-ordination and control of military forces.
2. An order given by a commander; that is, the will of the commander expressed for the purpose of bringing about a particular action.
3. A unit, or units, an organization, or an area under the command of one individual.
4. To dominate by a field of weapon fire or by observation from a superior position. *** Axis.** A line along which a headquarters will move. *** Channel.** *See* **Chain of command. * Destruct signal.** A signal used to operate intentionally the destruction signal in a missile. *** Guidance.** A guidance system wherein intelligence transmitted to the missile from an outside force causes the missile to traverse a directed flight path. Correction signals may be sent by radar, radio, infra-red or laser means or by wire. *** Net.** A communications network which connects an echelon of command with some or all of its subordinate echelons for the purpose of command control. *** Off the Line of Sight** (COLOS). Denotes a missile flying above and parallel to the sight line. A complex equipment used in NIKE/HERCULES (*qv*). *** Post** (CP). A unit or subunit's headquarters where the commander and the staff perform their activities. In combat, a unit or subunit's headquarters is often

divided into echelons; the echelon in which the unit or subunit commander is located or from which he operates is called a command post. *** Post Exercise** (CPX). An exercise involving the commander, his staff, and communications within and between headquarters. *** to Line of Sight** (CLOS). A term used in Guided Weapon Systems to include ACLOS (*qv*), MCLOS (*qv*) and SACLOS (*qv*). *** Vehicle.** A vehicle primarily designed as one from which a Commander can control his forces. *See also* **Area *; Base *; Full *; Functional *; National *; Operational *; Territorial *.**

Commandant. The title given to the Commander of a military school or establishment *eg* Commandant of the Staff College.

Commander (s). *See* **Executing *** (nuclear weapons); **Exercise *; Major NATO * National Force *; National territorial *; Releasing *** (nuclear weapons).

Commander's concept. *See* **Concept of operations.**

Commanding Officer (CO). Normally confined to the Commander of a regiment or battalion but can be used to designate the commander of a smaller independent unit.

Commando. A Royal Marine unit of battalion strength trained for offensive operations.

Commer. A heavy duty load carrying vehicle.

Commercial loading. *See* **Administrative loading.**

Commission. The warrant signed by or on behalf of the Sovereign authorizing a man or woman to exercise command in the Army.

Commodity loading. A method of loading in which various types of cargoes are loaded together, such as ammunition, rations, or boxed vehicles, in order that each commodity can be discharged without disturbing the others. *See also* **Loading.**

Common control (artillery). Horizontal and vertical map or chart location of points in the target area and position area, tied in with the horizontal and vertical control in use by two or more units. May be established by firing, survey, or combination of both, or by assumption. *See also* **Control point; Field control; Ground control.**

Common infrastructure. Infrastructure essential to the training of NATO forces or to the implementation of NATO operational plans which, owing to its degree of common use or interest and its compliance with criteria laid down from time to time by the North Atlantic Council is commonly financed by NATO members. *See* **Infrastructure.**

Common item. An item of *matériel* applicable to two or more types of equipment.

Common user item. An item of *matériel* in use by more than one Service.

Communication centre (COMMCEN). An agency charged with the responsibility for receipt, transmission, and delivery of messages.

Communication zone. Rear part of theatre of operations (behind but contiguous to the combat zone) which contains the lines of communications, establishments for supply and evacuation, and other agencies required for the immediate support and maintenance of the field forces. *See also* **Combat zone.**

Communications intelligence (COMINT). Information or intelligence about enemy or potential enemy communication systems.

Communications satellite. An orbiting vehicle, which relays signals between communications stations. They are of two types:

1. Active Communications Satellite. — A satellite which receives, regenerates, and retransmits signals between stations.
2. Passive Communications Satellite. — A satellite which reflects communications signals between stations.

Company. An infantry unit of about 100 men organized into three or more platoons normally commanded by a major; the equivalent of a squadron or battery in cavalry and artillery.

Comparative cover. Photographic coverage of the same area or object taken at different times, to show any changes in details. *See also* **Cover.**

Compartment marking. In an aircraft, a system of marking a cabin into compartments for the positioning of loads in accordance with the weight and balance requirements.

Compass. *See* **Deviation; Grid magnetic angle; Magnetic *; Magnetic north; Magnetic variation. * Direction.** The horizontal direction expressed as an angular distance measured clockwise from compass north. *** North.** The uncorrected direction indicated by the north seeking end of a compass needle. *** Rose.** A graduated circle, usually marked in degrees, indicating directions and printed or inscribed on an appropriate medium.

Compatability. Capability of two or more items or components of equipment to exist or function in the same system or environment without mutual interference. *See also* **Interchangeability.**

Compilation. Selection, assembly, and graphic presentation of all relevant information required for the preparation of a map or chart. Such information may be derived from other maps or charts or from other sources. *** Diagram.** A diagram giving details of the source material from which the map or chart has been compiled; this does not necessarily include reliability information. *See also* **Reliability diagram.**

Compliment. The military mark of respect shown to all persons in authority. It includes individual saluting, turning out a guard, presenting arms, etc.

Complete round. A basic munition, such as a shell, when all the components, explosive and non-explosive, necessary for it to function, are included.

Compo. Short for composite ration. A ration made up of a number of elements all having nutritive value which has largely superseded the bully beef and biscuits of a previous generation.

Component life. A period of acceptable usage after which the likelihood of failure sharply increases and before which the components are removed in the interests of reliability of operation.

Compromised. A term applied to classified matter, knowledge of which has, in whole or in part, passed to an unauthorized person or persons, or which has been subject to the risk of such passing.

Computed air release point. A computed air position where the first paratroop or cargo item is released to land on a specified impact point.

Conbat. An infantry heavy anti-armour weapon of 120 mm calibre.

Concealment. The protection from observation only. *See also* **Cover; Camouflage.**

Concentrated fire. Fire from a number of weapons directed at a single point or small area. *See also* **Fire.**

Concentration area.
1. An area, usually in the theatre of operations, where troops are assembled before beginning active operations.
2. A limited area on which a volume of gunfire is placed within a limited time.

Concept of operations. A verbal or graphic statement, in broad outline, of a commander's assumption or intent in regard to an operation or series of operations. The concept of operations is frequently embodied in campaign and operation plans; in the latter case particularly when the plan covers a series of connected operations to be carried out simultaneously or in succession. The concept is designed to give an overall picture of the operation. It is included primarily for additional clarity of purpose. Frequently referred to as 'commander's concept'.

Condensation trail. A visible cloud streak, usually brilliantly white in colour, which trails behind a missile or other vehicle in flight under certain conditions. Also known as 'vapour trail'.

Cone of silence. An inverted cone-shaped space directly over the aerial towers of some forms of radio beacons in which signals are unheard or greatly reduced in volume. *See also* **'Z' marker beacon.**

Confidential report. An annual return forwarded to the Military Secretary giving a commander's assessment of the character, efficiency and capability of each individual officer under his command. It is routed through the next senior formation where a second opinion is recorded. It is used to assess an officer's suitability for promotion.

Confirmation of information (intelligence). An information item is said to be confirmed when it is reported for the second time, preferably by another independent source whose reliability is considered when confirming information.

Confusion reflector(s). A reflector of electromagnetic radiations used to create echoes for confusion purposes. Radar confusion reflectors include such devices as chaff, rope and corner reflectors.

Consol. A long-range radio aid to navigation, the emissions of which, by means of their radio frequency modulation characteristics, enable bearings to be determined.

Console. A grouping of controls, indicators, and similar electronic or mechanical equipment, used to monitor readiness of, and/or control specific functions of, a system, such as missile checkout, countdown, or launch operations.

Consolidation of position. Organizing and strengthening a newly captured position so that it can be used against the enemy.

Constant of the cone.
1. For Lambert Conical Orthomorphic projection, *see* **Grid convergence factor.**
2. *See also* **Convergence factor.**

Consumable item. An item of *matériel* (other than one included in explosives stores ranges) that is consumed or used to destruction in service or which is regarded as expended on issue. It is therefore subject to minimal accounting procedures after issue from main stock.

Consumption rate. The average quantity of an item consumed or expended during a given time interval, expressed in quantities by the most appropriate unit of measurement.

Contact lost. A target tracking term used to signify that a target believed to be still within the area of visual, sonar or radar coverage is temporarily lost but the termination of track plotting is not warranted.

Contact point.
1. In land warfare, a point on the terrain, easily identifiable, where two or more units are required to make contact.
2. In close air support, a position at which the strike leader makes initial radio telephone contact with the forward air controller. *See also* **Air control team; Pull-up point; Turn-in point.**

Contact print. A print made from a negative or a diapositive in direct contact with sensitized materials.

Contact report. A report of visual, radio,

sonor or radar contact with the enemy. The first report, giving the information immediately available, when the contact is first made, is known as an 'initial contact report'. Subsequent reports containing additional information are referred to as 'amplifying reports'.

Contain. To stop, hold or surround the forces of the enemy or to cause the enemy to centre his activity on a given front and to prevent his withdrawing any part of his forces for use elsewhere.

Containerization. The system of handling by the process of packing unit loads individual packages and/or individual items of *matériel* into a freight container.

Contamination. The deposit and/or absorption of radioactive material, biological, or chemical agents on and by structures, areas, personnel, or objects. *See also* **Induced radiation; Residual radiation.**

Contamination control line. A line established by competent authority identifying the area contaminated to a specific level of the contaminant of interest.

Contamination control point. That portion of the contamination control line used by personnel to control entry to and exit from the contaminated area.

Contingency plan. A plan for contingencies which can reasonably be anticipated in an area of responsibility.

Continuation training. The training of individuals as effective members of their subunit after they have completed recruit training and, hopefully, before they take part in collective training (*qv*).

Continuous fire.
1. Fire conducted at a normal rate without interruption for application of adjustment corrections or for other causes.
2. In artillery and naval gunfire support, loading and firing as rapidly as possible, consistent with accuracy, within the prescribed rate of fire for the weapon.

Firing will continue until the command 'check firing' or 'end of mission' is given.

Continuous illumination fire. A type of fire in which illuminating projectiles are fired at specific time intervals to provide uninterrupted lighting on the target or specificed area. *See also* **Co-ordinated illumination fire.**

Continuous processor. Equipment which processes film or paper in continuous strips.

Continuous running. In transport terminology denotes that a vehicle runs the whole distance from start to finish of a route but that the driver is changed at predetermined points on it.

Continuous strip camera. A camera in which the film moves continuously past a slit in the focal plane. producing a photograph in one unbroken length by virtue of the continuous forward motion of the aircraft.

Continuous strip photography. Photography of a strip of terrain in which the image remains unbroken throughout its length along the line of flight.

Contour-flying. The flight of an aircraft close to the ground so as to avoid enemy radar. Slang term is 'hedge hopping'.

Contour interval. Difference in elevation between two adjacent contour lines.

Contour line. A line on a map or chart connecting points of equal elevation.

Contractor. A heavy duty tractor capable of carrying a payload in excess of 75 tons.

Control.
1. Authority which may be less than full command exercised by a commander over part of the activities of subordinate or other organizations.
2. In photogrammetry, a system of accurately established positions used to determine the distances and directions or differences in elevation between points on the earth.

* Area. A controlled airspace extending upwards from a specified height above the surface of the earth without an upper limit unless one is specified. *See also* **Airway; Controlled airspace; Terminal * area. * Point:**
1. A position along a route of march at which men are stationed to give information and instructions for the regulation of supply or traffic.
2. A position marked by a buoy, boat, aircraft, electronic device, conspicuous terrain feature, or other identifiable object which is given a name or number and used as an aid to navigation or control of units, ships, boats or aircraft.
3. A point located by ground survey with which a corresponding point on a photograph is matched, as a check, in making mosaics. *** Stick steering.** Control of an aircraft through the automatic flight control system by manipulation of the control stick. *** System (missile).** A system that serves to maintain altitude stability and to correct deflections. *See also* **Guidance system (missile). * Zone.** A controlled airspace extending upwards from the surface of the earth. *See also* **Airway, Controlled airspace; Terminal * area. * and Reporting centre (CRC).** A subordinate air control element of the tactical air control centre from which radar control and warning operations are conducted within its area of responsibility. *** and Reporting system.** An organization set up for:
1. early warning, tracking, and recognition of aircraft and tracking of surface craft, and
2. control of all active air defences. It consists primarily of a chain of radar reporting stations and control centres and an observer organization, together with the necessary communications network.

Controlled airspace. An airspace of defined dimensions within which air traffic control service is provided.

Controlled exercise. One in which constraints are imposed on some or all of the participating units by the Directing Staff.

Controlled humidity storage. A type of storage in which the relative humidity is regulated to remain within set limits.

Controlled interception. An aircraft intercept action wherein the friendly aircraft are controlled from a ground, ship, or airborne station. *See also* **Air interception. Controlled Mosaic.** A mosaic corrected for scale, rectified, and laid to ground control to provide an accurate representation of distances and direction. *See also* **Mosaic; Rectification.**

Controlled passing. A traffic movement procedure whereby two lines of traffic travelling in opposite directions are enabled to traverse alternately a point or section of route which can take only one line of traffic at a time.

Controlled response. The process of limited escalation, whereby each enemy move is countered by raising only slightly the tempo of the conflict. Equally applicable to diplomacy and operations.

Controlled route. A route, the use of which is subject to traffice or movement restrictions. *See also* **Route.**

Controlled stores. Stores which owing to scarcity or costliness are only issued after special approval has been obtained.

Conventional war. Also known as General war and denotes a state of warfare in between Counter Insurgency Operations (*qv*) and one where nuclear weapons are used.

Conventional weapon. Any weapon without a NBC (*qv*) warhead.

Convergence factor. The ratio of the angle between any two meridians on the chart to their actual change of longitude. *See also* **Grid, Map, True convergence.**

Conversion. A change in the identification or condition under which an item of *matériel* is held on charge. *** Angle.** The angle between a great circle bearing and

a rhumb line bearing of a point, measured at a common origin. *** Scale.** A scale indicating the relationship between two different units of measurement. *See also* **Scale.**

Convoy. A group of vehicles organized for the purpose of control and orderly movement with or without escort protection. *** Escort.** An escort to protect a convoy of vehicles from being scattered, destroyed, or captured. *** Loading.** The loading of troop units with their equipment and supplies in vessels of the same movement group, but not necessarily in the same vessel. *See also* **Loading. * Route.** The specific route assigned to each convoy by the appropriate routing authority.

Co-ordinated attack. A carefully planned and executed offensive action in which the various elements of a command are employed in such a manner as to utilize their powers to the greatest advantage to the command as a whole.

Co-ordinated illumination fire. A type of fire in which the firing of illuminating and high explosive projectiles is co-ordinated to provide illumination of the target and surrounding area only at the time required for spotting and adjusting the high explosive fire. *See also* **Continuous illumination fire.**

Co-ordinates. Linear or angular quantities which designate the position that a point occupies in a given reference frame or system. Also used as a general term to designate the particular kind of reference frame or system such as plane rectangular co-ordinates or spherical co-ordinates. *See also* **Geographic Co-ordinates; Georef; Grid co-ordinates.**

Co-ordinating authority. The authority granted to a commander or individual assigned responsibility for co-ordinating specific functions or activities involving forces of two or more countries, of two or more Services or two or more forces of the same Service. He has the authority to require consultation between the agencies involved or their representatives, but does not have the authority to compel agreement. In case of disagreement between the agencies involved, he will attempt to obtain essential agreement by discussion. If he is unable to obtain essential agreement, he should refer the matter to the appointing authority.

Co-ordinating point. Designated point at which, in all types of combat, adjacent units/formations must make contact for purposes of control and co-ordination.

Cordon. Used in internal security (*qv*) operations to denote the line of troops surrounding an area to be penetrated by patrols or search parties.

Coriolis effect. The apparent deflection of a body in motion in one co-ordinate system when the motion is measured in a second co-ordinate system which is rotating in respect to the first. Thus, any particle moving on earth exhibits this deflection with respect to an earth frame. The deflection is to the right of the velocity vector in the northern hemisphere.

Coriolis force. A force phenomenon for which compensation must be made when navigation relative to earth is considered; an acceleration affecting a particle moving over a rotating surface.

Corner reflector. A device normally consisting of three metallic surfaces or screens perpendicular to one another, designed to act as a radar target or marker.

Cornet. Formerly the junior commissioned rank in the cavalry, now replaced by Second Lieutenant.

Corporal (cpl). A junior non-commissioned rank usually held by a soldier in command of an infantry section or equivalent in other arms.

Corps. A functional branch of the army, *eg* Royal Armoured Corps, Royal Army Ordnance Corps. * **Troops.** Troops assigned or attached to a Corps, but not from one of the divisions that make up the Corps. *See also* **Army Corps.**

Corps of Royal Engineers (RE). The primary duty of this corps is to provide technical engineer support to infantry and armour *eg* mine laying and gapping, bridge building, etc. It is organized in regiments and squadrons, some of which have further specialist skills *eg* airfield construction. At its head is the Engineer in Chief (E in C); at Corps HQ the Commander Corps Royal Engineers (CCRE) and at Divisional HQ the Commander Royal Engineers (CRE).

Correlation. In air defence, the determination that an aircraft appearing on a radarscope, on a plotting board, or visually is the same as that on which information is being received from another source. * **Factor.** The ratio of a ground dose rate to a reading taken at approximately the same time at survey height over the same point on the ground.

Countdown. The step-by-step process leading to initiation of missile testing, launching, and firing. It is performed in accordance with a pre-designated item schedule.

Counter air. Air operations conducted to attain and maintain a desired degree of air superiority by the destruction or neutralization of enemy forces.

Counterattack. Attack by a part or all of a defending force against an enemy attacking force, for such specific purposes as regaining ground lost or cutting off or destroying enemy advance units, and with the general objective of denying to the enemy the attainment of his purpose in attacking. In sustained defensive operations, it is undertaken to restore the battle position and is directed at limited objectives.

Counter battery fire (CB). Fire directed by one's own artillery or mortars to neutralize enemy fire. Also called counter bombardment.

Counter-espionage. A category of counter-intelligence, the objective of which is the detection and neutralization of foreign espionage. *See also* **Counter-intelligence.**

Counterfire. Fire intended to destroy or neutralize enemy weapons. *See also* **Fire.**

Counter-guerrilla warfare. Operations and activities conducted by armed forces, para-military forces, or non-military agencies against guerrillas.

Counter-insurgency operations. Those military, para military, political, economic, psychological, and socio-logical activities undertaken by a government, independently or with the assistance of friendly nations, to prevent or defeat subversive insurgency, and to restore the authority of the central government.

Counter-intelligence. That phase of intelligence covering all activity devoted to destroying the effectiveness of inimical foreign intelligence activities and to the protection of information against espionage, personnel against subversion, and installations or materials against sabotage. *See also* **Counter-espionage; Counter-sabotage; Counter-subversion.**

Countermarch. A drill movement whereby a column of troops changes direction by 180° whilst still retaining its original order of march.

Counter penetration. Action to counter enemy penetration of our own defended zone or area.

Counterpreparation fire. Intensive prearranged fire delivered when the imminence of the enemy attack is discovered.

Countersabotage. Action designed to destroy the effectiveness of sabotage activities through the process of identifying, penetrating, manipulating, and neutralizing or repressing individuals, groups, or organizations conducting or capable of conducting such activities. *See also* **Counter-intelligence.**

Countersign. A secret challenge and its reply. *See also* **Challenge; Password; Reply.**

Countersubversion. That part of counter-intelligence which is devoted to destroying the effectiveness of subversive activities through the detection, identification, exploitation, penetration, manipulation, deception, and repression of individuals, groups or organizations conducting or capable of conducting such activities. *See also* **Counter-intelligence.**

Countersurveillance. All active or passive measures taken to prevent hostile surveillance of a force, area or place.

Country cover diagrams. A small scale index, by country, depicting the existence of air photography for planning purposes only.

Coupled. A flight control state in which an aircraft is controlled through the automatic flight control system by signals from guidance equipment.

Course of action.
1. Any sequence of activities which an individual or unit may follow.
2. A possible plan open to an individual or commander which would accomplish, or is related to the accomplishment of, his mission.
3. The scheme adopted to accomplish a job or mission.
4. A line of conduct in an engagement.

Court Martial. A legally constituted court for the purpose of trying persons subject to military law.

Court of Enquiry. A board of officers assembled by any officer in command to elicit information which will help him to form a just conclusion.

Coverage.
1. The action by land, air, or sea forces to protect by offence, defence, or threat of either or both.

2. Shelter or protection, either natural or artificial. *See also* **Concealment.**
3. To maintain a continuous receiver watch with transmitter calibrated and available, but not necessarily available for immediate use.
4. The ground area represented on imagery, photomaps, mosaics, maps, and other geographical presentation systems. *See also* **Comparative cover.**

Coverage. *See* **Cover.**

Covered storage. A type of storage which affords partial protection against the weather.

Covering fire.
1. Fire used to protect troops when they are within range of enemy small arms.
2. In amphibious usage, fire delivered prior to the landing to cover preparatory operations such as underwater demolition or minesweeping. *See also* **Fire.**

Covering force.
1. A force operating apart from the main force for the purpose of intercepting, engaging, delaying, disorganizing, and deceiving the enemy before he can attack the force covered.
2. Any body or detachment of troops which provides security for a larger force by observation, reconnaissance, attack, or defence, or by any combination of these methods.

Cover search. In air photographic reconnaissance, the process of selection of the most suitable existing cover for a specific requirement.

Covertrace (reconnaissance). One of a series of overlays showing all air reconnaissance sorties covering the map sheet to which the overlay refers.

Crab angle. The angle between the aircraft track or flight line and the fore and aft axis of a vertical camera, which is in line with the aircraft heading.

Craftsman (cfn). The equivalent of infantry private soldiers in technical corps.

Crash locator beacon. An automatic radio beacon which will help searching forces to locate a crashed aircraft. *See also* **Personal locator beacon.**

Crater. The cavity formed in the ground by the explosion of a shell, mine or bomb.

Creeping barrage. A barrage in which the fire of all units participating remains in the same relative position throughout and which advances in steps of one line at a time.

Crew portable. A weapon or item which can be moved about the battlefield by its operating crew, either as a single item, or broken down in specific loads. The need for it to be broken down must be stated.

Critical altitude. The altitude beyond which an aircraft or airbreathing guided missile ceases to perform satisfactorily. *See also* **Altitude.**

Critical supplies and materials. Those supplies vital to the support of operations, which owing to various causes are in short supply or are expected to be in short supply. *See also* **Regulated item.**

Cross-servicing. That servicing performed by one service or national element for other services or national elements and for which the other services or national elements may be charged.

Crotale. A French automatic short range surface to air missile system. Also in use in South Africa and Lebanon.

Cruising altitude. A level determined by vertical measurement from mean sea level, maintained during a flight or portion thereof.

Cruising level. A level maintained during a significant portion of a flight. *See also* **Altitude.**

Crusader. A high speed, long distance articulated truck.

Cryptanalysis. The study of encrypted texts. The steps or processes involved in converting encrypted text into plain text without initial knowledge of the key employed in the encryption.

Cryptomaterial. All material, including documents, devices, equipments, and apparatus essential to the encryption, decryption, or authentication of tele-communications. When classified, it is designated CRYPTO and subject to special safeguards.

Cryptoparts. The divisions of a message as prescribed for security reasons. The operating instructions for certain crypto-systems prescribe the number of groups which may be encrypted in the system, using a single message indicator. Crypto-parts are identified in plain language. They are not to be confused with message parts.

Culture. Features of the terrain that have been constructed by man; included are such items as roads, buildings and canals; boundary lines, and, in a broad sense, all names and legends on a map.

Cupola. The revolving turret of an AFV.

Currency. The up-to-dateness of a map or chart as determined by comparison with the best available information at a given time.

Current intelligence. Intelligence of all types and forms of immediate interest which is usually disseminated without the delays necessary to complete evaluation or interpretation.

Cut-off.
1. The deliberate shutting off of a reaction engine.
2. A safety device on a single shot rifle.
3. A unit is cut-off if it has lost touch with all friendly forces through enemy action.
* Velocity. The velocity attained by a missile at the point of cut-off.

Cymbeline. A lightweight portable radar for mortar location and for the adjust-ment for artillery fire.

Daily messing rate. The standard amount per person authorized for messes obtaining food from normal sources of supply; *ie* part Service, part NAAFI and part private traders.

Damage assessment. The determination of the effect of attacks on targets.

Damage control. Measures necessary aboard ship to preserve and re-establish watertight integrity, stability, manoeuvrability, and offensive power; to control list and trim; to effect rapid repairs of *matériel*; to limit the spread of, and provide adequate protection from, fire; to limit the spread of, remove the contamination by, and pro-vide adequate protection from, toxic agents; and to provide for care of wounded personnel. *See also* **Area damage control; Rear area security.**

Damages. A charge levied on a unit or subunit to make good deficiences or injuries done to Government property other than through fair wear and tear.

Danger area. A specified area above, below, or within which there may exist potential danger.

Dangerous cargo. Cargo which, because

of its dangerous properties, is subject to special regulations for its transport.

Data link. A communications link suitable for transmission of data.

Date line. *See* **International date line.**

Date-time group. The date and time, expressed in digits and zone suffix, at which a message is prepared for transmission. (Expressed as six digits followed by the zone suffix; first pair of digits denoting the date, second pair the hours, third pair the minutes), *eg* 061215Z meaning a quarter of an hour after noon on the sixth of the month by Greenwich mean time.

Datum. Any numerical or geometrical quantity or set of such quantities which may serve as a reference or base for other quantities. Where the concept is geometric, the plural form is 'datums' in contrast to the normal plural 'data'.
* Level. A horizontal plane to which elevations, heights, or depths on a map or chart are related. *See also* **Altitude.**
* Point. Any reference point of known or assumed co-ordinates from which calculation or measurements may be taken.

Day of supply. *See* **One day's supply.**

Dazzle. Temporary loss of vision or a temporary reduction in visual acuity, by access light or moving light.

D-day. The day on which an operation commences or is due to commence. This may be the commencement of hostilities or any other operation. *See also* **K-day;** **M-day.**

Dead space.
1. An area within the maximum range of a weapon, radar, or observer, which cannot be covered by fire or observation from a particular position because of intervening obstacles, the nature of the ground, or the characteristics of the trajectory, or the limitations of the pointing capabilities of the weapon.

2. An area or zone which is within range of a radio transmitter, but in which a signal is not received.
3. The volume of space above and around a gun or guided missile system into which it cannot fire because of mechanical or electronic limitations.

Dead zone. *See* **Dead space.**

Debarkation. The unloading of troops with their supplies and equipment from a ship. A debarkation schedule provides for the timely and orderly debarkation of troops and equipment and emergency supplies for the waterborne ship-to-shore movement.

Decay (radioactive). The decrease in the radiation intensity of any radioactive material with respect to time. *** Curves.** Lines on a graph representing the decrease of radioactivity with the passage of time. *** Rate.** The rate of disintegration of radioactive material with respect to time.

Decentralized control. In air defence, the normal mode whereby a higher echelon monitors unit actions, making direct target assignments to units only when necessary to ensure proper fire distribution or to prevent engagement of friendly aircraft. *See also* **Centralized control.**

Deception. Those measures designed to mislead the enemy by manipulation, distortion, or falsification of evidence to induce him to react in a manner prejudicial to his interests.

Decision. In an estimate of the situation, a clear and concise statement of the line of action intended to be followed by the commander as the one most favourable to the successful accomplishment of his mission.

Declassify. To cancel the security classification of an item of classified matter. *See also* **Downgrade.**

Declination. The angular distance to a body on the celestial sphere measured North or South through 90° from the celestial equator along the hour circle of the body. Comparable to latitude on the terrestrial sphere. *See also* **Magnetic declination; Magnetic variation.**

Decompression sickness. A syndrome including bends, chokes, neurological disturbances, and collapse, resulting from exposure to reduced ambient pressure and caused by gas bubbles in the tissues, fluids and blood vessels.

Decontamination. The process of making any person, object, or area safe by absorbing, destroying, neutralizing, making harmless, or removing, chemical or biological agents, or by removing radioactive material clinging to or around it. * **Station.** A building or location suitably equipped and staffed where personnel and their clothing are decontaminated from the effects of toxic attack.

Decorations. Medals awarded for gallantry in action *eg* Victoria Cross, Military Cross, etc.

Decoy. A model, electromagnetic reflector or other device which is used to deceive sensors. *See also* **Chaff.** * **Airfield.** A genuine but unwanted landing ground rigged up with dummy aircraft and lighting devices to give the effect of an active operational base.

Decrab. To yaw an aircraft so as to align the plane of the landing gear wheels with the direction of the aircraft's momentum.

Deep fording. The ability of a self-propelled gun or ground vehicle equipped with built-in waterproofing and/or a special waterproofing kit, to negotiate a water obstacle with its wheels or tracks in contact with the ground.

Deep supporting fire. Fire directed on objectives not in the immediate vicinity of our forces, for neutralizing and destroying enemy reserves and

weapons, and interfering with enemy command, supply, communications and observations. *See also* **Supporting fire.**

Defaulter. A soldier sentenced to confinement to barracks for some military offence.

Defector. A person who for political or other reasons has repudiated his country and may be in possession of information of sufficient interest to justify special treatment.

Defence. The formation adopted to repulse an enemy attack. * **in depth.** The siting of mutually supporting defence positions designed to absorb and progressively weaken attack, prevent initial observations of the whole position by the enemy, and to allow the commander to manoeuvre his reserve. * **Readiness condition.** A number or code word indicating the readiness posture of a unit for actual operations or exercises.

Defensive coastal area. A part of a coastal area and of the air, land, and water area adjacent to the coast line within which defence operations may involve land, sea and air forces.

Defensive fire (DF). Those close defensive fire (DF) tasks which cover the most dangerous approaches to a position. Guns allotted to such tasks remain laid on them whenever they are not otherwise engaged.

Defensive task. A specific pre-arranged fire task allotted to supporting arms and usually indicated by a code word.

Defensive minefield (land mine warfare). Minefield laid in accordance with an established plan to prevent a penetration between positions and to strengthen the defence of the positions themselves. *See also* **Minefield** (land mine warfare).

Deficiency. A quantity disclosed by physical check as being less than the quantity indicated on the appropriate records.

Defilade.
1. Proection from hostile observation and fire provided by an obstacle such as a hill, ridge, or bank.
2. A vertical distance by which a position is concealed from enemy observation.
3. To shield from enemy fire or observation by using natural or artificial obstacles.

Defile. A narrow passage between natural obstacles.

Definition. In imagery interpretation, the degree of clarity and sharpness of an image.

Defoliating agent. A chemical which causes trees, shrubs and other plants to shed their leaves prematurely.

Defoliant operations. The employment of defoliating agents (*qv*) on vegetated areas in support of military operations.

Delay (radar).
1. The ground distance from a point directly beneath the aircraft to the beginning of the area of radar scan.
2. The electronic delay of the start of the time base used to select a particular segment of the total.

Delaying action. An engagement mounted to hold up the enemy's advance by making him deploy (*qv*) from a march to an attack formation.

Deliberate attack. An attack mounted against prepared enemy positions with time for reconnaissance at the lowest level of command.

Deliberate breaching (land mine warfare). A major minefield operation requiring extensive planning, especially trained personnel, and positive methods of locating and removing each mine to create demined lanes through minefields. *See also* Breaching.

Deliberate crossing. A crossing of a river or stream that requires extensive planning and detailed preparation. *See also* Hasty crossing.

Deliberate defence. A defence normally organized when out of contact with the enemy or when contact with the enemy is not imminent and time for organization is available. It normally includes an extensive fortified zone incorporating pillboxes, forts, and communications systems. *See also* Hasty defence.

Delivery error. The inaccuracy associated with a given weapon system resulting in a dispersion of shots about the aiming point. *See also* Circular error probable; Deviation; Dispersion; Dispersion error; Horizontal error.

Delivery system. A loose expression to denote the mechanics of transmitting a warhead from its launching point to its target when tube artillery is not used.

Demand. A request for materials sent by a demanding unit to a supply source.

Demanding unit. The unit, organization or installation initiating a demand.

Demilitarized zone. A defined area in which the stationing, or concentrating of military forces, or the retention or establishment of military installations of any description, is prohibited.

Demolition. The destruction of structures, facilities or equipment by use of fire, water, explosives, mechanical, or other means. * **Belt.** A selected land area sown with explosive charges, mines and other available obstacles to deny use of the land to enemy operations, and as a protection to friendly troops. It may be of two sorts: *primary*. A continuous series of obstacles across the whole front, selected by the divisional or a higher commander. (The preparation of such a belt is normally a priority

engineer task.) *subsidiary.* A supplement to the primary belt to give depth in front or behind or to protect the flanks.
* Firing party. The party at the site which is technically responsible for the demolition. *** Guard.** A local force positioned to ensure that a target is not captured by an enemy before orders are given for its demolition and before the demolition has been successfully fired. The commander of the guard is responsible for the operational command of all troops at the site, including the firing party. He is responsible for transmitting the order to fire to the firing party.

Demonstration. An attack or show of force on a front where a decision is not sought, made with the aim of deceiving the enemy. *See also* **Amphibious demonstration; Diversion; Diversionary attack.**

Denial measures. Action to hinder or deny the enemy the use of space, personnel, or facilities. It may include destruction, removal, contamination, or erection of obstacles.

Density (land mine warfare). The average number of mines per specified unit of measure of front of the minefield.

Departure airfield.
1. An airfield from which aircraft depart.
2. An airfield on which passengers or cargo are emplaned for flights.

Departure point. A navigational check point used by aircraft as a marker for setting course.

Deploy.
1. The extension or widening of the front of a military unit, extending from a close order to a battle formation.
2. In a strategic sense, the relocation of forces to desired areas of operation.

Depot. A supporting but not a fighting unit, *eg* Infantry depot where recruits are trained; Ordnance depot where stores are held.

Depth.
1. The vertical distance from the plane of the hydrographic datum to the bed of the sea, lake or river.
2. *See* **Defence.**
* Contour. A line connecting points of equal depth below the hydrographic datum. *** Curve.** *See* **Depth contour.**

Deputy Provost Marshal (DPM–. A senior officer of military police.

Descriptive name. Written indication on maps and charts, used to specify the nature of a feature (natural or artificial) shown by a general symbol.

Deserter. An officer or soldier absent from his unit who does not intend to return to duty.

Design approved firm. A firm approved by the Ministry as suitable to act as a Design Authority for specified classes of *matériel.*

Design approved authority. The Authority empowered by the Ministry of Defence to approve the specification of a design.

Design approved fee. The amoutn payable to the owner of a design for the right to make or have made *matériel* to that design.

Desired ground zero (DGZ). A point on the surface of the earth, below, at, or above the centre of a nuclear burst. *See also* **Actual ground zero; Ground zero.**

Despatch route. A roadway over which full control, both as to priorities of use and the regulation of movement of traffic in time and space is exercised. *See also* **Route.**

Despatcher. Assigned parachute jumping instructor (PJI) who controls parachutists from the time they enter the aircraft until they exit.

Destruct (missile). Intentional destruction of a missile or similar vehicle for safety or other reasons. * **System** (missile). A system which, when operated by external command or preset internal means, destroys the missile or similar vehicle.

Destruction fire. Fire delivered for the sole purpose of destroying material objects. *See also* **Fire.**

Detachment.
1. A part of a unit separated from its main organization for duty elsewhere.
2. A temporary military or naval unit formed from other units or parts of units.

Detail.
1. The basic graphic representation of features.
2. Small party of servicemen assigned to a specific duty, *eg* firing party or fatigues.

Detailed report (photographic interpretation). A comprehensive, analytical, intelligence report written as a result of the interpretation of photography usually covering a single subject, target, or target complex, and of a detailed nature.

Detour. Deviation from those parts of a route, where movement has become difficult or impossible, to ensure continuity of movement to the destination.

Development area. An area in Great Britain suffering from or threatened with high or persistent unemployment, so designated under the Industrial Development Act 1966. Similar provision exists for Northern Ireland. Such areas receive a degree of preference in the award of Government contracts.

Development cost plan. An estimate of likely cost and resources required for development work, broken down intp required constituents and spread over the timescale of the development, presented in such a form that achievements to a given date can be compared with the estimate to that date.

Deviation.
1. The distance by which a point of impact or burst misses the target.
2. The angular difference between magnetic and compass headings. *See also* **Circular error probable; Delivery error; Dispersion error; Horizontal error.**

Dew line. The Distant Early Warning Line is a radar system extending from Iceland to the Aleutian Islands to give the American forces warning of a Soviet attack across the Polar icefield.

Diaphragm. The physical element of an optical system which regulates the quantity of light traversing the system. The quantity of light determines the brightness of the image without affecting its size.

Diapositive. A positive photograph on a transparent medium. *See also* **Transparency.**

Died of wounds received in action. A battle casualty who dies of wounds or other injuries received in action, after having reached any medical treatment facility. It is essential to differentiate these cases from battle casualties found dead or who died before reaching a medical treatment facility (the 'killed in action' group). It should be noted that reaching a medical treatment facility while still alive is the criterion. *See also* **Killed in action.**

Differential. An arrangement of gears enabling driving wheel or tracks of vehicles to revolve at different speeds when a vehicle is turning a corner.

Diffraction loading. The force (or loading) on the structure during the envelopment process.

Diffusion (light). The scattering of light rays either when reflected from a rough surface or during the transmission of light through a translucent medium.

Digger. (Australian slang). An Australian soldier.

Digital Plotter Map (DPM). A large scale automated display device that allows Field Direction Control personnel to plan operations, monitor activities and retain an overview of the tactical situation.

Direct action fuse. *See* **Impact action fuse; Proximity fuse; Self-destroying fuse; Time fuse; Variable time fuse.**

Direct damage assessment. A direct examination of an actual strike area by air observation, air photography, or by direct observation.

Direct fire. Fire directed at a target which is visible to the aimer.

Direct laying. Occurs when a weapon's sights are laid directly on the target. Also called 'open sights'.

Direct support. The support provided by a unit or formation not attached or under command of the supported unit or formation, but required to give priority to the support required by that unit or formation. *See also* **Support.**

Direct support artillery. Artillery whose primary task is to provide fire requested by the supported unit.

Direct supporting fire. Fire delivered in support of part of a force, as opposed to general supporting fire which is delivered in support of the force as a whole. *See also* **Supporting fire.**

Directing staff. A group of officers who by virtue of experience, qualifications, and thorough knowledge of the exercise instructions, are selected to direct, conduct, or control an exercise. Their knowledge of both Blue and Orange roles will usually preclude them from specific Blue or Orange duties.

Direction of attack (ground forces). A specific direction or route which the main attack or centre of mass of the unit will follow. The unit is restricted and required to attack as indicated and is not normally allowed to by-pass the enemy. The direction of attack is used primarily in counter-attacks or to ensure that supporting attacks make maximum contribution to the main attack.

Directional radar prediction. A prediction made for a particular heading.

Director.
1. An officer in charge but not in command, *eg* Director of Army Training (DAT) formulates all army training policy and implements it through each Arms Director. *eg* Director of artillery, Director of infantry, etc.
2. **Artillery director.** An instrument used to direct artillery fire.

Director (directorate) of Army Legal Services (DALS). An officer on the Adjutant General's Staff, who has representatives at lower formation level. They advise and assist on all legal matters such as the preparation of cases for court martial, instruct in military law and act as legal advisers to commanders on whose staff they serve. They are quite distinct from the Judge Advocate General's Department.

Directive.
1. A military communication in which policy is established or a specific action is ordered.
2. A plan issued with a view to placing it in effect when so directed or in the event of a stated contingency arising.
3. Broadly speaking, any communication which initiates or governs action, conduct or procedure.

Dirty. In bomb disposal/counter insurgency operations an area in which it is thought that explosive devices may exist is classified as 'dirty' until it has been cleared by the bomb disposal organization.

Disarmed mine. A mine which has been rendered inoperative by breaking a link in the firing sequence. *See also* **Mine.**

Discrepancy. Any difference between the actual quantity, condition, identification or price of *matériel* and the associated records.

Disembarkation schedule. *See* **Debarkation.**

Dismountable. An item carried and used in/on a vehicle but which can equally be dismounted and used on the ground; the degree of portability required must be. stated.

Dispersed movement pattern. A pattern for ship-to-shore movement which provides additional separation of landing craft both laterally and in depth. This pattern is used when nuclear weapon threat is a factor.

Dispersion.
1. A scattered pattern of hits, by bombs dropped under identical conditions or by projectiles fired from the same weapon or group of weapons with the same firing data.
2. In anti-aircraft gunnery, the scattering of shots in range and deflection about the mean point of impact. As used in flak analysis the term includes scattering due to all causes, and the mean point of impact is assumed to be the target.
3. The spreading or separating of troops, *matériel*, establishments or activities which are usually concentrated in limited areas, to reduce vulnerability to enemy action.
4. In chemical operations, the dissemination of agents in liquid or aerosol form from bombs and spray tanks. *See also* **Circular error probable; Delivery error; Deviation; Horizontal error. * Error.** The distance from the point of impact or burst of a round to the mean point of impact or burst. * **Pattern.** The distribution of a series of rounds fired from a weapon or a group of weapons under conditions as nearly identical as possible; the points of burst or impact being dispersed about a point called the 'mean point of impact'.

Displaced person. A civilian who is involuntarily outside the national boundaries of his country. *See also* Evacuees; Refugee.

Disposal. A generic term covering action taken to dispense with *matériel* declared surplus to, or unsuitable for, all known Ministry of Defence requirements.

Disposition. Distribution of the elements of a command within an area, usually the exact location of each unit headquarters and the deployment of the forces subordinate to it. *See also* **Deployment; Dispersion.**

Dissemination (intelligence). The timely distribution of information and/or intelligence in the most suitable form to those who need it.

Dissident. An individual who takes covert or overt action against a government.

Distributed fire. Fire so dispersed as to engage most effectively an area target.

Distribution point (DP). A point at which supplies and/or ammunition, obtained from supporting supply points by a division or other unit, are broken down for distribution to subordinate units. Distribution points usually carry no stocks; items drawn are issued completely as soon as possible after arrival.

District. A geographical area within which all troops, unless specifically excluded, come under the command of the District Headquarters, usually commanded by a Major General.

Diversion.
1. The act of drawing the attention and forces of an enemy from the point of the principal operation; an attack, alarm, or feint which diverts attention. *See also* **Demonstration.**
2. A change made in a prescribed route for operational or tactical reasons. Except in the case of aircraft, a diversion

order will not constitute a change of destination.

* Order. A formal instruction to a contractor or other manufacturing or repair authority to consign *matériel* already on order to an address different from that specified in the relevant contract or order.

Diversionary attack. An attack wherein a force attacks, or threatens to attack, a target other than the main target for the purpose of drawing enemy defences away from the main effort. *See also* **Demonstration.**

Division.
1. A major administrative and tactical unit/formation which combines in itself the necessary arms and services required for sustained combat, larger than a regiment/brigade and smaller than a corps.
2. An organizational part of a headquarters that handles military matters of a particular nature, such as personnel, intelligence, plans and training, or supply and evacuation.
3. An administrative grouping of infantry regiments of a similar background, whether territorial or functional. *eg* Guards Division.

Divisional Administrative Area (DAA). All administrative units in or attached to a division are co-located in one area, known as the DAA, unless their function requires that they be elsewhere. It is controlled by the AA & QMG (*qv*) of the division.

Divisional Maintenance Area (DMA). Ideally, in a fast moving modern war, replenishment stocks are kept loaded on their vehicles until issued to units. When this is not possible they are off-loaded into a DMA.

Dodge. A 14 ton heavy duty truck.

Door bundle. A bundle for manual ejection in flight normally followed by parachutists.

Doppler effect. The phenomenon evidenced by the change in the observed frequency of a sound or radio wave caused by a time rate of change in the effective length of the path of travel between the source and the point of observation.

Dose rate contour line. A line on a map, diagram or overlay joining all points at which the radiation dose rate at a given time is the same.

Dosimetry. The measurement of radiation doses. It applies to both the devices used (dosimeters) and to the techniques.

Doughboy. US slang for an American soldier (WWI).

Downgrade. To reduce the security classification of a classified document or an item of classified matter or *matériel*. *See also* **Declassify.**

Draftee. *See* **Transient.**

Dragon. (US). A one man, shoulder fired ATGW (*qv*). The operator keeps the target in view during the flight of the missile which receives corrections through a wire link.

Dragoon. Originally a mounted infantryman. Regiments of Dragoons gradually became ordinary cavalry and are now part of the Royal Armoured Corps.

Drainage system. Rivers, streams, and other inland water features.

Drawbar pull. The pulling force exerted at the drawbar of a ground vehicle.

Drawing key. An image or preliminary drawing used as a guide for scribing or drawing. *See also* **Blue key.**

Dress n. uniform. *eg* Battle *, Ceremonial *, Combat *, Fatigue *, Mess *, Service *, appropriate to the activity being pursued. v. to align in ceremonial order.

Drift. In ballistics a change in the path taken by a projectile due to gravitational and atmospheric conditions. * **Angle.** The angle measured in degrees between the heading of an aircraft and the track made good.

Drifter. RAF parachute jumping instructor who jumps first on a troop training flight to assess wind direction accurately.

Drill. n. The instruction given to a recruit to enable him to obey correctly words of command given on the parade ground, comprising foot drill and arms drill. Ceremonial drill is carried out on public occasions *eg* Trooping the Colour, Changing the Guard, etc. * **Mine** (land mine warfare). A completely inert replica of a mine used for training in handling, loading, fusing and other drill purposes.

Driver (dvr). A soldier in charge of a vehicle, equivalent rank to private in some arms.

Driving Sprocket. Wheel, usually toothed, which transfers power from the gearbox output or tank final drive to the tank's tracks.

Drone. A land, sea, or air vehicle which is remotely or automatically controlled.

Drop altitude. The altitude above mean sea level at which airdrop is executed. *See also* **Altitude.**

Drop height. The vertical distance between the dropping zone and the aircraft.

Dropmaster. *See* **Air despatcher** (cargo).

Drop message. A message dropped from an aircraft to a ground or surface unit.

Dropping zone (DZ). A specified area upon which parachute troops, equipment, or supplies are air dropped.

Drum magazine. A circular magazine which holds the rounds to be fed into the chamber.

Drum Major. The Warrant or Non commissioned officer in charge of the Battalion Corps of Drums. On parade he carries a staff and leads the Corps.

Drummer (dmr). An infantry soldier in the Battalion Corps of Drums. Light infantry and rifle regiments have the equivalent rank of bugler. A drummer may play any instrument in the Corps. *eg* fife, bass drum, etc.

Dry gap bridge. A bridge, fixed or portable, which is used to span a gap that does not normally contain water, *eg* anti-tank ditches, road craters, etc.

Dual carriageway. *See* **Dual lane highway.**

Dual lane highway. Any highway in which opposing streams of traffic are physically separated by a divider.

Dud. Explosive munition which has not been armed as intended or which has failed to explode after being armed.

Dues in. The quantities of an item of *matériel*, not yet brought on charge, but recorded as expected from all sources.

Dumb craft. A river craft which is not self-propelled and must therefore be towed.

Dummy message. A message sent for some purpose other than its content, which may consist of dummy groups or may have a meaningless text.

Dump. A temporary storage area, usually in the open, for bombs, ammunition, equipment, or supplies. * **Party.** A body of men detailed to collect, stack and distribute supplies dropped by air or delivered by fixed wing aircraft.

Duplicate negative. A negative reproduced from an original negative or diapositive.

Dynamic pressure. Pressure resulting from some medium in motion, such as the air following the shock front of a blast wave.

Early resupply. The shipping of supplies during the period between D-day and the beginning of 'planned resupply'. *See also* Elements of resupply.

Earmark. A quantity of an item of *matériel* reserved for a specific purpose.

Earmarked for assignment. Forces which nations have agreed to assign to the operational command or operational control of a NATO commander at some future date. In designating such forces, nations specify when these forces will be available in terms agreed to in the echelon or category systems. * **on Mobilization.** Forces specifically designated by nations for assignment to a NATO Commander in the event of mobilization or war. In designating such forces, nations specify, in the terms agreed to in the echelon system, when these forces will be available. *See also* NATO forces.

Earthworks. Any defensive work in which movement of earth is the principal ingredient.

Easting. Eastward (that is left to right) reading of grid values.

Echelon.
1. A subdivision of a headquarters, *ie* forward echelon, rear echelon.
2. Separate level of command. As compared to a brigade, a division is a higher echelon, a battalion is a lower echelon.
3. A fraction of a command in the direction of depth, to which a principal combat mission is assigned; *ie* attack echelon, support echelon, reserve echelon.
4. A formation in which the subdivisions are placed one behind another, extending beyond and unmasking one another wholly or in part.

5. Transport: F echelon consists of those vehicles essential to a unit for fighting *eg* AFV (*qv*); A echelon vehicles required for immediate support and replenishment of F echelon *eg* those carrying ammunition and POL (*qv*); B echelon vehicles carrying 'on call' stores.

Echeloned displacement. Movement of a unit from one position to another without discontinuing performance of its primary function.

Economic mobilization. The process of preparing for and carrying out such changes in the organization and functioning of the national economy as are necessary to provide for the most effective use of resources in a national emergency.

Economic potential. The total capacity of a nation to produce goods and services.

Economic warfare. Aggressive use of economic means to achieve national objectives.

Economy of force. The principle on which a commander uses the correct mix of arms in the right quantities to achieve his objective with the minimum of casualties *eg* wasted effort.

Edition. In cartography, a particular issue of a map or chart which is different from other issues. * **Designation.** The number, letter, date, or symbol distinguishing one edition from another.

Effective Strength. The actual number of men posted to and doing duty with a unit, *ie* excluding men sick, on leave or otherwise absent. * **of enemy forces.** That part, including logistic component, of the initial strength which is currently capable of combat employment.

Ejector. A projection in the body of a small arm which throws the expended cartridge out after being withdrawn from the chamber by the extractor.

Electronic counter-countermeasures (ECCM). That major subdivision of electronic warfare involving actions taken to ensure our own effective use of elctro-magnetic radiations despite the enemy's use of countermeasures.

Electronic countermeasures (ECM). That major subdivision of electronic warfare involving actions taken to prevent or reduce the effectiveness of enemy equipment and tactics employing, or affected by, electro-magnetic radiations and to exploit the enemy's use of such radiations.

Electronic deception. The deliberate radiation, reradiation, alteration, absorption, or reflection of electro-magnetic radiations in a manner intended to mislead an enemy in the interpretation of data received by his electronic equipment or to present false indications to electronic systems. *See also* **Electronic countermeasures.**

Electronic Jamming. The deliberate radiation, reradiation, or reflection of electro-magnetic signals, with the object of impairing the use of electronic devices by the enemy. *See also* **Jamming.**

Electronic silence. The deliberate prohibition of electronic radiations, normally applied for a stated period to specific equipments or frequency bands.

Electronic Tactical Display (ETD). A radar screen showing tactical dispositions by electronic means.

Electronic warfare (EW). That division of the military use of electronics involving actions taken to prevent or reduce an enemy's effective use of radiated electro-magnetic energy and actions taken to ensure our own effective use of radiated electro-magnetic energy.

Elements of resupply. *See* **Early resupply; Improvised (early) resupply; Initial (early) resupply; Planned resupply; Resupply.**

Elevation. The vertical distance of a point or a level, on, or affixed to, the surface of the earth, measured from mean sea level. *See also* **Altitude; Height.**
* of security. Minimum elevation permissible for firing above friendly troops without endangering their safety. This concept can only be applied to certain equipment having a flat trajectory.
* Tint. *See* **Hypsometric tinting.**

Elint. Information and intelligence on electronic matters.

Embarkation. The loading of troops with their supplies and equipment into a ship.
* Area. An area ashore, including a group of embarkation points, in which final preparations for embarkations are completed and through which assigned personnel and loads for craft and ships are called forward to embark. *** Order.** An order specifying dates, times, routes, and methods of movement to shipside for troops with their supplies and equipment.

Emergency burial. A burial, usually on the battlefield, when conditions do not permit evacuation for internment in a cemetery. *See also* **Burial.**

Emergency in war. An operational contingency in a limited area caused by a critical aggravation of combat operations and requiring special and immediate action by National and Allied Commanders. The existence of such an emergency shall be determined by the Allied Commander responsible for the limited area involved, in consultation with the National Commander concerned.

Emergency risk (nuclear). A degree of risk where anticipated effects may cause some temporary shock, casualties, and may significantly reduce the unit's combat efficiency. *See also* **Moderate risk (nuclear).**

Emergency substitute. A product which may be used, in an emergency only, in place of another product, but only on the advice of technically qualified personnel of the nation using the product, who will specify the limitations. *See also* **Acceptable alternate product; NATO unified product; Standardized product.**

Emplacement.
1. A prepared position for one or more weapons or pieces of equipment, for protection against hostile fire or bombardment, and from which they can execute their tasks.
2. The act of fixing a gun in a prepared position from which it may be fired.

Encipher. To convert a plain text message into unintelligible language by means of a cipher system.

Endoscope. A long slim optical instrument used to inspect the inside of tubes, *eg* the barrels of rifles and guns.

Endurance. The time an aircraft can continue flying, or a ground vehicle can continue operating, under specified conditions, *eg* without refuelling.
* Distance. Total distance that a ground vehicle can be self-propelled at any specified endurance speed.

Enemy capabilities. Those courses of action of which the enemy is physically capable and which, if adopted, will affect the accomplishment of our mission. The term 'capabilities' includes not only the general courses of action open to the enemy, such as attack, defence, or withdrawal, but also all the particular courses of action possible under each general course of action. Enemy capabilities are considered in the light of all known factors affecting military operations including time, space, weather, terrain, and the strength and disposition of enemy forces. In strategic thinking, the capabilities of a nation represent the courses of action within the power of the nation for accomplishing its national objectives in peace or war.

Enfilade Fire. Fire originating from a flank.

Engagement control. In air defence, that degree of control exercised over the operational functions of an air defence unit that are related to detection, identification, engagement, and destruction of hostile targets.

Engin Blundé de Reconnaissance (EBR). A large and complicated French armoured car.

Enlargement. A negative, diapositive, or paper print made at a larger scale than the original.

Enlist. v. To join the army in the rank of private or equivalent.

Enlisted man. US. Private soldier.

Ensign. Originally the junior commissioned rank in the infantry, now replaced by Second Lieutenant.

Entac. An Anti-tank Guided Weapon System (ATGW) in use in NATO and other countries.

Envelop. To surround an enemy force.

Epaulette. A shoulder decoration worn by certain ranks in ceremonial dress.

Equal area projection. One in which equal areas on the ground are represented by equal areas on the map.

Equerry. An officer, by tradition mounted, who accompanies the Sovereign on State occasions.

Equipment. The accessories, other than arms, required by a soldier to carry out his task. Personal equipment, that which each individual carries on his person or in first line transport. Unit equipment. A pool of equipment kept on unit charge for allotment as required. *** Collecting point (ECP).** An area in or near a BAA (*qv*) where casualties are collected from forward units for backloading for repair.

Equivalent airspeed. Calibrated airspeed corrected for compressibility error. *See also* **Airspeed.**

Equivalent focal length. The distance measured along the optical axis of the lens from the rear nodal point to the plane of best average definition over the entire field used in a camera. *See also* **Focal length.**

Escalation. The sequence of events and the appropriate responses which increase the tempo of conflict, whether diplomatic or physical.

Escort.
1. To convoy.
2. A combatant unit or units assigned to accompany and protect another force.
3. Aircraft assigned to protect other aircraft during a mission.
4. An armed guard that accompanies a convoy, a train, prisoners, etc.
5. An armed guard accompanying persons as a mark of honour.

Espionage. Actions directed toward the acquisition of information through clandestine operations.

Essential Elements of information (intelligence) (EEI). The critical items of information regarding the enemy and his environment required in order to make timely decisions.

Essential supply cargo. A commodity which is essential for the prosecution of the war in the survival period, or for national survival in that period, and which should be discharged as soon as circumstances permit. This will comprise such things as food, refined petroleum, oils, and lubricants, and medical stores. *See also* **Cargoes.**

Establishment.
1. An installation, together with its personnel and equipment, organized as an operating entity.

2. The table setting out the authorized numbers of men and major equipments in a unit/formation; sometimes called 'table of organization' or 'table of organization and equipment'. *See also* **Base.**

Estimate of the situation. A logical process of reasoning by which a commander considers all the circumstances affecting the military situation and arrives at a decision as to the course of action to be taken in order to accomplish his mission.

Estimated Time of Departure (ETD). Used in movement tables and orders when an exact time cannot be given.

Evacuation control ship. In an amphibious operation, a ship designated as a control point for landing craft, amphibious vehicles, and helicopters evacuating casualties from the beaches. Medical personnel embarked in the evacuation control ship effect distribution of casualties throughout the attack force in accordance with ships' casualty capabilities and specialized medical facilities available, and also perform emergency surgery.

Evacuees. Civilians, either residents or transients, who have been ordered to move by competent authority, and whose movement and accommodation are planned and controlled. *See also* **Displaced person; Refugee.**

Evaluation (intelligence). Appraisal of an item of information in terms of credibility, reliability, pertinency, and accuracy. Appraisal is accomplished at several stages within the intelligence process with progressively different contexts. Initial evaluations, made by case officers and report officers are focused upon the reliability of the source and the accuracy of the information as judged by data available at, or close to, their operational levels. Later evaluations by intelligence analysts, are primarily concerned with verifying accuracy of information and may, in effect, convert information into intelligence. Appraisal or evaluation of items of information or intelligence is indicated by a standard letter-number system. The evaluation of the reliability of sources is designated by a letter from A to F, and the accuracy of the information is designated by numerals 1 to 6. These are two entirely independent appraisals, and these separate appraisals are indicated in accordance with the system indicated below. Thus information adjudged to be 'probably true' received from a 'usually reliable source' is designated 'B2', while information of which the 'truth cannot be judged' received from a 'usually reliable source' is designated 'B6'.

Reliability of Source	Accuracy of Information
A – completely reliable	1 – confirmed by other sources
B – usually reliable	2 – probably true
C – fairly reliable	3 – possibly true
D – not usually reliable	4 – doubtful
E – unreliable	5 – improbable
F – reliability cannot be judged	6 – truth cannot be judged

Evasion and escape. The procedures and operations whereby military personnel and other selected individuals are enabled to emerge by devious routes from an enemy-held or hostile area to areas under friendly control.

Exaggerated stereoscopy. *See* **Hyperstereoscopy.**

Exchequer and Audit Department reference sheet. An official request submitted by the Exchequer and Audit Department to the Accounting Officer for information on, or explanation of, apparent shortcomings revealed during the course of their audit.

Executing commander (nuclear weapons). A commander to whom nuclear weapons are released for delivery against specific targets or in accordance with approved plans. *See also* **Releasing commander** (nuclear weapons).

Exercise (ex). A military manoeuvre or simulated war-time operation involving planning, preparation, and execution. It is carried out for the purpose of training and evaluation. It may be a combined, unified, joint, or single service exercise, depending on participating organizations. **Command post exercise.** *See under* **Command. Skeleton exercise,** one in which commanders and essential personnel only, *eg* drivers, take part. **Tactical exercise,** without troops, *see* TEWT * **Commander.** A commander taking part in the exercise who will issue appropriate operation orders to forces placed under his control. He may be allocated responsibilities regarding controlling, conducting, and/or directing the exercise in addition to that of command. * **Planning Directive.** The instructions given by the officer who has initiated the exercise to his staff to give guidance in its preparation. It amplifies the Directive **Specification** which embodies the fundamental requirements and scope of the exercise.

Exon. *See* **Queen's Bodyguard of the Yeomen of the Guard.**

Expected approach clearance time. The time at which it is expected that an arriving aircraft will be cleared to commence approach for a landing.

Expeditionary Force Institutes (EFI). The uniformed branch of NAAFI (*qv*).

Expendable supplies and materials. Items which are consumed in use, such as ammunition, or which lose their identity such as certain repair parts, or which are of low intrinsic value, unworthy of full accounting procedures.

Experimental model. A model constructed in order to determine how certain assumptions made in design will work out in practice or to explore particular areas of uncertainty.

Exploitation.
1. Taking full advantage of success in battle and following up initial gains.
2. Taking full advantage of any information that has come to hand for tactical or strategic purposes.

Explosive ordnance. Bombs and warheads; guided and ballistic missiles; artillery, mortar, rocket and small arms ammunition; all mines; demolition charges; pyrotechnics; clusters and dispensers; cartridge and propellant actuated devices; electro-explosive devices; clandestine and improvised explosive devices; and all similar or related items or components explosive in nature. This definition includes all munitions containing explosives, nuclear fission or fusion materials and biological and chemical agents. * **Disposal.** The detection, identification, field evaluation, rendering-safe, recovery and final disposal of unexploded explosives. It may also include the rendering-safe and/or disposal of explosives which have become hazardous by damage or deterioration when the disposal of such explosives is beyond the capabilities of personnel normally assigned the responsibility for routine disposal.

Explosive ordnance reconnaissance. Reconnaissance involving the investigation, detection, location, verification, marking, identification and reporting of suspected unexploded explosives in order to determine further action.

Exposure dose. The measurement of radiation at a given point in relation to its ability to produce ionization. The unit of measurement of the exposure dose is the roentgen.

External audit. The examination of a department's accounts by the Comptroller and Auditor General (Exchequer and Audit Department).

Extra Regimental Employment (ERE). An appointment held by an officer or soldier on the staff or in an establishment which does not count against the strength of his parent unit.

Extraction parachute. An auxiliary parachute designed to release and extract and deploy cargo from aircraft in flight and deploy cargo parachutes.

Extractor. The claw which removes the expended cartridge from the chamber of a small arm.

Ex-works contract. A contract under which formal delivery of the articles is effected at the contractor's works.

Facility. An activity which provides a specific kind of operating assistance to naval, ground or air forces thereby facilitating any action or operation. *See also* **Base.**

Facings. The name given to the cuffs and collar of the ceremonial and mess dress of a regiment. The colour of the facings differs according to the Regiment, *eg* Royal Artillery scarlet, Royal Regiments of Infantry blue.

Facsimile. A system of telecommunications for the transmission of fixed images with a view to their reception in a permanent form.

Fair drawing. A drawing complete in all respects in the style and form specified for reproduction.

Falcon. A tracked British self-propelled armoured anti-aircraft vehicle mounting two 30 mm guns.

Fallout. The precipitation to earth of radioactive particulate matter from a nuclear cloud; also applied to the particulate matter itself. * **Contours.** Lines joining points which have the same radiation intensity that define a fallout pattern, represented in terms of roentgens per hour. * **Pattern.** The distribution of fallout as portrayed by fallout contours. * **Wind vector plot.** A wind vector diagram based on the wind structure from the surface of the earth to the highest altitude of interest.

False colour film. A colour film with at least one emulsion layer sensitive to radiation outside the visible region of the spectrum (*eg* infra red), in which the representation of colours is deliberately altered.

False origin. A fixed point to the south and west of a grid zone from which grid distances are measured eastward and northward.

False parallax. The apparent vertical displacement of an object from its true position when viewed stereoscopically, due to movement of the object itself as well as to change in the point of observation.

False stereo. An imaginary impression of stereoscopic relief.

Fan camera photography. Photography taken simultaneously by an assembly of three or more cameras, systematically installed at fixed angles relative to each other so as to provide wide lateral coverage with overlapping images.

Fan marker beacon. A type of radio beacon, the emissions of which radiate in a vertical, fan-shaped pattern. The signal can be keyed for identification purposes. *See also* **Radio beacon; Z Marker beacon.**

Fanfare. A flourish of trumpets.

Farrier. An artificer who shoes the horses of the mounted squadron of the Household Cavalry. Before mechanization farriers were borne on the strength of all units which had horses or mules on their establishment.

Fascine. A roll of wooden palings, usually large. Usually designed to be dropped by

a tank into a trench, enabling it to cross.

Fatigues. A task of a non-combative, and usually unpopular, nature carried out by soldiers.

Feather bonnet. The ceremonial head-dress of Highland Regiments.

Feature. In cartography, any object or configuration of ground or water represented on the face of a map or chart. * **Line overlap.** A series of overlapping air photographs which follow the line of a ground feature. *eg* river, road, railway, etc.

F echelon. The vehicles and men of a unit required in action.

Felix. The bomb disposal organization.

Ferret. A British four-wheeled armoured car, normally mounting one 7.62 mm machine-gun.

Feu de Joie. A discharge of blank ammunition on a ceremonial occasion. It consists of three discharges commencing on the right of the line, each man firing as soon as the man on his right has done so.

Fibrescope. A flexible endoscope (*qv*).

Fiducial marks. *See* **Collimating marks.**

Field Ambulance. A mobile RAMC unit which collects and treats sick and wounded and either returns them to their unit or evacuates them for further treatment.

Field army.
1. The largest administrative and tactical organization of a land force made up of a number of corps and divisions.
2. All the military forces of a nation or group of allied nations exclusive of the naval and airforces thereof, except in the case of certain nations whose airforces are included in their army.

Field Army Support Command (FASCOM). The US organization supplying logistic support to a field army.

Field Artillery Computer Equipment (FACE). An equipment at the gun site which computes the information fed into it by the FO and includes gun and target positional data, allowance for rotation of the earth, meteorology, wear of gun barrels and variation of projectile weight. It can calculate its own exact position on the ground in less than ten seconds.

Field control. A series of points whose relative positions and elevations are known. These positions are used in basic data in mapping and charting. Normally, these positions are established by survey methods, and are sometimes referred to as 'trig control'. *See also* **Common control; Control point; Ground control.**

Field defences. Protective works of a temporary nature, capable of construction by all arms with a minimum of engineer support.

Field Dressing Station (FDS). A fully mobile element of the Casualty Clearing Station (CCS) (*qv*) which cares for less serious cases and can be used for other duties by reason of its mobility.

Field exercise. An exercise conducted in the field under simulated war conditions in which troops and armaments on one side are actually present, while those of the other side may be imaginary or in outline. *See also* **Command post exercise.**

Field Fortifications. Emplacements and shelters of a temporary nature which can be constructed with reasonable facility by units requiring no more than minor engineer supervisory and equipment participation.

Field Marshal. The highest rank in the Army. A Field Marshal never retires. He remains on the active list until death. but his pay is reduced when he ceases to be employed.

Field of fire (f of f). The area which a weapon or group of weapons may cover effectively with fire from a given position.

Field of view. The angle between two rays passing through the perspective centre (rear nodal point) of a camera lens to the two opposite sides of the format. Not to be confused with 'angle of view' (*qv*).

Field rank (Officer). Officers above the rank of Captain and below that of Major General.

Field workshop REME. Each armoured or infantry brigade has one field workshop attached to it which is equipped to carry out field repairs to every type of vehicle and equipment in the brigade. It is fully mobile and self administered. It includes a stores section RAOC.

Fife. A small wind instrument used in the corps of drums and played by a drummer.

Fighter cover. The maintenance of a number of fighter aircraft over a specified area or force for the purpose of repelling hostile air activities. *See also* **Airborne alert.**

Fighter engagement zone (air defence). That part of the Air Defence Area not covered by the Missile and LLAD (*qv*) Zone(s). Within a fighter zone friendly fighter interceptors have freedom of action to identify and if necessary engage other aircraft. Provision may have to be made for the safe passage of friendly aircraft through the zone by the establishment of safe zones.

Fighting compartment. Space inside a tank which encloses those members of the crew who man the armament.

Fighting patrol. *See* **Combat patrol.**

File. When a unit is formed in line the front rank man and the rear rank man behind him constitute a file.

Filler point. *See* **Charging point.**

Film badge. A photographic film packet to be carried by personnel, in the form of a badge, for measuring and permanently recording (usually) gamma-ray dosage.

Final assault position. The place on the ground where attacking troops form up before making physical contact with the enemy.

Final controller. A radar controller employed in the transmission of GCA talk-down instructions to the pilot of an aircraft on the final approach to the runway, and in passing monitoring information to the pilot when using a landing aid other than GCA.

Final drive. Mechanism which transfers power from the gearbox to the driving sprocket of a tank.

Fire and movement. The tactic of dividing an attacking force into two parties, one delivering fire whilst the other advances. Roles are changed at suitable intervals according to the ground and the size of the units engaged.

Fireball. The luminous sphere of hot gases which forms a few millionths of a second after detonation of a nuclear weapon and immediately starts expanding and cooling.

Fire control radar. Radar used to provide target information inputs to a weapon fire control system.

Fire control system.
1. Group of interrelated fire control equipments and/or instruments designed for use with a weapon or group of identical weapons.
2. A system including radar equipment installed in interceptor aircraft used to assist or effect an air-to-air interception.
3. A system including radar equipment designed to ensure that surface-to-air missiles are used as effectively and efficiently as possible.

Fire for effect.
1. Fire which is delivered after the mean point of impact or burst is within the desired distance of the target or adjusting/ranging point.
2. Term in a fire message to indicate the adjustment/ranging is satisfactory and fire for effect is desired.

Fire message. *See* **Call for fire.**

Fire mission.
1. Specific assignment given to a fire unit as part of a definite plan.
2. Order used to alert the weapon/battery area and indicate that the message following is a call for fire.

Fire plan. A tactical plan for using the weapons of a unit or formation so that their fire will be co-ordinated.

Fire selector lever. US. *See* **Change lever.**

Fire storm. Stationary mass fire, generally in built-up urban areas, generating strong, inrushing winds from all sides; the winds keep the fires from spreading while adding fresh oxygen to increase their intensity.

Fire support area. An appropriate manoeuvre area assigned to fire support ships from which to deliver gunfire support of an amphibious operation. *See also* **Naval support area.**

Fire support co-ordination. The planning and executing of fire so that targets are adequately covered by a suitable weapon or group of weapons. * **Centre.** A single location in which are centralized communications facilities and personnel incident to the co-ordination of all forms of fire support. * **Line (FSCL).** A line established by the appropriate ground commander to insure co-ordination of fire not under his control but which may affect current tactical operations. The FSCL should follow well-defined terrain features. The establishment of the FSCL is normally co-ordinated with the appropriate tactical air commander and other supporting elements.

Fire support group. A temporary grouping of ships under a single commander charged with supporting troop operations ashore by naval gunfire. A fire support group may be further subdivided into fire support units and fire support elements.

Fire task. *See* **Fire mission.**

Firepower.
1. The amount of fire which may be delivered by a position, unit, or weapon system.
2. Ability to deliver fire.

Firepower umbrella. An area of specified dimensions defining the boundaries of the airspace over a naval force at sea within which the fire of ships' anti-aircraft weapons can endanger aircraft, and within which special procedures have been established for the identification and operation of friendly aircraft. *See also* **Air defence operations area.**

Firm price. A price which is not subject to variation.

First key plan. A plan of the layout of a projected Advanced Base or Maintenance Area, made from maps and from such information of the terrain as may be available when access to the area is not possible.

Fission. The process of the nucleus of a heavy element splitting up into the nuclei of lighter elements, thereby releasing a substantial amount of energy.
* Products. A general term for the complex mixture of substances produced as a result of nuclear fission. *** to yield ratio.** The ratio of the yield derived from nuclear fission to the total yield; it is frequently expressed in percentage.

Fix. A position determined from terrestrial, electronic, or astronomical data.

Fixed ammunition. Ammunition in which the cartridge case is permanently attached to the projectile. *See also* **Ammunition.**

Fixed defence. Protective works of a permanent nature, the construction of which involves the employment of specialists.

Fixed medical treatment facility. A medical treatment facility which is designed to operate for an extended period of time at a specific site.

Fixed price. An agreed price which may or may not be subject to variation as provided for in the contract.

Fixer network system. A combination of radio or radar direction-finding installations which, operating in conjunction, are capable of plotting the position relative to the ground of an aircraft in flight.

Flame thrower. A weapon that projects incendiary fuel and has provision for ignition of this fuel.

Flank. The extreme right or left of a body of troops on a military position.
* Guards. A security element operating to the flank of a moving or stationary force to protect it from enemy ground observation, direct fire and surprise attack.

Flap. (Slang). A mild state of emergency. 'There is a flap on' indicates that an unexpected order requiring action has been received.

Flare. The change in the flight path of an aircraft so as to reduce the rate of descent for touchdown.

Flash blindness. Temporary or permanent impairment of vision resulting from an intense flash of light. It includes loss of night adaptation and dazzle, and may be associated with retinal burns. *See also* **Dazzle.**

Flash burn. A burn caused by excessive exposure (of bare skin) to thermal radiation.

Flash suppressor. Device attached to the muzzle of the weapon which reduces the amount of visible light or flash created by burning propellant gases.

Flechette (round). A bullet which has a long thin central core of hard metal which tumbles (*ie* ceases to fly straight) on impact and causes an incapacitating wound. It's lethality is beyond question, but it tends to be inaccurate in flight.

Flight (air).
1. A subdivision of a squadron.
2. Any airborne period in an aircraft.
* **Following.** The task of maintaining contact with specified aircraft for the purpose of determining en route progress and/or flight termination. * **Information centre.** A unit established to provide flight information service and alerting service. * **Information region.** An airspace of defined dimensions within which flight information service and alerting service are provided. *See also* **Air traffic control centre.** * **Levels.** Surfaces of constant atmospheric pressure which are related to a specific pressure datum, 1013.2 mb (29.92 in), and are separated by specific pressure intervals. (Flight levels are expressed in three digits that represent hundreds of feet; *eg* flight level 250 represents a barometric altimeter indication of 25,000 feet and flight level 255 is an indication of 25,500 feet.) * **Line.** In air photographic reconnaissance, the prescribed ground path over which an air vehicle moves during the execution of its photo mission. * **Plan.** Specified information provided to air traffic services units, relative to the intended flight of an aircraft. * **Readiness firing.** Short duration tests relating to a rocket system carried out with the propulsion device in operation, the rocket being fixed on the launcher. Such tests are carried out in order to define the state of preparation of the rocket system and of the launching facilities before the flight test.* **Sister.** *See* **Nursing officer.** * **Surgeon.** A physician specially trained in aviation medical practice whose primary duty is the medical examination and medical care of aircrew.
* **Test.** Test of an aircraft, rocket, missile, or other vehicle by actual flight or launching. A flight test is planned to achieve specific test objectives and gain operational information.

Floating lines. In photogrammetry, lines connecting the same two points of detail on each print of a stereo pair, used to determine whether or not the points are intervisible. The lines may be drawn directly into the prints or superimposed by means of strips of transparent material.

Floating mark or dot. A mark seen as occupying a position in the three dimensional space formed by the stereoscopic fusion of a pair of photographs, used as a reference mark in examining or measuring a stereoscopic model.

Floating reserve. In an amphibious operation, reserve troops which remain embarked until needed. *See also* **General reserve.**

Flotation. The capability of a vehicle to float in water.

Flume. An inclinded channel for conveying water.

Flush fitting. A fitting having the whole of the top surface level with the surrounding paved surface.

Fly-in-Scale. *See* **Scale** (logistic).

Flying bridge. Consists of one or more barges attached to a cable fastened to both banks of a river. By correct angling of the barges they will be pushed from bank to bank by the force of the current.

Flying time. The total time from the moment an aircraft becomes airborne until it touches down.

Focal length. *See* **Calibrated focal length; Equivalent focal length; Nominal focal length.**

Focal plane. The plane, perpendicular to the optical axis of the lens, in which images of points in the object field of the lens are focused.

Fog. Obscurity of the atmosphere reducing surface visibility to less than 1,100 yards, caused by particles of condensed moisture (or of smoke) held in suspension in the air.

Follow-up (amphibious). The landing of reinforcements and stores after the assault and assault follow-on echelons have been landed. * **Echelon** (air transport). Elements moved into the objective area after the assault echelon.
* **Scale.** *See* **Scale** (logistic).

Foot Guards. The Grenadier, The Coldstream, The Scots, The Irish and the Welsh Guards.

Force. Army Cadet Force (ACF). A voluntary body of youths composed of contingents based on a territorial or school basis who undergo military training under adult officers and instructors as part of the youth movement of the country. **Combined Cadet Force (CCF)** as for ACF but confined to certain schools and includes Naval and/or Air Force contingents.

Forces allocated to NATO. Those forces made available to NATO by a nation under the categories of:
1. assigned.
2. earmarked for assignment.
3. earmarked for assignment on mobilization.

Foreshore flats. An area of sand, gravel, mud, etc, which is bare or awash at low tide but covered at high tide.

Foresight. The blade at the end of the barrel of a small arm which is aligned with the backsight on to the target for a correct aim.

Format.
1. In photography, the size and/or shape of a negative or of the print therefrom.

2. In cartography, the shape and size of a map or chart.

Formation.
1. An ordered arrangement of troops and/or vehicles for a specific purpose.
2. An ordered arrangement of two or more units or aircraft proceeding together.

Forming up place (FUP). The last position occupied by an assault echelon before crossing the start line/line of departure.

Form line. A line joining all points of approximately equal elevation. Form lines are not normally annotated with elevation figures.

Forward aeromedical evacuation. That phase of evacuation which provides airlift for patients between points within the battlefield, from the battlefield to the initial point of treatment, and to subsequent points of treatment within the combat zone.

Forward air controller (FAC). An officer who, from a forward position, directs the action of combat aircraft engaged in close air support of ground forces.

Forward airhead maintenance area (FAMA). The maintenance area located forward of the MRT airhead. It is established when the forward troops have moved beyond the economical range of VTOL aircraft being used for logistic support or one day's turn round in the second line transport from the AMA/FMA.

Forward battle zone (FBZ). The area in which opposing forces are in actual contact, or where an immediate threat of such contact exists. In static warfare it is easy to define but during mobile operations an FBZ can be created almost anywhere by the incursion of airborne forces.

Forward brigade administrative area (Fwd BAA). Units 'A' Echelon (*qv*) vehicles, some DPs (*qv*), an ADS (*qv*) and other supporting units may be so located near Brigade HQ in a Forward BAA under command of an officer of Brigade HQ who will co-ordinate movement and defence.

Forward defended locality (FDL). *See* **Forward Edge of the Battle Area.**

Forward Edge of the battle area (FEBA). The foremost limits of a series of areas in which ground combat units are deployed, excluding the areas in which the covering or screening forces are operating, designated to co-ordinate fire support, the positioning of forces, or the manoeuvre of units.

Forward lap. *See* **Overlap.**

Forward Maintenance Area (FMA). *See* **Airhead Maintenance Area.**

Forward motion compensation. *See* **Image motion compensation.**

Forward observer (FO). An oberver operating with front line troops and trained to adjust ground or naval gunfire and air bombardment and pass back battlefield information.

Forward Repair Team (FRT). A REME detachment of the Brigade Workshop which supplements the work of the LAD (*qv*) and undertakes repairs beyond the capacity of the latter.

Forward slope. Any slope which descends towards the enemy.

Four-round illumination diamond. A method of firing illuminating shells to cover and illuminate a large area.

Fox. A British four-wheeled armoured car, developed from the Ferret, normally mounting a 30 mm Rarden cannon.

Fraction package. A package containing less than the originally authorized quantity of stores.

Frag. v. (US slang). Embarrass or intimidate officers by enlisted men.

Frame. In photography, any single exposure contained within a continuous sequence of photographs.

Free air overpressure. The unreflected pressure, in excess of the ambient atmospheric pressure, created in the air by the blast wave from an explosion.

Free drop. The dropping of equipment or supplies from an aircraft without the use of parachutes. *See also* **Airdrop; Air movement; Free fall; High velocity drop; Low velocity drop.**

Free fall. A parachute manoeuvre in which the parachute is manually activated at the discretion of the jumper or automatically at a pre-set altitude.

Free field overpressure. *See* **Free air overpressure.**

Free issue. The issue of *matériel* other than to a public account which under specific authority, is made without a charge.

Free rocket. A rocket not subject to guidance or control in flight.

Freedom fighters. *See* **Guerilla.**

Freight. Cargo transported, including mail and unaccompanied baggage.
* **Container.** A receptacle designed to contain unit loads, individual packages and/or individual items of *matériel* so that they may be transported with a minimum of handling, even when several methods of transportation are used.

Frog.
1. NATO code name for a family of USSR battlefield support tactical missiles.
2. The piece of equipment which attaches the bayonet to the belt of a soldier.

Front.
1. The lateral space occupied by troops measured from the extremity of one

flank to the extremity of the other flank.

2. The direction of the enemy.

3. The line of contact of two opposing forces.

4. When a combat situation does not exist or is not assumed, the direction toward which the command is faced.

Frontage. The linear extent of ground occupied or dominated by a unit.

Frontal attack. Where the main thrust is directed at the enemy's front.

Fug. A Soviet designed light armoured car in use in some satellite countries.

Full command. The military authority and responsibility of a superior officer to issue orders to subordinates. It covers every aspect of military operations and administration and exists only within national services. The term command, as used internationally, implies a lesser degree of authority than when it is used in a purely national sense. It follows that no NATO Commander has full command over the forces that are assigned to him. This is because nations, in assigning forces to NATO, assign only operational command or operational control. *See also* **Command.**

Functional Command. Denotes a command without territorial limits to which units are allotted by the nature of their duties as opposed to their physical location.

Furlough. An obsolescent term for leave of absence.

Furnished married quarter hiring. A house or flat taken on individual short-term lease, of usually not more than three years, to accommodate an entitled family. It is furnished by the owner and the rent paid from the Defence Lands Vote.

Fuse. *See* **Boresafe fuse; Impact action fuse; Proximity fuse; Self-destroying fuse; Shuttered fuse; Time fuse; Variable time fuse.**

Fusilier (Fus). A private soldier in the Royal Regiment of Fusiliers.

Fusion. The process of the nuclei of light elements combining to form the nucleus of a heavy one, thereby releasing an immense amount of energy.

FV 432. A tracked British armoured personnel carrier capable of carrying ten infantrymen in full battle order.

G-Day. The day and the hour (G-hour) when the order to carry out an operation is issued. All subsequent timings are based on it.

G-Hour. *See* **G-day.**

G 1098. The inventory of arms and equipment which are, or should be, held on charge by a unit.

Gabion. A hollow cylinder which can be filled with earth to revet a trench.

Gainful. NATO codename for a USSR anti-aircraft missile system.

Galil. The new Israeli rifle firing the US 5.56 mm cartridge designed to replace the Uzi (*qv*) and other small arms.

Galosh. NATO code name for a Russian surface to air missile similar to the US Spartan (*qv*).

Ganef. NATO codename for a USSR surface-to-air missile.

Gap filler radar. A radar used to supplement the coverage of long range radar in areas where coverage is inadequate.

Gap marker (land mine warfare). Used to mark a minefield gap. A gap marker at the entrance to, and exit from, the gap will be referenced to a land mark or

intermediate marker. *See also* **Marker**
(land mine warfare).

Garrison force. All units assigned to a
base or area for defence, development,
operation, and maintenance of facilities.

General. The rank immediately below
that of Field Marshal. Below him is a
Lieutenant General and below that again
a Major General. The rank of Brigadier
General was abolished after the First
World War and that of Brigadier sub-
stituted.

General purpose machine-gun (GPMG).
The present replacement for both the
heavy and the light machine-guns of the
past.

General reserve. Reserve of troops under
the control of the overall commander.
See also **Floating reserve.**

General service (GS). Slang, roughly
equivalent to 'general purpose' and
applicable to any common issue equipment: *eg* overcoat. When applied to a
person indicates that he is strict and
conscientious.

General staff (G or GS). The senior
division of the staff. It is divided into a
number of branches *eg* Staff Duties
(*qv*), Operations, Intelligence,
Training, etc.

General support artillery. Artillery
which fires in general support of an
operation and not specifically in support
of a designated unit.

Geneva Convention. A code of behaviour
in war-time governing the treatment of
sick, wounded and prisoners agreed by
the European powers in 1864-65, subsequently much amended and signed by
most civilized nations.

Gentlemen-at-Arms. Members of Her
Majesty's Bodyguard of the Honourable
Corps of Gentlemen-at-Arms. A small

bodyguard of retired officers of field
rank in attendance on the Sovereign on
State occasions commanded by a Captain
under whom there is a Lieutenant, a
Standard Bearer, a Clerk of the Cheque
and Adjutant and a Harbinger.

Geographic co-ordinates. The quantities
of latitude and longitude which define
the position of a point on the surface of
the earth with respect to the reference
spheroid. * **Meridian.** A general term
applying alike to an astronomical or
geodetic meridian.

Georef. A grid system used in reporting
positions, using the earth's graticule of
latitude and longitude as the grid. *See
also* **Co-ordinates.**

Glacis. The cleared area sloping down
from a line of trenches or other fortifications. * **Plate.** Frontal hull armour
of a tank.

Glide. In a flight control system, a
control mode in which an aircraft is
automatically positioned to the centre
of the glide slope course.
* **Path.**
1. The flight path of an aircraft or
winged missile as it glides downward, the
line of which forms an angle with the
longitudinal axis of the aircraft or
missile.
2. The line to be followed by an aircraft
as it descends from horizontal flight to
land upon the surface. Also called 'glide
slope'.

Go around. In an automatic flight
control system, a control mode which
terminates an aircraft approach and
programmes a climb. *See also* **Overshoot.**

Go green (US slang). To transfer a
telephone conversation from an ordinary
to a secure line. Derived from the colour
of the instrument which is connected to
the latter. To speak confidentially.

Gog. NATO code name for a USSR anti-
aircraft guided missile system.

Gorget. Originally the piece of body armour worn as a protection to the throat, now commemorated by the gorget patches of cloth worn by officers of star rank on their lapels.

Graphic. Any and all products of the cartographic and photogrammetric art. A graphic may be either a map, chart or mosaic or even a film strip that was produced using cartographic techniques; *** Scale.** A graduated line by means of which distances on the map, chart or photograph may be measured in terms of ground distance. *See also* **Scale.**

Graticule. In cartography, a network of lines representing the earth's parallels of latitude and meridians of longitude. *** Ticks.** In cartography, short lines indicating where selected meridians and parallels intersect.

Gravity extraction. The extraction of cargoes from the aircraft by influence of their own weight.

Grazing fire. Fire which is approximately parallel to the ground and does not rise above the height of a man standing.

Great circle. A circle on the surface of the earth, the plane of which passes through the centre of the earth. *** Route.** The route which follows the shortest arc of a great circle between two points.

Green Archer. A radar and computer system designed for the rapid location of enemy mortar positions and for observation and correction of friendly fire.

Greenwich mean time. Mean solar time at the meridian of Greenwich.

Grenade. A metal or plastic container filled with explosive which bursts either on impact or by the operation of a time fuse. May be thrown by hand or fired from a rifle.

Grenadier. Literally a man who throws

a grenade. Previously each regiment had a grenadier company but now all infantry soldiers are taught to throw grenades. A member of the Grenadier Guards is frequently referred to as a grenadier.

Grid. *See* **Military grid. * Bearing.** The direction of an object from a point, expressed as a horizontal angle, measured clockwise with reference to grid north. *** Convergence.** The horizontal angle at a place between true north and grid north. It is proportional to the longitude difference between the place and the central meridian. *** Convergence factor.** The ratio of the grid convergence angle to the longitude difference (see grid convergence). In the Lambert Conical Orthomorphic projection this is constant and is sometimes called the 'constant of the cone'. *See also* **Convergence. * Co-ordinates.** Plane-rectangular co-ordinates based on and mathematically adjusted to a map projection in order that geographic positions (latitudes and longitudes) may be readily transformed into plane co-ordinates and the computations relating to them made by the ordinary methods of plane surveying. *** Co-ordinate system.** A plane-rectangular co-ordinate system usually based on, and mathematically adjusted to, a map projection in order that geographic positions (latitudes and longitudes) may be readily transformed into plane co-ordinates and the computations relating to them may be made by the ordinary methods of plane surveying. *See also* **Co-ordinates. * Interval.** The distance represented between the lines of a grid. *** Magnetic angle.** Angular difference in direction between grid north and magnetic north. It is measured east or west from grid north. Grid magnetic angle is sometimes called 'grivation' and/or 'grid variation'. *** North.** The northerly or zero direction indicated by the grid datum of directional reference. *** Ticks.** Small marks on the neatline of a map or chart indicating additional grid reference systems included on that sheet. Grid ticks are sometimes shown on the interior grid

lines of some maps for ease of referencing.
* Variation. *See* **Grid magnetic angle.**

Griffon. NATO code name for a Soviet
surface-to-air missile.

Grivation. *See* **Grid magnetic angle.**

Grooves. The helical spirals in a barrel
of a weapon (*qv*) which give spin to the
projectile.

Gross weight. Weight of a ground vehicle
including fuel, lubricants, coolant,
vehicle tools and spares, cargo and
operating personnel. *See also* **Net weight.**

Ground alert. The status of aircraft on
the ground which are fully armed and
serviced, with their combat crews at
hand and ready to leave on a mission at
very short notice.

Ground attack (GA). Offensive action by
aircraft against ground targets using
cannons, bombs, rockets or air to ground
missiles.

Ground control. A system of accurate
measurements used to determine the
distances and direction or differences in
elevation between points on the earth.
See also **Common control; Control
point; Field control; Traverse.**

Ground controlled approach. The technique or procedures for talking down
− through the use of both surveillance
and precision approach radar − an
aircraft during its approach so as to
place it in a position for landing.

Ground effect machine. A machine
which normally flies within the zone of
the ground effect or ground cushion.

Ground liaison officer (GLO). An officer
especially trained in air reconnaissance
and/or offensive air support activities.
These officers are normally organized
into teams under the control of the
appropriate ground force commander
to provide liaison to air force and navy

units engaged in training and combat
operations.

Ground liaison section (GLsect). An
Army unit consisting of a variable
number of Army officers, other ranks,
and vehicles responsible for Army/Air
liaison under control of Army headquarters.

Ground Nadir. The point on the
ground vertically beneath the perspective
centre of the camera lens. On a true
vertical photograph this coincides with
the principal point.

Ground observer organization. A corps
of ground watchers deployed at suitable
points throughout an air defence system
to provide visual and aural information
of aircraft movements.

Ground position. The position of the
earth vertically below an aircraft.
* indicator. An instrument which
determines and displays automatically
the dead-reckoning position of an
aircraft.

Ground pressure. The main parameter
determining a tank's performance on
soft ground. Usually expressed in pounds
per square inch (psi) of the area of
track laid by the tank on level ground.

Ground return. The reflection from the
terrain as displayed and/or recorded as
an image.

Ground signals. A system of visual
signals displayed on an airfield to give
local Air Traffic Rules information to
pilots in the air. *See also* **Signal area.**

Ground speed. In a flight control system,
a control mode in which the ground
speed of an aircraft is automatically
controlled to a computed value.

Ground zero (GZ). The point on the
surface of land or water at, or vertically
below or above, the centre of the

burst of a nuclear weapon. *See also*
**Actual ground zero; Desired ground
zero.**

Group burial. A burial in a common grave
of two or more individually unidentified
remains. *See also* **Burial.**

Guard of Honour. In US **Honor Guard.**
A body of men drawn up in line to
receive a Royal or distinguished person.
Its strength varies according to the rank
of the visitor.

Guardsman. A soldier of the Foot
Guards. The equivalent of private in
line regiments.

Guard task. Usually given to armour to
carry out screen tasks and also to delay
the enemy for a specific period so as to
provide time, usually for the preparation
of the main battle area, and to inflict
casualties.

Guerilla. A man or woman who has
joined with others to take up arms against
an established government. Known
variously as Freedom Fighters, Patriots,
Assassins, Thugs, etc., according to
choice and political affiliation. * **Warfare.**
Military and para-military operations
conducted in enemy held or hostile
territory by irregular, predominantly
indigenous forces.

Guidance. In weapon systems denotes
the method employed by the operator
to induce the missile to home on to its
target. *See also* **Beam Riding Guidance;
Command guidance; Homing guidance
and Inertial guidance.** * **Station equipment.** The ground-based portion of a
missile guidance system necessary to
provide guidance during missile flight.
* **System** (missile). A system which
evaluates flight information, correlates
it with target data, determines the
desired flight path of the missile and
communicates the necessary commands
to the missile flight control system.
See also **Control system** (missile).

Guided missile (GM). An unmanned

vehicle moving above the surface of the
earth, whose trajectory or flight path is
capable of being altered by an external
or internal mechanism. *See also* **Aerodynamic missile; Ballistic missile.**
* (Air-to-air). An air-launched guided
missile for use against air targets.
* (Air-to-surface). An air-launched
guided missile for use against surface
targets. * (Surface-to-air). A surface-
launched guided missile for use against
air targets. * (Surface-to-surface). A
surface-launched guided
use against surface targets.

Guided weapons (GW), are those in
which the missile is guided on to its
target (*see* **Guidance**) as opposed to
artillery or mortars where the firer has
no control after initiating the flight path.
(*see* **Guided Missile).**

Guideline. NATO code name for a USSR
medium range anti-aircraft guided weapon
system.

Guide signs. Signs used to indicate
locations, distances, directions, routes,
and similar information.

Guidons. *See under* **Standards.**

Guild. NATO code name for a USSR
anti-aircraft guided missile system.

Gun. An artillery piece, which is breech
loaded as opposed to a mortar which is
muzzle loaded, and a rifle which is hand
held. **Anti-aircraft** *. A ground artillery
piece designed for use against aircraft.
Anti-tank *, a ground artillery piece
firing armour piercing (*qv*) ammunition
designed for use against tanks. * **Ship.**
Helicopter armed with weapons suitable
for offensive action. * **Carriage.** A
mobile or fixed support for a gun. It
sometimes includes the elevating and
traversing mechanisms. Sometimes called
'carriage'. * **Position officer (GPO).** The
artillery officer in charge of the gun site,
responsible for laying and firing the guns
as directed by the Battery Commander
or FO (*qv*). * **Target line.** An imaginary

straight line from the gun(s) to the target. * **Trunnions.** Supporting projections which act as a pivot for a gun in elevation.

Gunfire. A hot drink served at reveille. Derived from the old custom of firing a gun at the beginning of the day as a time signal.

Gunner. A soldier of the Royal Artillery. The equivalent of private in line regiments.

Gun-type weapon. A device in which two or more pieces of fissionable material, each less than a critical mass, are brought together very rapidly so as to form a supercritical mass which can explode as the result of a rapidly expanding fission chain.

Hachuring. A method of representing relief upon a map or chart by shading in short disconnected lines drawn in the direction of the slopes.

Half-life. The time required for the activity of a given radioactive species to decrease to half of its initial value due to radioactive decay. The half-life is a characteristic property of each radioactive species and is independent of its amount or condition. The effective half-life of a given isotope is the time in which the quantity in the body will decrease to half as a result of both radioactive decay and biological elimination.

Half-residence time. As applied to delay fallout, it is the time required for the amount of weapon debris deposited in a particular part of the atmosphere, to decrease to half of its initial value.

Half thickness. Thickness of absorbing material necessary to reduce by one-half the intensity of radiation which passes through it.

Halftone. Any photomechanical printing surface or the impression therefrom in which detail and tone values are represented by a series of evenly spaced dots of varying size and shape, varying in direct proportion to the intensity of the tones they represent. * **Screen.** A grating of opaque lines on glass, crossing at right angles, producing transparent apertures between intersections. Used in a process camera to break up a solid or continuous tone image into a pattern of small dots.

Half-track. A vehicle drawn by tracks in the rear half and steered by wheels in the front. Obsolescent.

Halt. Given as a word of command it brings movement to stop.

Harassing (air). The attack of any target within the area of land battle not connected with interdiction or close air support. It is designed to reduce the enemy's combat effectiveness. * **Fire** (HF). Fire designed to disturb the rest of the enemy troops, to curtail movement and, by threat of losses, to lower morale.

Harbour. An area behind the lines where tanks retire after battle for rest and maintenance although protection and concealment will be maintained.

Hard. A prepared surface on the bank of a river from which ferries, boats and amphibious vehicles can be launched.

Harden. To give protection from nuclear attack to an area or installation.

Hardened site. A site constructed to withstand the blast and associated effects of a nuclear attack and likely to be protected against a chemical, biological, or radiological attack.

Hard missile base. A launching base that is protected against a nuclear explosion.

Hardstand.
1. A paved or stablized area where

vehicles are parked.
2. Open ground having a prepared surface and used for the storage of material.

Harpon. A French wire guided surface to surface or air to surface missile system for anti-tank and similar purposes.

Hasty breaching (land mine warfare). The creation of lanes through enemy minefields by expedient methods such as blasting with demolitions, pushing rollers or disabled vehicles through the minefields when the time factor does not permit detailed reconnaissance, deliberate breaching or by-passing the obstacle. *See also* **Breaching.**

Hasty crossing. A crossing of a river or stream using crossing means at hand or readily available without pausing to make elaborate preparations. *See also* **Deliberate crossing.**

Hasty defence. A defence normally organized while in contact with the enemy or when contact is imminent and time available for the organization is limited. It is characterized by improvement of the natural defensive strength of the terrain by utilization of foxholes, emplacements, and obstacles. *See also* **Deliberate defence.**

Haversack. The small container attached to a soldier's equipment in which he can carry his razor, soap, spare socks, etc.

Hawk. A US mobile surface to air guided weapon system.

Hazard signs (road transport). Signs used to indicate traffic hazards. Military hazard signs are used in a communications zone area only in accord with existing agreement with national authorities.

Haze. Obscurity in the atmosphere caused by smoke or dust particles held in suspension, resulting in a visibility of between 1,110 and 2,200 yards.

Heading. The direction in which the longitudinal axis of an aircraft is pointed, usually expressed in degrees from North (true, magnetic, compass or grid). *** Hold.** In a flight control system, a control mode which automatically maintains an aircraft heading that exists at the instant of completion of a manoeuvre. *** Select.** A flight control system feature which permits selection or pre-selection of desired automatically controlled heading or headings of an aircraft.

Head up display. A method of representing to a driver or pilot an accurate visual display of command or situation information which is superimposed on his normal field of view.

Headquarters. The complex of offices from which a commander and his staff direct operations and exercise command. It will vary in size from the huge general headquarters of an army to the slit trench which serves a platoon as its headquarters.

Heavy-lift ship. A ship specially designed and capable of loading and unloading heavy and bulky items. It has booms of sufficient capacity to accommodate a single lift of 100 tons.

Hedgehog. The all round defence of an area with anti-tank, anti-personnel and anti-aircraft capability.

Hedgehopping. Slang for contour flying (*qv*).

Height.
1. The vertical distance of a level, a point, or an object considered as a point, measured from a specified datum.
2. The vertical dimension of an object. *See also* **Altitude; Elevation.**

Height datum. *See* **Altitude datum.**

Height delay. *See* **Altitude delay.**

Height hole. *See* **Altitude hole.**

Height of burst.
1. The vertical distance from the earth's surface or target to the point of burst.
2. For nuclear weapons, the optimum height of burst for a particular target (or area) is that at which it is estimated a weapon of a specified energy yield will produce a certain desired effect over the maximum possible area.

Helicopter(s). Any rotary winged aircraft. *** Assault force.** A task organization combining helicopters, supporting units, and helicopter-borne troops. *** Lane.** A safety corridor in which helicopters fly to or from their destination during helicopter operations. **Scout *.** A lightly armed helicopter used to seek and identify an enemy which can then be engaged by other units. *** Wave.** *See* **Wave.**

Helipad. A prepared area designated and used for take-off and landing of helicopters. Includes touchdown or hover point.

Heliport. A facility for operating, basing, servicing, and maintaining helicopters.

Helve. The wooden handle of entrenching and cutting tools *eg* picks, axes, etc.

Herbicide. A chemical compound which will kill or damage plants.

Hide. An area in which a force conceals itself before operations or before moving into battle positions. Particularly applicable to armour.

High altitude. Conventionally, an altitude above 10,000 metres. (33,000 feet). *See also* **Altitude. * Burst.** The explosion of a nuclear weapon which takes place at a height in excess of 100,000 feet. *See also* **Types of burst.**

High angle fire. Fire delivered at elevations greater than the elevation of maximum range; fire, the range of which decreases as the angle of elevation is increased.

Higher control. On exercises the staff responsible for formulating the plans and issuing orders supposed to emanate from an imaginary Headquarters superior to that being exercised. *See also* **Lower control.**

High explosive (HE). Used loosely as a generic term for any propellant charge but more explicitly for a shell which bursts as opposed to solid shot, gas or shrapnel.

High explosive anti-tank (HEAT). An explosive charge which penetrates armour on impact. Unlike AP (*qv*) a HEAT round can be fired from weapons with a low mv (*qv*).

High explosive squash head. (HESH). An anti-tank round. On striking a hard surface the casing is squashed and the charge explodes causing the interior armour to throw off lethal slabs of metal.

High speed motorway. A highway designed for high speed vehicular traffic, often, although not necessarily, a dual lane highway.

High velocity drop. A drop procedure in which the drop velocity is greater than 30 feet per second (low velocity drop) and lower than free drop velocity.

Highway. A main road or thoroughfare. *** Clover leaf.** An intersection of two or more highways, the plan pattern of which resembles the shape of a clover leaf.

Hill shading. A method of representing relief on a map by depicting the shadows that would be cast by high ground if light were shining from a certain direction.

Hi-valu. The term used to describe the monetary level at which an item of *matériel* may be selected for an intensified method of management control.

Hold.
1. A cargo storage compartment aboard ship.
2. To maintain or retain possession of by force, as a position or an area.
3. In an attack, to exert sufficient pressure to prevent movement or redisposition of enemy forces.
4. As applied to air traffic, to keep an aircraft within a specified space or location which is identified by visual or other means in accordance with Air Traffic Control instructions.

Hold fire. (Air defence). An emergency order meaning 'CEASE FIRE' or 'DO NOT OPEN FIRE' is cancelled only by 'RELEASE'. It is possible that a 'HOLD FIRE' order, qualified by a track number, is received too late with a missile already launched at that target. In such a case the missile is destroyed. This order may be qualified by the following either singly or in combination:
1. Bearing(s).
2. Height(s).
3. Range(s).
4. Time(s).
5. Sector or area.
6. Track number.

Holdee. *See* **Transient.**

Holding and reconsignment point. A rail or motor centre with considerable capacity, to which cars or trucks may be sent and at which they may be held until their destination becomes known or until the proper time arrives for them to be moved farther toward their destination. Also, a place where railroad cars or trucks may be unloaded and the cargo held for future transshipment.

Holding attack. An attack designed to hold the enemy in position, to deceive him as to where the main attack is being made, to prevent him from reinforcing the elements opposing the main attack, and/or to cause him to commit his reserves prematurely at an indecisive location.

Holding pattern programmer. Automatic control of an aircraft to fly the programmed holding pattern.

Holding point. A specified location, identified by visual or other means, in the vicinity of which the position of an aircraft in flight is maintained in accordance with air traffic control clearances.

Hole up. US slang for dig in, assume a defensive position.

Holster. The case which holds a revolver and is attached to a man's equipment.

Homing. The technique of tracking along a position line towards the point of origin of a radio, radar or other navigational aid. * **Guidance** in guided weapons systems is a system in which the flight path of the missile is determined by inbuilt guidance equipment, which reacts to some particular radiant characteristic of the target. *See also* **Active * Guidance; Passive * Guidance; Semi active * device. * Adaptor.** A device which, when used with an aircraft radio receiver produces aural and/or visual signals which indicate the direction of the transmitting radio station with respect to the heading of the aircraft.

Homogeneous area. An area which has uniform radar reflecting power at all points.

Honest John (HJ). A US unguided surface to surface rocket weapon system, giving place to Lance (*qv*).

Horizontal action mine. A mine designed to produce a destructive effect in a plane approximately parallel to the ground.

Horizontal error. The error in range, deflection, or in radius, which a weapon may be expected to exceed as often as not. Horizontal error of weapons making a nearly vertical approach to the target is described in terms of circular error probable. Horizontal error of weapons producing elliptical dispersion pattern is expressed in terms of probable error. *See also* **Circular error probable; Delivery error; Deviation; Dispersion error.**

Horizontal Loading. Loading of items of like character in horizontal layers throughout the holds of a ship. *See also* **Loading.**

Horse Artillery. The Royal * is the *corps d'élite* of the Royal Regiment of Artillery. It maintains one horsed battery for ceremonial purposes. When on parade with its guns the RHA assumes the right of the line.

Hostage. A person held as a pledge that certain terms or agreements will be kept. (The taking of hostages is forbidden under the Geneva Conventions 1949.)

Hostile track (air defence). The classification assigned to a track which, based upon established criteria, is determined to be an enemy airborne, ballistic, and/or orbiting threat.

Hot. An acronym for *Haut subsonique Optiquement teleguidé dur Tube,* a heavy anti-tank weapon developed by France and Germany.

Hot spot. Region in a contaminated area in which the level of radioactive contamination is considerably greater than in neighbouring regions in the area.

H-Hour. The specific hour on D-day on which hostilities commence. When used in connection with planned operations, it

is the specific hour on which the operation commences. **G** * *see* **G Day.**

P-Hour. The time planned for the first drop of a parachute force. Times relative to the designated hour are denoted by plus or minus.

Household Troops consist of the Life Guards, Blues and Royals and the five regiments of Foot Guards (*qv*).

Hovercraft. Any aircraft, *eg* helicopter, VTOL, with the capacity to hover.

Hovering. A self-sustaining manoeuvre whereby a fixed, or nearly fixed position is maintained relative to a spot on the surface of the earth * **Ceiling.** The highest altitude at which the helicopter is capable of hovering in standard atmosphere. It is usually stated in two figures: hovering in ground effect and hovering out of ground effect.

Hover pilot. The man at the controls of a hovercraft.

Howitzer (How). An artillery ordnance with a high trajectory.

Hueycobra. A US armed helicopter.

Hull down. A tactical position in which the tank exposes only its gun to the target thereby shielding its hull from view relative to the target.

Hussars. Formerly light cavalry, now part of the Royal Armoured Corps.

Hydrographic chart. A nautical chart showing depths of water, nature of bottom, contours of bottom and coastline, and tides and currents in a given sea or sea and land area.

Hydrography. The science which deals with the measurements and description of the physical features of the oceans, seas, lakes, rivers, and their adjoining coastal areas, with particular reference to their use for navigational purposes.

Hyperfocal distance. The distance from the lens to the nearest object in focus when the lens is focused at infinity.

Hypergolic fuel. Fuel which will spontaneously ignite with an oxidizer, such as aniline with fuming nitric acid. It is used as the propulsion agent in certain missile systems.

Hypersonic. Of or pertaining to speeds equal to, or in excess of, 5 times the speed of sound. *See also* **Speed of sound.**

Hyperstereoscopy. Stereoscopic viewing in which the relief effect is noticeably exaggerated, caused by the extension of the camera base. Also known as 'exaggerated stereoscopy'.

Hypsometric tinting. A method of showing relief on maps and charts by colouring in different shades those parts which lie between different levels. Sometimes referred to as 'elevation tints'; 'altitude tints'; 'layer tints'.

Icecrete. A mixture of gravel and frozen snow used as protection from fire or the elements in Arctic warfare.

Identification. The indication by any act or means of your own friendly character or individuality. * **Friend or foe** (IFF). A system using radar transmissions to which equipment carried by friendly forces automatically responds, for example, by emitting pulses, thereby distinguishing themselves from enemy forces. It is the primary method of determining the friendly or unfriendly character of aircraft and ships by other aircraft or ships and by ground forces employing radar detection equipment and associated Identification, friend or foe units.

Idler wheel. An unpowered wheel which carries the track of a tank. It is often adjustable so that it can act as a track tensioner.

Illegal absentee. A service officer or soldier, male or female, who is subject to the Army Act and has been absent without leave or other sufficient cause for a period of 21 days or more.

Imacon. An ultra high speed camera.

Image displacement. In a photograph, any dimensional or positional error.

Image motion compensation. The process of synchronizing the relative movement of the ground image, caused by all vehicle motion, with a recording sensor during exposure.

Imagery. Collectively, the representations of objects reproduced electronically or by optical means on film, electronic display devices, or other media. * **Interpretation.** The process of location, recognition, identification, and description of objects, activities, and terrain represented on imagery. * **Interpretation key.** Any diagrams, charts, tables, lists, or sets of examples, etc, which are used to aid imagery interpreters in the rapid identification of objects visible on imagery. * **Sortie.** One flight by one aircraft for the purpose of recording air imagery.

Immediate. When used in a signal or letter gives precedence over all other communications. * **Air support.** Air support to meet specific requests which arise during the course of a battle and which by their nature cannot be planned in advance. *See also* **Air support.** * **Decontamination.** Decontamination carried out by the individual as part of the CW immediate action drill. * **Operational readiness.** The state in which any arm or Service is ready in all respects for instant combat.

Immediately vital cargo. A cargo already loaded, which the consignee country regards as immediately vital for the prosecution of the war or for national survival, and delivery of which may be authorized by the national authorities of the flag of ship carrying the cargo, notwithstanding the risk to the ship. *See also* **Cargoes.**

Impact action fuse. A fuse that is set in action by the striking of a projectile or bomb against an object, *eg* percussion fuse, contact fuse, Synonymous with 'direct action fuse'. *See also* **Fuse.**

Impact area. An area having designated boundaries within the limits of which all ordnance is to make contact with the ground.

Impact point. The point on the drop zone where the first parachutist or airdropped cargo item should land.

Implosion weapon. A device in which a quantity of fissionable material, less than a critical mass, has its volume suddenly decreased by compression, so that it becomes supercritical and an explosion can take place. The compression is achieved by means of a spherical arrangement of specially fabricated shapes of ordinary high explosive which produce an inwardly-directed implosion wave, the fissionable material being at the centre of the sphere.

Imprint. Brief note in the margin of a map giving all or some of the following: date of publication, printing, name of publisher, printer, place of publication, number of copies printed, and related information.

Improvised (early) resupply. The onward movement of commodities which are available on land and which can be readily loaded into ships. *See also* **Elements of resupply.**

Incident (exercise). An occurrence injected by directing staffs into the exercise which will have an effect on the forces being exercised, or their facilities, and which will require action by the appropriate commander and/or staff being exercised.

Indefinite call sign. A call sign which does not represent a specific facility, command, authority, activity, or unit, but which may represent any one or any group of these. *See also* **Call sign.**

Indent. v. and n. A form of requisition used when stores are required.

Index contour line. A contour line accentuated by a heavier line weight to distinguish it from intermediate contour lines. Index contours are usually shown as every fifth contour with their assigned values, to facilitate reading elevations.

Index to adjoining sheets. *See* **Map index.**

Indicated airspeed. The airspeed shown by an airspeed indicator. * **Hold.** In a flight control system, a control mode in which desired indicated airspeed of an aircraft is maintained automatically.

Indicated altitude. The altitude as indicated or shown by an altimeter.

Indications (intelligence). Information in various degress of evaluation, all of which bears on the intention of a potential enemy to adopt or reject a course of action.

Indigo. An Italian land mobile surface to air tactical guided missile.

Indirect air support. Support given to land or sea forces by air action against objectives other than enemy forces engaged in tactical battle. It includes the gaining and maintaining of air superiority, interdiction and harassing. *See also* **Air support.**

Indirect approach. The tactic, advocated notably by Sir Basil Liddell Hart, of attacking the soft parts of an enemy defensive position and bypassing the heavily defended areas.

Indirect damage assessment. A revised target analysis based on new data such as actual weapon yield, burst height, and ground zero obtained by means other than direct assessment.

Indirect fire. Fire delivered at a target which cannot be seen by the aimer.

Indirect laying. When the target is invisible from the gun site, the gun is laid upon it by using some other fixed object from which adjustments can be made.

In direct support of. Applies to artillery only. Support is guaranteed to the supported formation or unit, but is also available to other callers when priority rights are not being exercised. The supporting unit is not under the command of the supported unit.

Individual training. The elementary military training given to a recruit before he joins his unit, carried out at corps and regimental depots (*qv*).

Induced radiation. Radiation produced as a result of exposure to radioactive materials, particularly the capture of neutrons. *See also* **Contamination; Residual radiation.**

Inertial Guidance in guided weapon systems is one in which the flight path to the target is determined by equipment measuring missile acceleration, self-contained within the missile.

Inertial navigation system. A self-contained navigational system capable of automatically determining dead-reckoning position through double integration of the outputs of accelerometers having pre-aligned gyro-stabilized axes.

Inert mine (land mine warfare). An inert replica of a standard mine. It is used for instructional purposes. *See also* **Mine.**

Infantry. Front line soldiers who fight dismounted as opposed to RAC (*qv*) who fight from armoured vehicles.

Infill. In cartography, the filling of an area or feature with colour, *eg* roads, town shapes, lakes, etc.

Infiltration. The movement through or into an area or territory occupied by either friendly or enemy troops or organizations. The movement is made, either by small groups or by individuals, at extended or irregular intervals. When used in connection with the enemy, it infers that contact is avoided.

Inflight report. A standard form of message whereby aircrews report mission results while in flight. It is also used for reporting any other tactical information sighted of such importance and urgency that the delay, if reported by normal debriefing, would negate the usefulness of the information.

Information (intelligence). Unevaluated material of every description, including that derived from observations, reports, rumours, imagery, and other sources which, when processed, may produce intelligence. * **Box.** A space on an annotated overlay, mosaic, map, etc., which is used for identification, reference, and scale information. * **Processing.** *See* **Intelligence cycle.**

Infra-red intruder system (IRIS) consists of an infra-red beam projected between a transmitter and a sensor to give warning of personnel or vehicles approaching within its arc.

Infrastructure. A term generally applicable to all fixed and permanent installations, fabrications, or facilities for the support and control of military forces. *See also* **Bilateral infrastructure; Common infrastructure; National infrastructure.**

Initial approach. That part of an instrument approach procedure consisting of the first approach to the first navigational facility associated with the procedure, or to a predetermined fix. When not associated with an instrument approach procedure, that portion of the flight of an aircraft immediately prior to arrival over the airfield of destination or over the reporting point from which the final approach to the airfield is commenced. * **Area.** An area of defined width lying between the last preceding navigational fix or dead reckoning position and either the facility to be used for making an instrument approach or a point associated with such a facility that is used for demarcating the termination of the initial approach area.

Initial contact report. *See* **Contact report.**

Initial (early) supply. The onward movement of ships which are already loaded with cargoes which will serve the requirements after D-day. This includes such shipping evacuation from major ports/major water terminals and subsequently dispersed to secondary ports/alternate water terminals and anchorages. *See also* **Elements of resupply.**

Initial issue. First combat supply; placed at the disposal of units of all arms of all Services in peace-time. In principle, it enables these units to fulfil their first missions without further supply. It can be transported by the organic transport of the unit. The data is expressed in number of rounds (or in lots in the case of explosives).

Initial point.
1. A well-defined point, easily distinguishable visually and/or electronically, used as a starting point for the bomb run to the target.
2. The first point at which a moving target is located on a plotting board.
3. (Airborne). A point close to the landing area where serials (troop carrier air formations) make final alterations in course to pass over individual drop or landing zones.
4. (Helicopter). An air control point in the vicinity of the landing zone from which individual flights of helicopters are directed to their prescribed landing sites.
5. A pre-selected point on the surface of the earth which is used as a reference. *See also* **Target approach point.**

Initial radiation. The radiation, essentially neutrons and gamma rays, resulting from a nuclear burst and emitted from the fireball within one minute after burst.

Initiation (nuclear). Action which sets off a chain reaction in a fissile mass which has reached the critical state (generally by the emission of a 'spurt' of neutrons).

Initiative. A commander who holds the initiative can impose his will on his opponent and force the latter to fight in accordance with his own wishes. Provided he can retain the initiative he will be the ultimate victor.

Inserted grouping (radar). The inclusion of one area of homogeneous surface material in an area of different material.

Inset. In cartography, a separate map positioned within the neatline of a larger map. Three forms are recognized:
1. an area geographically outside a sheet but included therein for convenience of publication, usually at the same scale;
2. a portion of the map or chart at an enlarged scale;
3. a smaller scale map or chart of surrounding areas, included for location purposes.

Instructional mine (land mine warfare). A completely inert replica of a mine used for classroom instruction in identification and functioning. It may be sectioned. *See also* **'Mine'.**

Instrument flight. Flight in which the path and altitude of the aircraft are controlled solely by reference to instruments.

Instrument landing system. A system of radio navigation intended to assist aircraft in landing which provides lateral and vertical guidance, including indications of distance from the optimum point of landing.

Instrument meteorological condition. Weather conditions which are such that flight in compliance with visual flight rules is precluded.

Instrument recording photography.
Photography of the presentation of
instrument data.

In support of. Assisting or protecting
another formation, unit, or organization while remaining under original
control. *See also* **Under command.**

Insurgency. Insurgency is a form of
rebellion, short of civil war, in which a
dissident faction that has the support
or acquiescence of a substantial part of
the population instigates the commission
of widespread acts of civil disobedience,
sabotage and terrorism in order to over-
throw the government.

Insurgents. Terrorists in organized
parties using quasi-military methods and
tactics.

Integrated logistic support. The pooling
of specified resources by nations for use
by the same nations as decided by their
co-ordinating agency or authority to
which the subscribing nations have
agreed. *See also* **Logistic assistance;**
Mutual aid; Reallocation of resources.

Integrated staff. A staff in a multi-
national headquarters in which one
officer only is appointed to each post
on the establishment of the headquarters,
irrespective of nationality and service.
See also **Combined staff; Joint staff;**
Parallel staff.

Integration. In photography, a process
by which the average radar picture
seen on several scans of the time base
may be obtained on a print, or the
process by which several photographic
images are combined into a single image.

Intelligence (Int). The product resulting
from the collection, evaluation, analysis,
integration and interpretation of all
available information which concerns
one or more aspects of foreign nations or
of areas of operations and which is
immediately or potentially significant to
military planning and operations. *See
also* **Basic *; Combat *; Counter *;**

Military *; Strategic *; Target *;
Technical *. * Collection plan. A plan
for gathering information from all
available sources to meet an intelligence
requirement. Specifically, a logical plan
for transforming the essential elements
of information into orders or requests
to sources within a required time limit.
* Cycle. The steps by which information
is assembled, converted into intelligence
and made available to users. These steps
are in four phases.
1. Direction – determination of
intelligence requirements, preparation of
a collection plan, issuance of orders and
requests to information collection
agencies, and a continuous check on the
productivity of collection agents.
2. Collection – the exploitation of
sources of information by collection
agencies and the delivery of this
information to the proper intelligence
processing unit for use in the production
of intelligence.
3. Processing – the step whereby information becomes intelligence through
evaluation, analysis, integration, and
interpretation.
4. Dissemination – the conveyance of
intelligence in suitable form (oral, graphic
or written) to agencies needing it.
* Estimate. An appraisal of the elements
of intelligence relating to a specific situation or condition with a view to
determining the courses of action open
to the enemy or potential enemy and
the probable order of their adoption.
* Officer, (IO). The Staff officer responsible for collecting and collating
information, and transposing it into
intelligence. *** Reporting.** The
preparation and conveyance of information by any means. More commonly,
the term is restricted to reports as they
are prepared by the collector and as
they are transmitted by him to his
headquarters and by this component
of the intelligence structure to one or
more intelligence-producing components. Thus, even in this limited
sense, reporting embraces both
collection and dissemination. The
term is applied to normal and specialist
intelligence reports. *See also* **Normal ***

reports; Specialist * reports; * Requirements. Any subject, general or specific, upon which there is a need for the collection of information, or the production of intelligence. *See also* **Essential elements of information.**

Intercept receiver. A receiver designed to detect and provide visual and/or aural indication of electromagnetic emissions occurring within the particular portion of the electromagnetic spectrum to which it is tuned.

Intercepting search. A type of search designed to intercept an enemy whose previous position is known and the limits of whose subsequent course and speed can be assumed.

Interchangeability. A condition which exists when two or more items possess such functional and physical characteristics as to be equivalent in performance and durability, and are capable of being exchanged one for the other without alteration of the items themselves or of adjoining items, except for adjustment, and without selection for fit and performance. *See also* **Compatibility.**

Inter-chart relationship diagram. *See* **Map index.**

Intercom. A telephone apparatus by means of which personnel can talk to each other within an aircraft, tank, ship, or activity.

Intercontinental ballistic missile (ICBM). Generally taken as one with a range in excess of 6,000 Km.

Interdict. To isolate. or seal off an area by any means; to deny the use of a route of approach.

Interdiction. Planned operations aimed at destroying or neutralizing the enemy's military potential and disrupting the movement of his forces into, out of and within the battle area. * **Fire.** Fire placed on an area or point to prevent the enemy from using the area or point.

Interface. A boundary or a point common to two or more similar or dissimilar command and control systems, sub-systems, or other entities against which, or at which, necessary information flow takes place.

Interior economy. A general term covering the whole administrative management of a unit.

Intermediate area illumination. Illumination in the area, extending in depth from the far boundary of the close-in (about 2,000 metres) to the maximum effective range of the bulk of division artillery weapons (about 10,000 metres).

Intermediate contour line. A contour line drawn between index contours (*qv*). Depending on the contour interval there are three or four intermediate contours between the index contours.

Intermediate marker (land mine warfare). A marker, natural, artificial or specially installed, which is used as a point of reference between the landmark and the minefield.

Intermediate range ballistic missile (IRBM) is one with a range between that of a MRBM and an ICBM, *ie* 2,500 – 6,000 Km.

Intermittent illumination. Firing illuminating shells at irregular intervals.

Internal audit. An independent examination and appraisal by Ministry of Defence auditors of accounting, financial and related operations.

Internal radiation. Nuclear radiation (alpha and beta particles and gamma radiation) resulting from radioactive substances in the body.

Internal security (IS). Any military role that involves primarily the maintenance or restoration of law and order and essential services in the face of civil disturbances and disobedience, using minimum force. It covers action dealing with minor civil disorders with no political undertones as well as riots savouring of revolt and even the early stages of rebellion.

International call sign. A call sign assigned in accordance with the provisions of the International Telecommunications Union to identify a radio station. The nationality of the radio station is identified by the first or the first two characters. (When used in visual signalling, international call signs are referred to as 'signal letters'.) *See also* **Call sign.**

International date line. The line coinciding approximately with the antimeridian of Greenwich, modified to avoid certain habitable land. In crossing this line there is a date change of one day.

International map of the world. A map series at 1:1,000,000 scale published by a number of countries to a common internationally agreed specification.

International military post. An appointment filled by an officer or soldier in an international organization. His pay remains the responsibility of his home country but in his work he is responsible to the international authority.

Interocular distance. The distance between the centres of rotation of the eyeballs of an individual or between the oculars of optical instruments.

Interoperability. The ability of systems, units or forces to provide services to and accept services from other systems, units or forces and to use the services so exchanged to enable them to operate effectively together.

Interphone. *See* **Intercom.**

Interrupted line. A broken, dashed, or pecked line usually used to indicate the indefinite alignment or area of a feature on the map.

Interval.
1. The space between adjacent individuals, ground vehicles, or units in a formation that are placed side by side, measured abreast.
2. The space between adjacent aircraft measured from front to rear in units of time or distance.
3. The time lapse between photographic exposures.

Intervention area. In limited war the area of operations, *eg* Port Said during the Anglo-French Suez expedition of 1956.

Inventory. A generic term applied to all the *matériel* within a specific field.
* Control. That phase of military logistics which includes managing, cataloguing, requirements determination, procurement, distribution, overhaul, and disposal of *matériel*. Synonymous with '*matériel* control'; '*matériel* management'; 'inventory management'; and 'supply management'.

Ionization. The process of producing ions by the removal or addition of electrons to atoms or molecules.

Ionosphere. The region of the atmosphere, extending from roughly 40 to 250 miles altitude, in which there is appreciable ionization. The presence of charged particles in this region profoundly affects the propagation of electro-magnetic radiations of long wavelengths (radio and radar waves). *See also* **Atmosphere.**

Iroquois Night Fighter and Night Tracker (INFANT). A US helicopter.

Irregular outer edge (land mine warfare). Groups of mines laid between the outer strip and the outer perimeter marking fence to improve the minefield by covering likely tank approaches and to deceive the enemy about the pattern and the extent of the minefield.

Isobar. A line along which the atmospheric pressure is, or is assumed to be, the same or constant.

Isocentre. In photography, the intersection of the interior bisector of the tilt angle with the film plane.

Isoclinal. A line drawn on a map or chart joining points of equal magnetic dip.

Isodose rate line. *See* **Dose rate contour line.**

Isogonal. A line drawn on a map or chart joining points of equal magnetic variation; the isogonic line.

Isogriv. A line drawn on a map or chart joining points of equal grivation.

Isothermal. Changes of volume, pressure or other properties, at constant temperature.

Issue in full. An issue made of the full quantity demanded.

Issue in satisfaction. An issue transaction considered to have been completed by the supply of a lesser quantity than that demanded.

Issue order. An instruction by a competent authority to a supply source to issue *matériel*.

J-Jour. French equivalent of D-Day (*qv*).

Jacket. A short uniform coat worn by officers of the Royal Horse Artillery. A man posted to a Royal Horse Artillery unit is said to get his jacket.

Jamming. *See* **Barrage jamming; Electronic countermeasures; Electronic**

jamming; **Spot jamming.**

Jamming report (JAMREP). A report initiated by units who suspect that their communications are being jammed by hostile action.

Javelot. A French mobile anti-aircraft multi-tube rocket firing system now under development.

Jet stream. A narrow band of high velocity wind in the upper troposphere or in the stratosphere.

Joint. Connotes activities, operations, organizations, etc., in which elements of more than one Service of the same nation participate. (When all Services are not involved, the participating Services shall be identified, *eg* * Army-Navy. *See also* **Combined.**
* **Amphibious operation.** An amphibious operation conducted by significant elements of two or more Services. * **Amphibious task force.** A temporary grouping of units of two or more Services under a single commander, organized for the purpose of engaging in an amphibious operation.
* **Common user items.** Items of an interchangeable nature which are in common use by two or more Services of a nation. * **Forward Air Controllers Training and Standards Unit** (JFACTSU). The Army/RAF unit which standardizes FAC (*qv*) doctrine and procedure within UKLF and BAOR and maintains close liaison with the German Air Force. * **Movements Co-ordinating Committee** (JMCC). Plans the policy for all movements by sea, air or land in the Communications zone (*qv*). It consists of representatives of the movement staff of all three Services. Action is implemented by its Joint Movements Staff (JMS) or a Priority of Movements (POM) staff.
* **Operations centre** (JOC). A joint agency normally set up at Army/Air Force Tactical Group headquarters and organized for the purpose of exchanging information, and for the co-ordination of the combat effort

of the air forces in tactical air support of ground force operations. It consists of an air section and a ground section, which is the agency to which the requests from the various ground forces headquarters are channelled, evaluated and, if approved, passed to the air control centre for action. * **Services Staff Manual** (JSSM). Contains instructions agreed by all three Services to regulate joint operations. * **Staff.** A staff formed of two or more of the Services of the same country. *See also* **Combined staff; Integrated staff; Parallel staff.** * **Strategic Target Planning Staff** (JSTPS). (US). The body responsible, under Congress, for planning the use of nuclear strategic weapons. * **Task Force.** A force composed of elements of two or more Services formed to undertake a specific task under a specified commander.

Judge Advocate General (JAG). A legal officer of the crown who is appointed by the Sovereign on the advice of the Lord Chancellor. He is assisted by a number of Deputy Judge Advocate Generals (DJAG) who attend courts martial. He reviews the proceedings of the courts. He is available to advise on general legal matters. *See also Director of Army Legal Services.*

Jump Speed. The airspeed of an aircraft at which parachutists can exit in safety. It varies with the design of the aircraft.

Jumpmaster (US.) The assigned parachute jumping instructor who controls parachutists from the time they enter the aircraft until they exit. *See also* **Despatcher; Stick commander** (Air transport).

Junction points. Points on or near boundaries at which physical contact will be made with flank units. These will normally be on bounds or objectives and will generally be selected from a map before an operation. They will have no tactical significance.

Kaman 43. A US helicopter specifically designed for fire-fighting duties on airfields.

Kanat. An underground aqueduct with breather tubes which project upward through the surface of the earth.

Kanone. A German SP anti-tank gun.

Kawasaki. A Japanese anti-tank wire guided missile system firing HEAT (*qv*) rounds.

K-day. The basic date for the introduction of convoy system on any particular convoy lane. *See also* **D-day; M-day.**

Kettle drums. Large circular basins of metal rounded at the bottom. Covered with vellum at the top and emblazoned with regimental honours they are used by cavalry bands when playing mounted.

Key. In cartography, a term sometimes loosely used as a synonym for 'legend'. *See also* **Blue key; Drawing key; Legend.** * **Area.** An area which is of paramount importance. * **Plan.** In an extensive operation or one in which unforseeable factors are anticipated the staff will formulate a first key plan in the early stages which will subsequently be modified by the second, etc., key plan. * **Point.** A concentrated site or installation, the destruction or capture of which would seriously affect the war effort or the success of operations. * **Symbol.** In psychological operations, a simple, suggestive, repetitive element (rhythm, sign, colour, etc,) which has an immediate impact on a target audience and which creates a favourable environment for the acceptance of a psychological theme. * **Terrain.** Any locality, or area, the seizure or retention of which affords a marked advantage to either combatant.

Kick-off drift. *See* **Decrab.**

Killed in action (KIA). A battle casualty who is killed outright or who dies of wounds or other injuries before reaching any medical treatment facility. *See also* **Died of wounds received in action.**

Killing zone (KZ). An area in which a commander plans to force the enemy to concentrate so as to destroy him with conventional or tactical nuclear weapons. Those killing zones where nuclear weapons are primarily planned to be used are termed nuclear killing zones (NKZ).

Kill probability. A measure of the probability of destroying a target.

Kiloton (Kt). Used of nuclear devices. One Kt is the equivalent of 1,000 tons of TNT.

Kiloton weapon. A nuclear weapon, the yield of which is measured in terms of thousands of tons of trinitroluene (TNT) explosive equivalents, producing yields from 1 to 999 kilotons. *See also* **Nominal weapon; Subkiloton weapon.**

Kiowa. A US turbine powered light observation helicopter.

Kit. Previously the term used to denote those articles issued to a soldier which he had to keep in repair. Currently it includes everything except his arms.

Laager. A close defensive formation adopted by tanks at night. Unarmoured vehicles are usually parked within this formation.

Label. *See* **Descriptive name.**

Lance. A US surface to surface guided battlefield support missile carrying either a nuclear or conventional warhead, which is superseding Honest John (*qv*). * **Bombadier,** the lowest non commissioned rank in the Royal Artillery. * **Corporal,** the same in other arms.

Land arm. A mode of operation in which automatic sequence is used to engage and disengage sub-systems of an aircraft automatic flight control system in order to execute the various flight phases in the terminal area necessary for completing an automatic approach and landing.

Land sparrow. A US landmobile air defence missile system.

Landing aids. Any illuminating light, radio beacon, radar device, communicating device, or any system of such devices for aiding aircraft in an approach and landing.

Landing area/ground (LG).
1. That part of the objective area within which are conducted the landing operations of an amphibious force. It includes the beach, the approaches to the beach, the transport areas, the fire support areas, the air occupied by close supporting aircraft, and the land included in the advance inland to the initial objective.
2. The general area used for landing troops and *matériel* either by airdrop or air landing. This area includes one or more drop zone or landing strip.
3. Any specially prepared or selected surface of land, water, or deck designated or used for take-off and landing of aircraft. *See also* **Airfield.**

Landing beach. That portion of a shore line usually required for the landing of a battalion landing team. However, it may also be that portion of a shore line constituting a tactical locality (such as the shore of a bay) over which a force larger or smaller than a battalion landing team may be landed.

Landing craft. A craft employed in amphibious operations, specifically designed for carrying troops and equipment and for beaching, unloading, and retracting. Also used for logistic cargo resupply operations. * **Assault (LCA).** As for the LCT (*qv*) but carrying infantry, and other, assault troops, obsolescent. * **Control officer.** A naval officer in control of the operations of all craft

and amphibians used in the ferry service between ship and shore in the build up stage of an amphibious assault.
* Mechanised (LCM) designed to carry a Chieftain tank or equivalent load from the Landing Platform Dock (LPD) (*qv*) to the beach. *** Recovery unit.** A naval unit which recovers or clears landing craft stranded on the beach in an amphibious operation.
* Tank (LCT). A vessel, becoming obsolescent, for carrying tanks and putting them ashore in the face of opposition. *** Vehicle and Personnel (LCVP)** are smaller vessels carried on Landing Platforms Helicopter (*qv*) to give the force the capacity to land over the beach when required.

Landing diagram. A graphic means of illustrating the plan for the ship-to-shore movement.

Landing force. A task organization of troop units, aviation and ground, assigned to an amphibious assault. It is the highest troop echelon in the amphibious operation. *See also* **Amphibious force.**

Landing ground (LG). *See under* **Landing area.**

Landing mat. A prefabricated, portable mat so designed that any number of planks (sections) may be rapidly fastened together to form surfacing for emergency runways, landing beaches, etc.

Landing Platform Dock (LPD), larger than a **Landing Platform Helicopter** (qv) it can carry a full squadron of battle tanks with personnel and equipment as well as a Royal Marine Commando.

Landing Platform Helicopter (LPH). A ship designed to carry one Royal Marine Commando Group complete with helicopters, vehicles, equipment and supplies.

Landing Platform Vehicle (LPV), is carried in the **Landing Platform** Helicopter for landing the vehicles of the force on arrival at the beach.

Landing point. A point within a landing site where one helicopter can land. *See also* **Airfield.**

Landing ship. An assault ship which is designed for long sea voyages and for rapid unloading over and on to a beach.

* Assault (LSA) designed to carry and disembark troops committed to an opposed landing. *** Dock.** A ship designed to transport and launch loaded amphibious craft and/or amphibian vehicles with their crews and embarked personnel and/or equipment and to render limited docking and repair services to small ships and craft. *** Logistics (LSL),** larger than the Landing Platform Dock (*qv*) designed to help and maintain a force ashore. It can carry pontoon equipment for the landing. *** Tank (LST),** designed to carry and disembark AFVs (*qv*) committed to an opposed landing.

Landing site. A site within a landing zone containing one or more landing points. (*qv*) *See also* **Airfield.**

Landing table. An executive order for an amphibious operation setting out the order of landing by craft loads.

Landing zone (LZ). A specified zone within an objective area used for the landing of aircraft. *See also* **Airfield.**
* Control party. A group of personnel specially trained and equipped to establish and operate communication and signal devices from the ground for traffic control of aircraft/helicopters for a specific landing zone. *See also* **Pathfinder aircraft. * Marking teams.** Teams whose duty it is to establish

navigational aids on a dropping/landing zone.

Landmark (land mine warfare). A feature. either natural or artificial, that can be accurately determined on the ground from a grid reference.

Land mine warfare. *See* **Mine warfare.**

Lands. The raised portions between the grooves (*qv*) in the barrel of a rifled weapon.

Lane marker(s) (land mine warfare). Used to mark a minefield lane. The entrance to and exit from the lane will be referenced to a landmark or intermediate marker. *See also* **Marker** (land mine warfare); **Minefield lane** (land mine warfare).

Lanyard. A plain or plaited cord worn round the shoulder to which a whistle or knife is attached carried in the breast pocket. Frequently coloured to denote to which unit or subunit the wearer belongs.

Laser. Acronym for Light Amplification by Stimulated Emission of Radiation; produces a concentrated beam of light on to a target. It is used in range finding and in training devices such as Simfire (*qv*).

Lashing. The fastening or securing of a load to its carrier to prevent shifting during transit. * **Points.** Strong points attached to aircraft, vehicles and vessels to which loads may be secured by lashings.

Last Post. The bugle or trumpet call traditionally sounded to signify the end of the day when all soldiers should be in barracks. Sounded also at military funerals as a farewell to the deceased.

Lateral gain. The amount of new ground covered laterally by successive photographic runs over an area.

Lateral route. A route, generally

parallel to the forward edge of the battle area, which crosses, or feeds into, axial routes. *See also* **Route.**

Latitude band. Any latitudinal strip, designated by accepted units of linear or angular measurement, which circumscribes the earth. Sometimes called 'latitudinal band'.

Latrine. The military word for a lavatory. In the field a trench dug down wind of a position. Abbreviation lats.

Lattice. A network of intersecting positional lines overprinted on a map or chart from which a fix may be obtained.

Launcher. A structural device designed to support and hold a missile in position for firing.

Launching site. Any site or installation with the capability of launching missiles from surface to air or surface to surface.

Launch pad. A concrete or other hard surface area on which a missile launcher is positioned.

Law. A US anti-tank rocket launcher.

Lay. To point: thus lay a gun, lay an aim, etc.

Laydown bombing. A very low level bombing technique wherein delay fuses and/or devices are used to allow the attacker to escape the effects of his bomb.

Layer tints. *See* **Hypsometric tinting.**

Lead aircraft.
1. An airborne aircraft designated to provide certain command and air control functions.
2. An aircraft in the van of two or more aircraft.

Lead collision. A vector, which if maintained by interceptor aircraft, will result in collision between the interceptor's armament and the target.

Lead pursuit. An intercept vector designed to maintain a course of flight at a predetermined point ahead of a target.

Leaf sight. The rear sight on certain rifles which can be raised or lowered to adjust the aim to the distance to the target.

Leapfrog. Form of movement in which like supporting elements are moved successively through or by one another along the axis of movement of supported troops.

Leave. A holiday away from work. Also used after illness, sock leave, or to settle private affairs, compassionate leave.

Left (or Right).
1. A term used to establish the relative position of a body of troops. The person using the terms left or right is assumed to be facing in the direction of the enemy regardless of whether the troops are advancing towards, or withdrawing from, the enemy.
2. A directional deviation used by an observer in adjusting gunfire.
3. Fire correction used by an observer to indicate that a lateral shift perpendicular to the spotting line is desired.

Left out of battle (LOB). Personnel kept back in a safe rear area when a unit is committed to action who will be ordered forward to replace casualties.

Legend. An explanation of symbols used on a map, chart, sketch, etc., commonly printed in tabular form at the side of the map, etc.

Lens coating. A thin transparent coating applied to a surface of a lens element.

Lens distortion. Image displacement caused by lens irregularities and aberrations.

Leopard. The main German battle tank.

Levee.
1. A natural or manmade embankment bordering a river.
2. The ceremony of presenting an officer to the Sovereign on first commissioning, promotion etc. Now obsolete.

Level of supply. The quantity of supplies authorized or directed to be held in anticipation of future demands.

Liaison. That contact or inter-communication maintained between elements of military forces to insure mutual understanding and unity of purpose and action. * **Officer (LO).** An officer, specially trained as such, to carry out these duties, and to convey his commander's orders to subordinates, obtain and transmit information to and from subordinate and flanking units and formations and generally to act as the eyes, ears and mouth of his commander.

Liberated territory. Any area, domestic, neutral or friendly, which, having been occupied by an enemy, is retaken by friendly forces.

Lieutenant. The rank next below Captain.

Lieutenant Colonel. The rank next below Colonel.

Lieutenant General. The rank next below General.

Lift off. The initial motion of a space vehicle or missile as it rises from the launcher.

Lifted item. An item of *matériel*, the use of which is curtailed by limitations imposed by its shelf life, in use life, or a combination of both.

Light Aid Detachment. A REME sub-unit attached to Regiments or battalions of teeth arm units to assist them in the repair and maintenance of their armament and vehicles.

Light Infantry. Formerly a body of strong and active soldiers used for scouting and skirmishing duties. Now a purely honorary title borne by certain regiments of infantry.

Light line (LL). A designated line forward of which vehicles are required to use black-out lights at night.

Light machine gun (LMG). A light, air cooled infantry automatic weapon supported by a bipod or fired from the hip or shoulder. Now being superseded by the General Purpose Machine Gun (GPMG) (*qv*).

Lights Out. The last bugle call of the day.

Limited War. A conflict of greater intensity than guerrilla war but one in which NBC weapons are not used.

Line. Infantry/cavalry of the Line are those Regiments not being Household Troops who formed the Line of battle.

Line ahead formation. A formation in which elements of troops, tanks, or vehicles are placed one behind the other. (Not applicable to ships or aircraft.)

Line item. An entry in a record which identifies an item of *matériel* irrespective of the quantity of that item.

Line of arrival. *See* **Line of impact.**

Line of departure.
1. A line designated to co-ordinate the departure of attack or scouting elements; a jump-off line.
2. A suitable marked offshore co-ordinating line to assist assault craft to land on designated beaches at scheduled times.

Line of impact. A line tangent to the trajectory at the point of impact or burst.

Linear building frontage. In air photo-graphic interpretation, the side elevation of structures of homogeneous area.

Linear Defence. A defensive position in which depth is sacrificed to length in order to prolong the front facing the enemy. Usually a recipe for defeat.

Linear scale. *See* **Graphic scale; Scale.**

Lines of communications (logistics). All the routes, land, water, and air, which connect an operating military force with one or more bases of operations, and along which supplies and reinforcements move.

Link (communications). A general term used to indicate the existence of communications facilities between two points.

Liquid propellant. Any liquid combustible fed to the combustion chamber of a rocket engine.

Litter. A basket or frame utilized for the transport of injured persons. * **Patient.** A patient requiring litter accommodation while in transit.

Little John. A US unguided ground to ground short-range rocket with a nuclear warhead.

Load (air). *See* **Payload;** *also* **Airlift; Airlift capability; Airlift requirement; Combat *; Planned *; Type *. * Adjuster.** A device used to calculate the centre of gravity of a loaded aircraft. * **Manifest** (air). A document specifying in detail the payload (*qv*) expressed in terms of passengers and/or freight carried in one aircraft for a specific destination. * **Sheet.** A summary of the load carried by an aircraft showing weight, destination, etc. A consolidation of the manifests. * **Spreader.** Material used to distribute the weight of a load over a given floor area to avoid exceeding designed stress.

Loading. The process of putting troops, equipment and supplies into ships, aircraft, trains, road transport, or other means of conveyance. *See also* **Administrative * ; Block stowage *; Combat *; Commodity *; Convoy *; Horizontal *; Preload *; Selective *; Unit *; Vertical *. * Plan.** All of the individually prepared documents which, taken together, present in detail all instructions for the arrangement of personnel and the loading of equipment for one or more units or other special grouping of personnel or *matériel* moving by highway, water, rail, or air transportation. *See also* **Load Manifest (air). * Point.** A point where one aircraft can be loaded. *** Site.** An area containing a number of loading points. *** Table.** The details of the stowage of the contents of a ship/craft/vehicle/wagon/aircraft, etc., for amphibious operations.

Loan. The authorized issue for a specific purpose and period of *matériel* which is normally subject to return in the same condition as loaned, fair wear and tear excepted.

Local mean time. The time interval elapsed since the mean sun's transit of the observer's anti-meridian.

Localizer. A directional radio beacon which provides to an aircraft an indication of its lateral position relative to a specific runway. *See also* **Instrument landing system; Beacon. * Mode.** In a flight control system, a control mode in which an aircraft is automatically positioned to and held at the centre of the localizer course.

Location diagram. *See* **Map index.**

Location statement. A table showing the position of units on the ground.

Lock on. Signifies that a tracking or target seeking system is continuously and automatically tracking a target.

Lodgement area. Following the invasion of a hostile coast and the establishment of a bridgehead ashore, the operations of invading forces are directed to the seizure of a lodgement area. This is an area which comprises adequate port, airfield, and communication facilities and sufficient space for the assembly and maintenance of the total forces destined to take part in the campaign.

Logistics. The science of planning and carrying out the movement and maintenance of forces. In its most comprehensive sense, those aspects of military operations which deal with:
1. design and development, acquisition, storage, movement, distribution, maintenance, evacuation, and disposition of *matériel*;
2. movement, evacuation, and hospitalization of personnel;
3. acquisition or construction, maintenance, operations, and disposition of facilities; and
4. acquisition or furnishing of services.

Logistic assessment. An evaluation of:
1. The logistic support required to support particular military operations in a theatre of operations, country, or area.
2. The actual and/or potential logistic support available for the conduct of military operations either within the theatre, country, or area, or located elsewhere.

Logistic assistance. A generic term used to denote types of assistance between and within military commands both in peace and war. *See also* **Integrated logistic support; Mutual aid; Reallocation of resources.**

Logistic Commands (US). Logistic support for a US Army is carried out by Theatre Army Logistic Commands (TALOG), Advance Logistic Commands (ADLOG) and Base Logistic Commands (BALOG).

Logistic support (medical). Medical care, treatment, hospitalization, evacuation, furnishing of medical services, supplies, *matériel,* and adjuncts thereto.

Loophole. A hole made in a building or wall through which a man can fire.

Loran. A long range radionavigation position fixing system using the time difference of reception of pulse type transmissions from two or more fixed stations. This term is derived from the words Long-Range electronic Navigation.

Lost. A shell or mortar bomb is said to be lost when its fall is not observed by the spotter.

Louvre. Ventilation inlet on an Armoured Fighting Vehicle (AFV) (*qv*) usually shielded by armour protection.

Low altitude bombing system mode. In a flight control system, a control mode in which the low altitude bombing manoeuvre of an aircraft is controlled automatically.

Low angle loft bombing. Type of loft bombing of free fall bombs wherein weapon release occurs at an angle less than 35 degrees above the horizontal.

Low angle fire. Fire delivered at angles of elevation below the elevation that corresponds to the maximum range of the gun and ammunition concerned.

Lower control. On exercises the staff representing the imaginary units under command of the Headquarters being exercised, who receive its orders and paint the picture (*qv*) of consequent events.

Lowering position. The position at which ships or craft stop or anchor in order to transfer the assault troops to assault craft.

Low stock. The level of stock below the appropriate provisioning level at which

action to accelerate receipt of dues in is indicated.

Low velocity drop. A drop procedure in which the drop velocity does not exceed 30 feet per second.

Lubber line. A datum line on an instrument indicating the fore-and-aft axis of an aircraft or ship.

Mach front. *See* **Mach stem.**

Mach hold. In a flight control system, a control mode in which a desired Mach number of an aircraft is maintained automatically.

Mach number. The ratio of the velocity of a body to that of sound in the surrounding medium.

Mach stem. The shock front formed by the fusion of the incident and reflected fronts from an explosion. The term is generally used with reference to a blast wave, propagated in the air, and reflected at the surface of the earth. In the ideal case, the mach stem is perpendicular to the reflecting surface and slightly convex (forward). Also called a 'Mach front'.

Mach trim compensator. In a flight control system, an automatic control sub-system which provides pitch trim of an aircraft as a function of mach number.

Machine gun (MG). A general term to cover belt or drum fed small arms in which firing and reloading is fully automatic. It differs from an automatic rifle by having a bipod or tripod for support and by having a greater capacity for sustained fire. MGs are frequently classified as Heavy (HMG), Medium (MMG), Light (LMG) and General Purpose (GPMG).

Magazine (mag).
1. Any store that is authorized for storage of explosives.

2. The part of a rifle or MG (*qv*) which holds the rounds before they are fed into the breech (*qv*).

Magnetic compass. An instrument that uses a pivoted magnetic needle or other magnetic sensing element to align itself with the earth's magnetic lines of force to indicate direction. *See also* **Deviation; Grid magnetic angle; Magnetic variation.**

Magnetic declination. The angle between the magnetic and geographical meridians at any place, expressed in degrees East or West to indicate the direction of magnetic North from true North. In nautical and aeronautical navigation, the term magnetic variation is used instead of magnetic declination and the angle is termed variation of the compass or magnetic variation. Magnetic declination is not otherwise synonymous with magnetic variation which refers to regular or irregular change with time of the magnetic declination, dip, or intensity. *See also* **Magnetic variation.**

Magnetic equator. A line drawn on a map or chart connecting all points at which the magnetic inclination (dip) is zero for a specified epoch.

Magnetic north. The direction indicated by the north seeking pole of a freely suspended magnetic needle, influenced only by the earth's magnetic field.

Magnetic variation. The horizontal angle at a place between the true North and magnetic north measured in degrees and minutes East or West according to whether magnetic North lies East or West of true North. *See also* **Declination.**

Main airfield. An airfield planned for permanent occupation in peace-time, at a location suitable for wartime utilization, and with operational facilities of a standard adequate to develop full use of its war combat potential. *See also* **Alternative airfield; Departure airfield; Redeployment airfield.**

Main attack. The principal attack or effort into which the commander throws the full weight of the offensive power at his disposal. An attack directed against the chief objective of the campaign or battle.

Main Battle Tank. (MBT). The heavy tank used as the principal breakthrough weapon.

Mainguard. Element of an advanced guard. *See also* **Advanced guard.**

Main line of resistance. A line at the forward edge of the battle position, designated for the purpose of co-ordinating the fire of all units and supporting weapons, including air and naval gun fire. It defines the forward limits of a series of mutually supporting defensive areas, but does not include the areas occupied or used by covering or screening forces.

Main supply route. The route or routes designated within an area of operations upon which the bulk of traffic flows in support of military operations.

Maintenance (*matériel*).
1. All action taken to retain materials in a serviceable condition or to restore it to serviceability. It includes inspection, testing, servicing, classification as to serviceability, repair, rebuilding and reclamation.
2. All supply and repair action taken to keep a force in condition to carry out its mission.
3. The routine recurring work required to keep a facility (plant, building, structure, ground facility, utility system, or other real property) in such condition that it may be continuously utilized at its original or designed capacity and efficiency, for its intended purpose.

Maintenance Area(s). The area in rear of the battle zone where stores can be assembled, repairs effected, casualties receive attention and troops rested. The route along which supplies of all sorts, ammunition, POL, (*qv*), rations, stores and reinforcements must pass from the port of entry to the FEBA (*qv*) is punctuated by maintenance areas. In the communications zone (*qv*) there are Rear * (RMA) (*qv*), Forward * (FMA) (*qv*), and Airhead * (*qv*). In the Corps Area the Corps * (CMA) and (under Divisional Control) the Divisional * (DMA) (*qv*) if formed. Evacuation is carried out in reverse. In the larger maintenance areas supporting installations and services are located in Composite Maintenance Groups (CMG) containing elements of each so as to spread equally the hazard of a nuclear strike.

Major. The rank next above captain and below Lieutenant Colonel.

Major General. The rank next below Lieutenant General and above Brigadier.

Major NATO commanders. Major NATO Commanders are Supreme Allied Commander Atlantic, Supreme Allied Commander Europe, and Allied Commander-in-Chief Channel. *See also* **Commander(s).**

Major nuclear power. Any nation that possesses a nuclear striking force capable of posing a serious threat to every other nation.

Malinger. To feign illness; (slang) to skive.

Mammoth major. A heavy duty vehicle which can be used as either a truck or a tractor.

Man movable. Items which can be towed, rolled, or skidded for short distances by an individual without mechanical assistance but which are of such size, weight, or configuration as to preclude being carried. Upper weight limit: approximately 424 pounds per individual.

Manpower and Personnel Administration (MPA). The branch of the A staff which

deals with the allocation of personnel, reinforcements, medical and related matters.

Mandator. A heavy duty truck.

Manning. A naval term adopted by the Army to denote the posting of officers and men to fill vacancies in establishments.

Manoeuvres. Large scale exercises with troops.

Manoeuvring area. That part of an airfield used for take-offs, landings and associated actions. *See also* **Aircraft marshalling area.**

Manpack. An item or component which can be carried by a man in addition to or as part of his fighting load and which may be used by him, even though it may reduce his fighting efficiency.

Manportable. An item designed for carriage operationally by one man without impairing his fighting efficiency.

Mantlet. The frontal plate of the turret of an AFV.

Manual Command to Line of Sight (MCLOS). In Guided Weapon Systems the missile is manually controlled on to the imaginary line joining target to target tracker by the operator using a command signal generator. This system is used in Vigilant.

Manual of Military Law (MML). A compendium giving the acts of Parliament which impose duties and obligations on members of the armed forces, additional to those of other citizens, (generally known as the Army Act,) together with explanations of how they are to be implemented. It lists the offences which are in contravention of the Act and the punishments which may be awarded. *See also* **Rules of Procedure.**

Map. A graphic representation, usually on a plane surface, and at an established scale, of natural or artificial features on the surface of a part or the whole of the earth or other planetary body. The features are positioned relative to a co-ordinate reference system.
* Convergence. The angle at which one meridian is inclined to another on a map or chart. *See also* **Convergence.**
* Index. A graphic key primarily designed to give the relationship between sheets of a series, their coverage, availability, and further information on the series.
* Reconnaissance (ground). The study of ground features such as roads, woods and waterways, on a map to obtain information needed in preparing a tactical plan for manoeuvre. *** Reference.** A means of identifying a point on the surface of the earth by relating it to information appearing on a map, generally the graticule or grid. *** Reference code.** A code used primarily for encoding grid co-ordinates and other information pertaining to maps. This code may be used for other purposes where the encryption of numerals is required. *** Series.** A collection of sheets having the same scale and cartographic specifications collectively identified by the producing agency. *** Sheet.** An individual map or chart either complete in itself or part of a series.

Marching Fire (US). An infantry tactic in which a line of infantrymen advance towards their objective firing all their weapons at any part of their front which could conceal an enemy. Not used by the British Army.

Marder. A German armoured personnel carrier.

Margin. In cartography, the area of a map or chart lying outside the border.

Marginal data. All explanatory information given in the margin of a map or chart which clarifies, defines, illustrates, and/or supplements the graphic portion of the sheet.

Marginal information. *See* **Marginal data.**

Marker.
1. A visual or electronic aid used to mark a designated point. *See also* **Beacon.**
2. The right (or left) hand man of the front rank of a line of soldiers is known as the right (or left) marker. *See also* **Gap marker** (land mine warfare); **Intermediate marker** (land mine warfare); **Lane marker** (land mine warfare); **Row marker** (land mine warfare); **Strip marker** (land mine warfare).

Marker ship. In an amphibious operation, a ship which takes accurate station on a designated control point. It may fly identifying flags by day and show lights to seaward by night.

Marking panel. A sheet of material displayed for visual communication usually between friendly units.

Marking teams. Personnel landed in the landing area with the task of establishing navigational aids. *See also* **Pathfinder aircraft.**

Marshalling.
1. The process by which units participating in an amphibious or airborne operation group together or assemble or move to temporary camps in the vicinity of embarkation points; complete preparation for combat or prepare for loading.
2. The process of assembling, holding and organizing supplies and/or equipment, especially vehicles of transportation, for onward movement. *See also* **Stage; Staging area.**

Martial contaminations. Areas contaminated by NBC (*qv*) agents or by minefields.

Masking.
1. In air defence, the use of additional transmitters to hide a particular electromagnetic radiation as to location of

source and/or purpose of the radiation.
2. In air transport, the method of covering or otherwise modifying interior projecting points of an aircraft so that strops or static lines cannot foul them when dropping parachutists.

Mass.
1. The concentration of combat power.
2. The military formation in which units are spaced at less than the normal distances and intervals.

Massed fire. *See* **Concentrated fire.**

Master plot. A portion of a map or overlay on which are drawn the outlines of the areas covered by an air photographic sortie. Latitude and longitude, map, and sortie information are shown.

Master switch. The switch which overrides all electric systems.

Materials handling. The movement of materials (raw materials, scrap, semi-finished, and finished) to, through, and from productive processes; in warehouses and storage; and in receiving and shipping areas.

Matériel. A generic term covering equipment, stores, supplies and spares.
* Control. The same as **inventory control** (*qv*). *** Distribution system.** The facilities, installations and organization for holding and distributing *matériel* between receipt into the system, issue to and receipt by the user.
* Management. *See* **Inventory control.**

Maximum effective range. The maximum distance at which a weapon may be expected to fire accurately to achieve the desired result.

Maximum landing weight. The maximum gross weight due to design or operational limitations at which an aircraft is permitted to land.

Maximum permissible concentration.
See **Radioactivity concentration guide.**

Maximum permissible dose. That radiation dose which a military commander or other appropriate authority may prescribe as the limiting cumulative radiation dose to be received over a specific period of time by members of his command, consistent with current operational military considerations.

Maximum price. The maximum amount as agreed with the contractor for specified work, services or supplies which the Authority is contractually liable to pay.

Maximum range. The greatest distance to which a weapon can throw its projectile irrespective of accuracy.

Maximum sustained speed (transport vehicles). The highest speed at which a vehicle, with its rated payload, can be driven for an extended period on a level first-class highway without sustaining damage.

Maximum take-off weight. The maximum gross weight due to design or operational limitations at which an aircraft is permitted to take-off.

M-day. The term used to designate the day on which mobilization is to begin.
See also **D-day; K-day.**

Meaconing. A system of receiving radio beacon signals and rebroadcasting them on the same frequency to confuse navigation. The meaconing stations cause inaccurate bearings to be obtained by aircraft or ground stations. *See also* **Beacon.**

Mean point of impact. The points whose co-ordinates are the arithmetic means of the co-ordinates of the separate points of impact of a finite number of projectiles fired or released at the same aiming point under a given set of conditions.

Mean sea level. The average sea level for a particular geographical location, obtained from numerous observations, at regular intervals, over a long period of time.

Measuring magnifier. A magnifying instrument incorporating a graticule for measuring small distances.

Medals. The generic term loosely used to cover all Orders, decorations and medals. Strictly speaking it should refer only to those medals which are a general issue. *eg* campaign medals for all those who took part, and long service and good conduct medals for old soldiers of impeccable character. The Military Medal is in fact a decoration awarded to an individual for gallantry in the field.

Medevac. A generic term covering the whole process of the evacuation of casualties.

Median lethal dose.
1. (nuclear). The amount of radiation over the whole body which would be fatal to 50% of the animals or organisms in question in a given period of time.
2. (chemical). The dose of toxic chemical agent which will kill 50% of exposed, unprotected personnel. It is expressed in milligram minutes per cubic centimetre.

Medical (med). The head of the Army Medical Service is the Director General of Medical Services (DGMS). Under him are the Deputy Directors of Medical Services (DDMS), Assistant Directors of Medical Services (ADMS) and Deputy Assistant Directors of Medical Services (DADMS).

Medium range ballistic missile (MRBM). Usually applied to a missile with a range up to 2,500 Km.

Megaton. A measure of power applied to nuclear warheads equivalent to one million short tons of Trinitrotoluene (TNT).

Megaton weapon. A nuclear weapon, the yield of which is measured in terms of

millions of tons of Trinitrotoluene (TNT) explosive equivalents.

Mess. n. Accommodation reserved for the use of certain ranks, *eg* Officers *, Sergeants *, Corporals *, usually consisting of a dining room, anteroom (*qv*) and single bedrooms. v. to mess with is to feed with.

Mess President. The Warrant Officer in charge of the Sergeants Mess. He is responsible to the RSM for the management and general tone of the mess.

Message. Any thought or idea expressed briefly in plain, coded, or secret language, prepared in a form suitable for transmission by any means of communication. communication.

Meteorological data. Meteorological facts pertaining to the atmosphere, such as wind, temperature, air density, and other phenomena which affect military operations.

Mickey mouse. US slang for petty, irritating or outdated regulations.

Micon. The Swiss Surface to Air Guided Weapon System (SAGW).

Midcourse guidance. The guidance applied to a missile between termination of the launching phase and the start of the terminal phase of flight.

Milan. A Franco-German wire guided, spin stabilized anti-tank missile system, whose full title is *Missile d'Infantrie Léger Antichar.*

Militant. A ten ton general-service load carrying vehicle.

Military. Pertaining to any one or more of the armed services, whether Army, Navy or Air Force. * **Aid to Civil Community (MACC).** A project carried out officially by an army unit to mitigate a disaster to or provide an amenity for the civilian

population, *eg* rescue work after an earthquake, or building a road.
* Assistant (MA). An officer on the personal staff of a senior commander who is in charge of his secretariat, briefs him when necessary on current military problems and protects him from being swamped by paper work.
* Currency. Currency prepared by a power and declared by its military commander to be legal tender for use by civilian and/or military personnel as prescribed in the areas occupied by its forces. It should be of distinctive design to distinguish it from the official currency of the countries concerned, but may be denominated in the monetary unit of either. *** Engineer services (MES).** Small units of Royal Engineers who control complex technical engineer work. *** Forwarding organization.** Any army organization designed to handle the movement of small consignments of stores and baggage of the Services between military stations within and between the overseas theatres and the United Kingdom. In wartime it is also responsible for handling casualty kits and effects of army personnel.
* Geographic documentation. Military geographic information which has been evaluated, processed, summarized, and published. *** Geographic information.** Comprises the information concerning physical aspects, resources, and artificial features which are necessary for planning and operations.
* Governor. The military commander or other designated person who, in an occupied territory, exercises supreme authority over the civil population subject to the laws and usages of war and to any directive received from his government or his superior. *** Grid.** Two sets of parallel lines intersecting at right angles and forming squares; the grid is superimposed on maps, charts, and other similar representations of the surface of the earth in an accurate and consistent manner to permit identification of ground locations with respect to other locations

and the computation of direction and distance to other points. *** Grid reference system.** A system which uses a standard-scaled grid square, based on a point of origin on a map projection of the surface of the earth in an accurate and consistent manner to permit either position referencing or the computation of direction and distance between grid positions. *** Intelligence.** *See* **Intelligence.**
* Load classification(s). The military load classification of a route, bridge, or raft is a class number which represents the safe load carrying capacity of the route, bridge, or raft and indicates the maximum vehicle class that can be accepted under normal conditions.
See also **Classification of bridges and vehicles; Route classification. * Necessity.** The principle where a belligerent has the right to apply any measures which are required to bring about the successful conclusion of a military operation and which are not forbidden by the laws of war. *** Nuclear power.** A nation which has nuclear weapons and the capability for their employment. *See also* **Nuclear power. * Police.** The Royal Corps of Military Police performs roughly the same duties in the field and in military installations as the civil police do in this country, *ie* control of traffic and prevention and detection of crime. They are familiarly known as Red Caps from the colour of their headdress.
* Provost Staff Corps (MPSC). Provides the staff of all military prisons, detention and corrective training centres. It is not part of the RMP. *** Platform.** A side loading platform generally at least 300 metres/1,000 feet long for military trains.
* Requirement. An established need justifying the timely allocation of resources to achieve a capability to accomplish approved military objectives, missions, or tasks. *** Secretary.** The General Officer responsible for promotions, appointments, honours, awards and ceremonial.

Military Knights of Windsor. A body of retired officers of field rank who are given apartments in Windsor Castle and have ceremonial duties to perform about the Sovereign.

Militia. Historically the able bodied men of a county liable to be embodied for home defence. Before World War II conscripts for the Regular army were called militia men.

Mine(s) (land mine warfare). An explosive or other material, normally encased, designed to destroy or damage vehicles, boats, or aircraft or designed to wound, kill or otherwise incapacitate personnel. It may be detonated by the action of its victim, by the passage of time, or by controlled means. * **Clearance.** The process of detecting and/or removing land mines by manual or mechanical means. * **Defence.** The defence of a position, area, etc., by mines. A mine defence system includes the personnel and equipment needed to plant, operate, maintain, and protect the minefields that are laid. * **Row.** A single row of clusters laid in a generally straight line. * **Strip.** Two parallel mine rows laid simultaneously six paces apart. * **Sweeping.** The technique of searching for, or clearing mines using mechanical or explosion gear, which physically removes or destroys the mine, or produces, in the area, the influence fields necessary to actuate it. * **Warfare.** The strategic and tactical use of mines and their countermeasures. * **Watching.** The mine countermeasures procedure which detects, finds the position of, and/or identifies mines during the act of laying by the enemy. *See also* **Anti-personnel** *; **Anti-tank** *; **Armed** *; **Disarmed** *; **Inert** *; **Phony** *; **Practice** *.

Minefield (land mine warfare). An area of ground containing mines laid with or without pattern. * **Gap** (land mine warfare). A portion of a minefield, in which no mines have been laid, of specified width to enable a friendly force to pass through the minefield in tactical formation. * **Lane.** An unmined (or demined) route through any minefield suitably marked. For lanes through

enemy minefields, the width will depend on the method of breaching and the purpose for which they are required. * **Marking.** Visible marking of all points required in laying a minefield and indicating the extent of such minefields. * **Record.** A complete written record of all pertinent information concerning a minefield, submitted on a standard form by the officer in charge of the laying operations. *See also* **Anti-airborne** *; **Anti-amphibious** *; **Anti-personnel** *; **Barrier** *; **Defensive** *; **Mixed** *; **Nuisance** *; **Phony** *; **Protective** *.

Minimum decision altitude. The minimum height above the landing surface at which the pilot can elect to go around without the risk of the aircraft touching down.

Minimum quality surveillance (petroleum). The minimum measures to be applied to determine and maintain the quality of bulk and packaged petroleum products in order that these products will be in a condition suitable for immediate use.

Minimum safe altitude. The altitude below which it is hazardous to fly owing to presence of high ground or other obstacles.

Minimum safe distance (nuclear). The sum of the radius of safety and the buffer distance.

Minimum warning time (nuclear). The sum of system reaction time and personnel reaction time.

Ministry of Defence (MoD). A civilian department of State which controls all three fighting services on behalf of the Minister of Defence.

Minor control. *See* **Photogrammetric control.**

Minuteman. A silo-launched solid-propellant ICBM (*qv*) developed by USA.

Misfire.
1. Fail to fire or explode properly.
2. Failure of a primer of the propelling charge or a projectile to function, wholly or in part.

Missile. A projectile which is guided to its target by electronic means.

Missile engagement zone. The airspace in which missiles may be given freedom of operation. Missile zones are promulgated by the Air Defence Commander and have the following characteristics.
1. The position of a zone will depend on the characteristics of the weapons deployed and may be of any shape and extend from the ground level to any altitude, or from one altitude to another.
2. No friendly aircraft may penetrate a missile zone unless under close control and approved by the Air Defence Commander, or via a safe lane.
3. Weapon restrictions may be applied within missile zones to allow the operation of friendly aircraft.

Mission.
1. The task given to a commander together with its purpose, thereby clearly indicating the action to be taken and the reason therefor.
2. The despatching of one or more aircraft to accomplish one particular task.

Mission review report (photographic interpretation). An intelligence report containing information on all targets covered by one photographic sortie.

Mixed (artillery fire). A report from an observer that rounds fired resulted in an equal number of air and impact bursts. * air, denotes that a larger number were airbursts and * graze that the majority were impact bursts.

Mixed minefield (land mine warfare). A minefield containing both anti-tank and anti-personnel mines. *See also* **Minefield** (land mine warfare).

Mobat. A heavy anti-armour weapon of 120 mm calibre.

Mobile air movements team. An airforce team trained for operational deployment on air movement/traffic section duties.

Mobile air operations team. RAF teams who may assist in the selection and preparation of helicopter landing sites, dropping zones and forward airstrips, and control aircraft at selected landing sites or air strips.

Mobile defence. An area of considerable depth in which mobile forces concentrate on favourable ground to destroy the enemy by selective counter strikes.

Mobile equipment. Equipment which is self-propelled or can be towed on its own wheels, tracks or skids.

Mobile servicing and repair detachment (MSRD). The theatre aircraft workshop detaches a MSRD to a divisional area to carry out repairs to aircraft which are unable to fly back to their parent workshop.

Mobility. A quality or capability of military forces which permits them to move from place to place while retaining the ability to fulfil their primary mission.

Mobilization (mob).
1. The act of preparing for war or other emergencies through assembling and organizing national resources.
2. The process by which the armed forces or part of them are brought to a state of readiness for war or other national emergency. This includes assembling and organizing personnel, supplies, and material for active military service.

Mock up. A model, built to scale, of a machine, apparatus, or weapon. It is used in studying the construction and in testing a new development, or in teaching personnel how to operate the actual machine, apparatus, or weapon. For example, a mock up of a ship, landing craft, and aircraft is used in training personnel to load, embark and debark.

Mode of transport. The various modes used for a movement. For each mode there are several means of transport.
1. Inland surface transportation (rail, road and inland waterways).
2. Sea transport (coastal and ocean).
3. Air transportation.
4. Pipelines.

Moderate risk (nuclear). A degree of risk where anticipated effects are tolerable, or at worst, a minor nuisance. *See also* **Emergency risk (nuclear).**

Modern Volunteer Army Program (US). The process by which the United States is converting from a drafted (conscripted) Army to a volunteer one.

Modification kit.
1. A modification set augmented by items supplied under separate Service arrangements.
2. An aggregation of items required for a modification entirely supplied under Service arrangements and not requiring a modification set.

Modification set. A set of items supplied and assembled by a manufacturer for the incorporation of a modification.

Moment. In air transport, the weight of a load multiplied by its distance from a reference point in the aircraft.

Monarch. A road tractor.

Monitoring.
1. The act of listening to, reviewing and/or recording enemy, one's own, or other friendly forces communications for the purpose of maintaining standards, improving communications, or for reference, as applicable.
2. The act of detecting the presence of radiation and the measurement thereof with radiation measuring instruments.

Mopping up. The liquidation of remnants of enemy resistance in an area that has

been surrounded or isolated, or through which other units have passed without eliminating all active resistance.

Morale. The state of mind of a man or a unit which measures the will to win at whatever cost. High morale is essential for victory. Low morale will ensure defeat.

Mortar. A high elevation ordnance throwing a comparatively light projectile. * **Report** (MORTREP). Similar to a shelling report (*qv*) but referring to hostile mortar fire.

Mosaic. An assembly of overlapping photographs that have been matched to form a continuous photographic representation of a portion of the surface of the earth. *See also* **Controlled mosaic; Semi-controlled mosaic; Uncontrolled mosaic.**

Mosquito. An Italian wire-guided roll-stabilised infantry anti-tank weapon system.

Most probable position. The position of an aircraft estimated from all the data available, bearing in mind the probability of error.

Motorized unit. A unit equipped with complete motor transportation that enables all its personnel, weapons, and equipment to be moved at the same time without assistance from other sources.

Mountable. An item used on the ground, but which can equally be mounted, carried and used on/in a vehicle; the degree of portability required is stated.

Mounting.
1. All preparations made in areas designated for the purpose, in anticipation of an operation. It includes the assembly in the mounting area, preparation and maintenance within the mounting area, movement to loading points, and subsequent embarkation

into ships, craft or aircraft if applicable.
2. A carriage or stand upon which a weapon is placed.
* Base. In limited war the area where troops, supplies, ammunition, vehicles, etc. are assembled before movement to the intervention area (*qv*). For example, Cyprus during the Anglo-French Suez expedition of 1956.

Movement. *See* **Fire and Movement.**
* Area. That part of an airfield reserved for the take-off, landing and manoeuvring of aircraft. *** Control.** The planning, routing, scheduling, and control of personnel and supply movements over lines of communication; also an organization responsible for these functions. *** Control check point.** A check point normally deployed in transit camps or concentration areas which is responsible for:
1. the assembling of troops, vehicles and equipment into loads;
2. supervising the preparation and documentation of such loads for air transportation;
3. the control of movement from the transit camp or concentration area to the airfield. *** Control officer.** An officer of the movement control organization responsible for the executive control of movement of military personnel and cargo by all means of transport.
* Credit. The allocation granted to one or more vehicles in order to move over a controlled route in a fixed time according to movement instructions.
* Priority. The relative precedence given to each movement requirement.
* Restriction. A restriction temporarily placed on traffic into and/or out of areas to permit clearance of, or prevention of congestion. *** Table.** A table giving detailed instructions or data for a move. When necessary, it will be qualified by the words Road, Rail, Sea, Air, etc., to signify the type of movement.
Normally issued as an annex to a movement order or instruction.

Moving target indicator. A radar presentation which shows only targets which are in motion. Signals from stationary targets are subtracted out of the return signal by the output of a suitable memory circuit.

Mufti. *See* **Plain clothes.**

Multiple independently targeted re-entry vehicle (MIRV). A missile whose multiple warheads can be separated to give a choice of impact targets.

Multiple married quarter hiring. Accommodation for entitled families built by private developers usually in the form of flats either to Mod order or as a commercial speculation. Leased by Mod for an agreed period of usually more than 3 years. This accommodation is furnished to scale by Mod and the rent paid from the Defence Lands Vote.

Multiple re-entry vehicle. (MRV). A missile whose warheads separate before re-entry into the atmosphere and reach the ground some distance apart from each other.

Muster. *See* **Roll.**

Mutual aid. Arrangements made at government level between one nation and one or more other nations to assist each other. *See also* **Integrated logistic support; Logistic assistance; Reallocation of resources.**

Mutual support. That support which units render each other against an enemy, because of their assigned tasks, their position relative to each other and to the enemy, and their inherent capabilities. *See also* **Cross servicing; Support.**

Muzzle brake. A device at the end of the barrel of a weapon to reduce recoil.

Muzzle velocity (mv). The velocity of a projectile with respect to the muzzle at the instant the projectile leaves the weapon.

M3/VTT. A French armoured personnel carrier.

Nadir. That point on the celestial sphere directly beneath the observer and directly opposite the zenith.

Nahal. Military agricultural settlements of Jews in Israel.

National command. A command that is organized by, and functions under the authority of, a specific nation. It may or may not be placed under a NATO Commander. *See also* **Command.**

National commander. All national commanders, territorial or functional, who are normally not in the Allied chain of command.

National component. Any national forces of one or more services under the command of a single national commander, assigned to any NATO Commander.

National force commanders. Commanders of national forces assigned as separate elements of subordinate Allied commands. *See also* **Commander(s).**

National forces for the defence of the NATO area. Non-allocated forces whose mission involves the defence of an area within the NATO area of responsibility. *See also* **NATO forces.**

National infrastructure. Infrastructure provided and financed by a NATO member in its own territory solely for its own forces (including those forces assigned to or designated for NATO). *See also* **Infrastructure.**

National military authority. The government agency, such as Ministry of Defence or Service Ministry, empowered to make decisions on military matters on behalf of its country. This authority may be delegated to a military or civilian group or individual at any level appropriate for dealing with Allied Commanders or their subordinates.

National Strategic Target List (NSTL) (US). A list of targets considered appro-

priate for nuclear attack in the event of war. It is maintained by JSTPS (*qv*).

National territorial commander. A national commander who is responsible for the execution of purely national functions in a specific geographical area. He remains a national territorial commander regardless of any Allied status which may be assigned to him. *See also* **Commander(s).**

NATO. *See* **North Atlantic Treaty Organization.** * **Air Defence Ground Environment** (NADGE). A computerized air defence system consisting of a 3,000 mile network from North of the Arctic Circle to Asia Minor which is capable of detecting, identifying and intercepting aircraft entering NATO air space. * **Forces.** *See* **Forces allocated to NATO; National forces for the defence of the NATO area; Other forces.** * **Intelligence subject code.** A numerical framework developed for indexing the subject matter of intelligence documents. In addition to the subject outline, it includes a system of alphabetical or numerical symbols for geographic areas which are used with the subject classification. * **Preparation time.** The time between the receipt of authorization from NATO political authorities for major NATO commanders to implement military measures to counter an impending attack and the start of the attack. * **Request for air transport support** (NARAT). A form on which a unit asks for replenishment of its requirements by air. Supplies are then airdropped or flown in by helicopters or fixed wing aircraft. * **Unified product.** A standardized product which is used or is fully suitable for use by all NATO nations for a given use. *See also* **Acceptable alternate product; Emergency substitute; Standardized product.** * **Warning time.** The time between recognition by a major NATO commander, or higher NATO authority that an attack is impending and the start of the attack.

Nautical chart. *See* **Hydrographic chart.**

Nautical twilight. *See* **Twilight.**

Naval assault group. The ships and craft organized to carry a tactically loaded military force.

Naval assault unit. The ships and craft required to carry and land in the assault a force not exceeding a tactically loaded army brigade group or the equivalent.

Naval augmentation group. A formed group of escort ships employed to augment the through escort of convoys when passing through areas known or suspected to be threatened by enemy forces.

Naval beach group. A permanently organized naval command, within an amphibious force, comprising a commander, his staff, a beachmaster unit, an amphibious constructions battalion, and board unit, designed to provide an administrative group from which required naval tactical components may be made available to the attack force commander and to the amphibious landing force commander to support the landing of one division (reinforced). *See also* **Shore party.**

Naval beach unit. *See* **Naval beach group.**

Naval gunfire liaison team. Personnel and equipment required to co-ordinate and advise ground/landing forces on naval gunfire employment.

Naval gunfire operations centre. The agency established in a ship to control the execution of plans for the employment of naval gunfire, process requests for naval gunfire support, and to allot ships to forward observers. Ideally located in the same ship as the Supporting Arms Co-ordination Centre. (*qv*)

Naval gunfire support commander. The commanding officer of the Amphibious Observation Regiment/Battery, Royal Artillery, who is on the staff of the naval task force commander as adviser on naval gunfire support.

Naval gunfire support forward observer (NGSFO). An officer of the amphibious observation unit who is specially trained to observe naval gunfire on shore targets; he calls for fire to meet the needs of the formation or unit to which he is attached.

Naval gunfire support liaison officer. An officer of the amphibious observation unit earmarked in a major war vessel as adviser to the captain.

Naval gunfire support senior liaison officer. An officer of the amphibious observation unit attached to the staff of the naval commander assault force as adviser on the provision of naval gunfire support.

Naval gunfire support staff officer. An officer of the amphibious observation unit who acts as adviser to a military formation commander, or the commander, Royal Artillery, ashore or afloat, on the suitability of targets for the various types of ship available to give supporting fire. He also controls NGSFOs on his front.

Naval support area. A sea area assigned to naval ships detailed to support an amphibious operation. *See also* **Fire support area.**

Navigational grid. A series of straight lines, superimposed over a conformal projection and indicating grid North, used as an aid to navigation. The interval of the grid lines is generally a multiple of 60 or 100 nautical miles. *See also* **Military grid.**

Navigation head. A trans-shipment point on a waterway where loads are transferred between water carriers and land carriers. A navigation head is similar in function to a railhead or truckhead.

Navigation mode. In a flight control system, a control mode in which the flight path of an aircraft is automatically maintained by signals from navigation equipment.

Navy Army and Air Force Institutes
(NAAFI). A non-profit making
organization which provides clubs, shops
and other facilities for Service men and
women. The US equivalent is PX.

Neatlines. The lines that bound the body
of a map, usually parallels and meridians.
Also called 'sheetlines'.

Negative. In photography:
1. (Black and white). An image on film,
plate, or paper, in which the normal tones
of the subject are reversed.
2. (Colour). An image on film, plate,
or paper in which colours appear as
their complements.

Negative photo plane. The plane in which
a film or plate lies at the moment of
exposure.

Negligible risk (nuclear). A degree of risk
where personnel are reasonably safe, with
the exception of dazzle or temporary loss
of night vision.

Nemesia. US codename for a project to
locate dormant missiles under water or in
unhardened silos on waste land which
could be activated in time of war.

Nerve Gases. Lethal chemical agents
which can be discharged from a shell
or missile.

Net (communications). An organization
of stations capable of direct communication on a common channel or frequency.
* Call sign. A call sign which represents
all stations within a net. *See also* **Call
sign.**

Net price. A price that has been reduced
by all applicable discounts.

Net weight. Weight of a ground vehicle
fully equipped and serviced for operation,
including fuel, lubricants, coolant, vehicle
tools and spares, but without crew,
personal equipment, traction devices, or
payload. *See also* **Gross weight.**

Neutralization fire. Fire which is delivered

to hamper and interrupt movement,
and/or the firing of weapons.

Neutron induced activity. Radioactivity
induced in the ground or an object as a
result of direct irradiation by neutrons.

'N'-Hour. That time planned for
the explosion of the first of a series of
tactical nuclear weapons, as part of a
specific ground forces operation, or in
the case of a single strike the time planned
for that explosion.

Nicknames (exercise). Nicknames may be
assigned formally or informally by any
appropriate authority to an event, project,
manoeuvre, exercise, test, or other
activity for purposes other than to
provide for the security of information.
Nicknames always consist of at least two
separate words and are short. Their most
common use is for naming manoeuvres
and exercises, *eg* Exercise Second
Thoughts.

Night effect. An effect mainly caused
by variations in the state of polarization
of reflected waves, which sometimes result
in errors in direction finding bearings.
The effect is most frequent at nightfall.

Nightsun. A helicopter borne search-
light frequently used to illuminate
at night.

Nike-Hercules (US). A surface to air missile
which is effective up to 150,000 ft.

Night vision device. A visual device which
enables the user to operate more
efficiently at night than he could with
the unaided eye.

No-fire line. A line short of which
artillery or ships do not fire except on
request or approval of the supported
commander, but beyond which they may
fire at any time without danger to friendly troops.

No Go Area. In Northern Ireland, urban
areas completely controlled by elements
hostile to troops.

No man's land. That area of ground between two opposing forces which is not physically occupied by either, but which both will endeavour to dominate by means of patrols, observation and similar methods.

Nominal focal length. An approximate value of the focal length, rounded off to some standard figure, used for the classification of lenses, mirrors, or cameras.

Nominal scale. *See* **Principal scale;** *also* **Scale.**

Nominal weapon. A nuclear weapon producing a yield of approximately 20 kilotons. *See also* **Kiloton weapons; Subkiloton weapons.**

Non accounting unit (*matériel*). A unit which is not required to maintain auditable records in respect of *matériel*, the task being carried out by its parent unit.

Non-battle casualty. A person who is not a battle casualty, but who is lost to his organization by reason of disease or injury, including persons dying from disease or injury, or by reason of being missing where the absence does not appear to be voluntary or due to enemy action or to being interned.

Non-commissioned Officer (NCO). A solider who holds a position of command or responsibility below warrant rank.

Non effective. Personnel held on the establishment of a unit but absent from it for any cause *eg* sickness, leave, etc.

Non-expendable supplies and material. Items which are not consumed in use and which retain their original identity during the period of use, such as weapons, and which normally require further accounting.

Non martial contaminations. Areas contaminated through natural use *eg* latrines, refuse dumps, etc.

Non-registered publication. A publication which bears no register number and for which periodic accounting is not required.

Non-scheduled units. Units of the landing force held in readiness for landing during the initial unloading period, but not included in either scheduled or on-call waves. This category usually includes certain of the combat support units and most of the combat service support units with higher echelon (division and above) reserve units of the landing force. Their landing is directed when the need ashore can be predicted with a reasonable degree of accuracy.

Non-vital cargo. A cargo of some value, loaded in peace-time but which is not immediately required in its country of destination. *See also* **Cargoes.**

Nord (French). The brand name of a family of guided missiles.

Normal impact effect. *See* **Cardinal point effect.**

Normal intelligence reports. A category of reports used in the dissemination of intelligence, which is conventionally used for the immediate dissemination of individual items of intelligence. *See also* **Intelligence reporting; Specialist intelligence report.**

North American Air Defence Command (NORAD). A joint US-Canadian organization to defend North America from attack from over the Polar regions.

North Atlantic Treaty Organization (NATO) (French OTAN). The organization of free democracies dedicated to preserve the Western way of life. Present members are Belgium, Canada, Denmark, Great Britain, Greece, Iceland, Italy, Netherlands, Norway, Portugal, Turkey, USA and West Germany.

Northern Army Group (NAG). The Army Group comprising Belgian, British, Dutch and German formations, supported by the Second Allied Tactical Air Force, (2TAF) stationed in North Germany.

Northing. Northward, that is from bottom to top, reading of grid values on a map.

Notice to airmen (NOTAM). A notice containing information concerning the establishment, condition or change in any aeronautical facility, service, procedures or hazard, the timely knowledge of which is essential to personnel concerned with flight operations.

No wind position. *See* **Air position.**

Nuclear airburst. The explosion of a nuclear weapon in the air, at a height greater than the maximum radius of the fireball. *See also* **Types of burst.**

Nuclear, Biological and Chemical (NBC) usually used as an adjective to denote the use of these agents as offensive weapons. * **Area of observation.** A geographical area consisting of several nuclear, biological, chemical zones of observation, comparable to the area of responsibility of an Army or Army Group or an Allied Tactical Air Force. * **Collection centre.** The agency responsible for the receipt, consolidation, and evaluation of reports of nuclear detonations, biological and chemical attacks, and resultant contamination within the nuclear, biological, chemical zone of observation and for the production and dissemination of appropriate reports and warnings. Agencies with similar functions, but with responsibilities for only part of the nuclear, biological, chemical zone of observation may be termed 'Sub Collection Centres'. * **Control centre.** The agency responsible for co-ordinating the efforts of all collection centres within the nuclear, biological, chemical area of observation. A control centre may assume the function of the collection centre for the area in which it is located. * **Zone of observation.** A geo-

graphical area which defines the responsibility for reporting and collecting information on enemy or unidentified nuclear detonations, biological or chemical attacks and resultant contamination. Boundaries of nuclear, biological, chemical zones of observation which may overlap, are determined by the organization of the forces concerned.

Nuclear cloud. An all-inclusive term for the volume of hot gases, smoke, dust, and other particulate matter from the nuclear bomb itself and from its environment, which are carried aloft in conjunction with the rise of the fireball produced by the detonation of the nuclear weapon.

Nuclear column. A hollow cylinder of water and spray thrown up from an underwater burst of a nuclear weapon, through which the hot, high-pressure gases formed in the explosion are vented to the atmosphere. A somewhat similar column of dirt is formed in an underground explosion.

Nuclear damage (land warfare).
1. **Light damage.** Damage which does not prevent the immediate use of equipment or installations for which it was intended. Some repair by the user may be required to make full use of the equipment or installations.
2. **Moderate damage.** Damage which prevents the use of equipment or installations until extensive repairs are made.
3. **Severe damage.** Damage which prevents use of equipment or installations permanently.

Nuclear damage assessment. The determination of the damage effect to the population, forces, and resources resulting from actual nuclear attack. It is performed during the trans-attack and post-attack periods. It does not include the function of evaluating the operational significance of nuclear damage assessments.

Nuclear defence. The methods, plans, and procedures involved in establishing and exercising defensive measures against the effects of an attack by nuclear weapons or radiological warfare agents. It encompasses both the training for, and the implementation of, these methods, plans and procedures. *See also* **Radiological defence.**

Nuclear Defence Affairs Committee (NDAC). The multi national committee within NATO (*qv*) which deals with nuclear matters.

Nuclear detonation, detection and reporting system. A system deployed to provide surveillance coverage of critical friendly target areas, and indicate place, height of burst, yield, and ground zero of nuclear detonations.

Nuclear free zone. An area in which nuclear weapons may not be stored or sited.

Nuclear incident. An unexpected event involving a nuclear weapon, facility, or component, but not constituting a nuclear weapon(s) attack.

Nuclear logistic movement. The transport of nuclear weapons or components of nuclear weapons in connection with supply or maintenance operations.

Nuclear nations. Military nuclear powers and civil nuclear powers. *See also* **Nuclear power.**

Nuclear Planning Group (NPG). The organization within NATO which is responsible for detailed guidance in the use of tactical nuclear missiles.

Nuclear power. Not used without appropriate modifier *eg See* **Major nuclear power; Military nuclear power; Nuclear nations.**

Nuclear radiation(s). Particulate and electro-magnetic radiation emitted from atomic nuclei in various nuclear processes. The important nuclear radiation, from the weapon standpoint, are alpha and beta particles, gamma

rays, and neutrons. All nuclear radiations are ionizing radiations, but the reverse is not true; X-rays for example, are included among ionizing radiations, but they are not nuclear radiations since they do not originate from atomic nuclei.

Nuclear safety line. A line selected, if possible, to follow well-defined topographical features and used to delineate levels of protective measures, degrees of damage or risk to friendly troops, and/or to prescribe limits to which the effects of friendly weapons may be permitted to extend.

Nuclear surface burst. An explosion of a nuclear weapon at the surface of land or water; or above the surface, at a height less than the maximum radius of the fireball. *See also* **Types of burst.**

Nuclear underground burst. The explosion of a nuclear weapon in which the centre of the detonation lies at a point beneath the surface of the ground. *See also* **Types of burst.**

Nuclear underwater burst. The explosion of a nuclear weapon in which the centre of the detonation lies at a point beneath the surface of the water. *See also* **Types of burst.**

Nuclear vulnerability assessment. The estimate of the probable effect on population, forces and resources from a hypothetical nuclear attack. It is performed predominantely in the preattack period; however, it may be extended to the trans-attack or postattack periods.

Nuclear warfare. Warfare involving the employment of nuclear weapons (*qv*).

Nuclear weapons. A device in which the explosion results from the energy released by reactions involving atomic nuclei, either fission or fusion or both.

Nuclear weapon(s) accident. Any unplanned occurrence involving loss or destruction of, or serious damage to,

nuclear weapons or their components
which results in an actual or potential
hazard to life or property.

Nuclear weapon employment time.
The time required for delivery of a
nuclear weapon after the decision to fire
has been made.

Nuclear weapon exercise. An operation
not directly related to immediate
operational readiness. It includes removal
of a weapon from its normal storage location, preparing for use, delivery to an
employment unit, the movement in a
ground training exercise to include
loading aboard an aircraft or missile and
return to storage. It may include any or
all of the operations listed above, but does
not include launching or flying operations. Typical exercises include aircraft
generation exercises, ground readiness
exercises, ground tactical exercises, and
various categories of inspections designed
to evaluate the capability of the unit to
perform its prescribed mission. *See also*
**Immediate operational readiness;
Nuclear weapon manoeuvre.**

Nuclear weapon manoeuvre. An
operation not directly related to immediate
operational readiness. It may consist of all
those operations listed for a nuclear
weapon exercise but is extended to
include fly-away in combat aircraft but
not to include expenditure of the weapon.
Typical manoeuvres include nuclear
operational readiness manoeuvres and
tactical air operations. *See also* **Immediate
operational readiness; Nuclear weapon
exercise.**

Nuclear weapons state. *See* **Military
nuclear power.**

Nuclear yields. The energy released in
the detonation of a nuclear weapon,
measured in terms of the kilotons or
megatons of trinitrotoluene (TNT)
required to produce the same energy
release.

Nudets (US). The American system of

seismic sensors which estimates the posi
tion and size of nuclear explosions.

Nuisance minefield (land mine warfare).
A minefield laid to delay and disorganize
the enemy and to hinder his use of an
area or route. *See also* **Minefield** (land
mine warfare).

Nullah. A small stream or watercourse.

Numbered wave. *See* **Wave.**

Numerical scale. *See* **Representative
fraction.**

Nurse. A male or female, in the ranks of a
nation's medical service or branch, who
possesses a nationally recognized
general nursing qualification. A nurse may
also be specially trained for aeromedical
duties and then be referred to as a 'flight
nurse'.

Nursing attendant. A male or female,
enlisted in the ranks of a nation's medical
service or branch, who does not possess a
nationally recognized general nursing
qualification. A nursing attendant may
be given special training to qualify him/
her for aeromedical duties.

Nursing officer. A male or female of
officer status possessing a nationally
recognized general nursing qualification
who also may be specially trained for
aeromedical duties. A female officer
so trained may be referred to as a flight
sister.

Objective. The physical object of the
action taken, *eg* a definite tactical feature,
the seizure and/or holding of which is
essential to the commander's plan.
* **Area.** A defined geographical area
within which is located an objective
to be captured or reached by the military
forces. This area is defined by competent
authority for purposes of command and
control.

Oblique. *See* **Oblique air Photograph.**

Oblique air photograph. An air photograph taken with the camera axis directed between the horizontal and vertical planes. Commonly referred to as an 'oblique'.
1. High Oblique. One in which the apparent horizon appears.
2. Low Oblique. One in which the apparent horizon does not appear.

Oblique fire. Fire brought to bear from a flank.

Observation post. A position from which military observations are made, or fire directed and adjusted, and which possesses appropriate communications; may be airborne.

Observed fire. Fire for which the points of impact or burst can be seen by an observer. The fire can be controlled and adjusted on the basis of observation.

Observed fire procedure. A standardized procedure for use in adjusting indirect fire on a target.

Observers (exercise). Representatives from nations who are invited to attend as observers at exercises, *eg* military attachés.

Observer-target line. An imaginary straight line from the observer or spotter to the target.

Observer target distance. The distance between the observer and the target measured along the observer-target line.

Obsolescent. A description applied to *matériel* expected to become obsolete and for which no further provision will therefore normally be made.

Obsolete. A description applied to *matériel* for which there is no further service use because due to revised requirements it is no longer satisfactory for the purpose for which it was originally obtained. It does not however mean that examples will not be found in units. Obsolete material is frequently retained,

for reasons of economy, until it can be replaced.

Obstruction. A building or other obstacle rising far enough above the surrounding surface to create a hazard to aircraft in flight.

Occupation of position. Movement into and proper organization of an area to be used as a battle position.

Offensive air support. All forms of air support not covered by tactical air transport, *eg* air protection, ground attack and air reconnaissance.

Officer (Offr). Commonly used to denote an officer holding the Sovereign's Commission, junior to whom are the ranks of warrant officer Class I or II (WO). Junior again to them is the noncommissioned officer (NCO).

Officer Cadet Training Unit (OCTU). A unit in which potential officers are instructed in the tactical and administrative duties and obligations of an officer.

Officer conducting the exercise. The officer responsible for the conduct of an allocated part of the exercise both from the Orange and Blue aspects. He will issue necessary supplementary instructions. In addition, he may be an exercise commander.

Officer Evaluation Report. US equivalent to Confidential Report (*qv*).

Officer scheduling the exercise. The officer who originates the exercise and orders it to take place. He will issue basic instructions which will include the designation of exercise areas, the allocation of forces, and the necessary coordinating instructions. He will also designate the officer conducting the exercise. (*qv*)

Offset bombing. Any bombing procedure which employs a reference or aiming point other than the actual target.

Offset distance (nuclear). The distance the desired ground zero or actual ground zero is offset from the centre of an area target or from a point target.

Offset post. An appointment which is eliminated from an establishment in order to provide the man power cover for another one.

Offsetting. A procedure related to stocktaking whereby a deficiency or surplus of one item of materiel is used to explain and adjust a surplus or deficiency of another item.

On call. The term used to signify that a prearranged concentration, air strike, or final protective fire may be called for. *See also* **Call for fire; Call mission.**
* Target. A target, other than a scheduled (*qv*) one, which has been registered and can be engaged when required. *** wave.** *See* **Wave.**

One day's supply. A unit or quantity of supplies adopted as a standard of measurement, used in estimating the average daily expenditure under stated conditions. It may also be stated in terms of a factor *eg*, rounds of ammunition per weapon per day.

O-O line An imaginary line which divides the responsibility for the co-ordination of artillery fire between the Corps or Force artillery commander and the commander of the Divisional artillery.

Operation(s) (Op). A military action or the carrying out of a strategic, tactical, service, training, or administrative military mission; the process of carrying on combat, including movement, supply, attack, defence and manoeuvres needed to gain the objectives of any battle or campaign. *** Order.** A directive, usually formal, issued by a commander to subordinate commanders for the purpose of effecting the co-ordinated execution of an operation. *** Plan.**
1. A plan for a single or series of connected operations to be carried out

simultaneously or in succession. It is usually based upon stated assumptions and is the form of directive employed by higher authority to permit subordinate commanders to prepare supporting plans and orders.
2. The designation 'plan' is usually used instead of 'order' in preparing for operations well in advance. An operation plan may be put into effect at a prescribed time, or on signal, and then becomes the operation order.

Operational chain of command. The chain of command established for a particular operation or series of continuing operations. *See also* **Administrative chain of command; Chain of command.**

Operational characteristics. The specific military qualities of performance and capability required of an item of equipment to enable it to meet an agreed operational need.

Operational command. The authority granted to a commander to assign missions or tasks to subordinate commanders, to deploy units, to re-assign forces, and to retain or delegate operational and/or tactical control as may be deemed necessary. It does not of itself include administrative command or logistical responsibility. May also be used to denote the forces assigned to a commander. *See also* **Command.**

Operational control. The authority granted to a commander to direct forces assigned so that the commander may accomplish specific missions or tasks which are usually limited by function, time, or location; to deploy units concerned, and to retain or assign tactical control of those units. It does not include authority to assign separate employment of components of the units concerned. Neither does it, of itself, include administrative or logistic control.

Operational interchangeability. Ability to substitute one item for another of different composition or origin without loss in effectiveness, accuracy, and safety of performance.

Operational missile. A missile which has been accepted by the using services for tactical and/or strategic use.

Operational readiness. The capability of a unit, weapon system or equipment to perform the missions or function for which it is organized or designed. May be used in a general sense or to express a level or degree of readiness.

Operational reserve. An emergency reserve of men and/or material established for the support of a specific operation.

Opportunity target. *See* **Target of opportunity.**

Optical axis. In a lens element, the straight line which passes through the centres of curvature of the lens surfaces. In an optical system, the line formed by the coinciding principal axes of the series of optical elements.

Optimum height. The height of an explosion which will produce the maximum effect against a given target. * **of burst.** For nuclear weapons, the optimum height of burst for a particular target (or area) is that at which it is estimated a weapon of a specified energy yield will produce a certain desired effect over the maximum possible area.

Orange forces. Denotes those forces used in an enemy role during NATO exercises. *See also* **Blue force(s).**

Orbit point. A geographically or electronically defined location over land or water, used in stationing airborne aircraft.

Order(s). A communication, written, oral, or by signal, which conveys instructions from a superior to a subordinate. Various forms are recognized: an operation order for a specific operation; routine orders which are issued daily, weekly or monthly; warning orders to

give prior information about impending events, etc. but whatever form is used the imperative is expressed by 'is to' or 'are to' never 'will' which only gives information or indicates the future tense. * **of Battle** (ORBAT). The identification, strength, command structure, and disposition of the personnel, units, and equipment of any military force. * **of battle card** (intelligence). A single, or master, standardized card containing basic information on each enemy ground force unit/ formation providing all pertinent order of battle information. * **Group.** A group assembled to receive a commander's orders. The basic composition of this group is normally prescribed in the SOP (*qv*) of the unit or formation concerned.

Orderly room. The office of the Commanding Officer of a Regiment, which accommodates his Adjutant and his orderly room staff.

Orders of Chivalry. *eg* the Bath, the British Empire, take precedence over most decorations (*qv*) except the Victoria Cross and the George Cross.

Ordnance.
1. A collective noun for guns; also denotes military stores. Master General of the Ordnance (MGO) is the member of the Army Board of the Defence Council responsible for the provision of warlike stores.
2. The Royal Army Ordnance Corps (RAOC) is responsible for the supply of most of the warlike stores (less Engineer and Medical), rations, ammunition, and POL used by the army. Under the Director of Ordnance Stores (DOS) there are the Deputy Directors of Ordnance Stores (DDOS) at Corps HQs; the Assistant Directors of Ordnance Stores (ADOS) are at Divisional HQ and are assisted by one or more Deputy Assistant Directors of Ordnance Stores (DADOS).

Ordnance Field Park (OFP). A completely mobile unit which carries and issues all the MT (*qv*) and technical stores which are in constant demand by units in order to maintain and repair their vehicles and equipment.

Oreo (US slang). n. A disparaging term given by coloured soldiers to coloured officers and NCOs who think and behave like their white colleagues.

Organic. Integral. A unit is organic to a formation when it has a permanent place in its order of battle (*qv*).

Organization of the ground. The development of a defensive position by strengthening the natural defences of the terrain and by assignment of the occupying troops to specific locations.

Originating medical facility. A medical facility that initially transfers a patient to another medical facility.

Orthomorphic projection. One in which the scale, although varying throughout the map, is the same in all directions at any point, so that very small areas are represented by correct shape and bearings are correct.

OTAN. French for NATO (*qv*).

Other forces. Forces not assigned or earmarked for assignment to a NATO command which may, at some future date, co-operate with NATO forces or be placed under the operational command or operational control of a NATO commander in certain circumstances which are specified.

Other rank(s) (OR). Any soldier below commissioned rank. Now obsolescent and being replaced by the word 'soldiers'.

Otway pit. A type of latrine (*qv*) with a flyproof cover.

Outflank. To move a force in such a way as to oppose it to the side instead of the front of an enemy position or column.

Out. A codeword given over the radio or telephone meaning that the conversation is finished.

Outline map. A map which presents just sufficient geographic information to permit the correlation of additional data placed upon it.

Outline plan. A preliminary plan which outlines the salient features or principles of a course of action prior to the initiation of detailed planning.

Over.
1. Artillery. The term used to denote that the missile has impacted beyond its target.
2. A code word used in radio transmissions meaning that the speaker has completed his message and awaits the recipient's reply.

Overhead clearance. The vertical distance between the route surface and any obstruction above it.

Overlap.
1. In photography, the amount by which one photograph includes the same area covered by another, customarily expressed as a percentage. The overlap between successive air photographs in adjacent parallel flight lines is called 'side lap'.
2. In cartography, that portion of a map or chart which overlaps the area covered by another of the same series.

Overlay. A printing or drawing on a transparent or translucent medium at the same scale as a map, chart, etc., to show details not appearing, or requiring special emphasis on the original.

Overpressure. The pressure resulting from the blast wave of an explosion. It is referred to as 'positive' when it exceeds atmospheric pressure and 'negative' during the passage of the wave when resulting pressures are less than atmospheric pressure.

Overprint. New material printed or stamped upon a map or chart to show data of importance or special use, in addition to that originally printed.

Overrrun control. Equipment enabling a camera to continue operating for a predetermined number of frames or seconds after normal cut-off.

Overshoot. A phase of flight wherein a landing approach of an aircraft is not continued to touch-down. *See also* **Go around.**

Pace (ground forces). The regulated speed of a column or element as set by the pace setter (*qv*) in order to maintain the average speed prescribed.

Pace setter. An individual, selected by the column commander, who travels in the lead vehicle or element to regulate the column speed and establish the pace necessary to meet the required movement order.

Package. The product of a complete series of packaging (*qv*) operations.

Packaged petroleum products. Petroleum products (generally lubricants, oils, greases, and speciality items) normally packaged by a manufacturer and procured, stored, transported, and issued in containers having a fill capacity of 45 Imperial Gallons (55 United States gallons) or less.

Packaging. The operations involved in the preparation of items of *matériel* for transportation, storage and delivery to the user. The term embraces preservation, identification and packing.

Pad. A landing area for a helicopter.

Padre. The colloquial word for an army chaplain.

Palisade. A barrier of wooden posts set in the ground.

Pallet. A flat base for combining stores or carrying a single item to form a unit load for handling, transportation, and storage by materials handling equipment.

Palletized unit load. Quantity of any item, packaged or unpackaged, which is arranged on a pallet (*qv*) in a specified manner and securely strapped or fastened thereto so that the whole is handled as a unit.

Palliasse. The rough straw or coir filled mattress issued to soldiers to sleep on. Now replaced by a conventional mattress. *See also* **Biscuit.**

Panel code. A prearranged code designed for visual communications, usually between friendly units, by making use of marking panels. *See also* **Marking panels.**

Panoramic air camera. An air camera which, through a system of moving optics or mirrors, scans a wide area of the terrain, usually from horizon to horizon. The camera may be mounted vertically or obliquely within the aircraft, to scan across or along the line of flight.

Panoramic ground camera. A camera which photographs a wide expanse of terrain by rotating horizontally about the vertical axis through the centre of the camera lens.

Parachute deployment height. The height above the intended impact point at which the parachute or parachutes are fully deployed.

Paradrag drop. Ultra low level airdrop using the drag of an arrester parachute to extract and halt airdrop loads.

Paradrop. Delivery by parachute of personnel or cargo from an aircraft in flight.

Parallactic angle. *See* **Angle of convergence.**

Parallax. In photography, the apparent displacement of the position of an object in relation to a reference point, due to a change in the point of observation.

Parallax difference. The difference in displacement of the top of an object in relation to its base, as measured on the two images of the object on a stereo pair of photographs.

Parallel staff. A staff in which one officer from each nation, or service, working in parallel is appointed to each post. *See also* **Combined staff; Integrated staff; Joint staff.**

Parados. Earth excavated from a trench (*qv*) and placed behind it to give protection from shells or bombs bursting in rear of the firer.

Parapet. Earth excavated from a trench (*qv*) and placed in front of it to give protection from fire.

Paratroop pathfinders. A small force of parachute troops dropped, when necessary, in advance of the main force to mark a drop zone or landing zone.

Partial issue. Issue of a lesser quantity than that demanded pending further action to supply the balance.

Passage of command. The outgoing unit commander is responsible for the defence of his assigned sector until command passes. The moment when command is to pass is determined by mutual agreement between the two unit commanders unless directed by higher headquarters. It normally occurs when the front line sub-unit commanders have assumed responsibility for their sectors and the incoming unit commander has sufficient communication facilities in operation to exercise control over his entire sector. (Applicable to 'Relief in place' only.)

Passage of lines. An operation in which an incoming unit attacks through a unit which is in contact with the enemy.

Sub-units of the unit being passed through remain in position until their fire has been masked, at which time they may undertake another mission.

Passive (surveillance). When no detectable energy is emitted by an equipment it is said to be passive.

Passive air defence. All measures, other than active defence, taken to minimize the effects of hostile air action. These include the use of cover, concealment, camouflage, dispersion, and protective construction. *See also* **Air defence.**

Passive defence. Measures taken to reduce the probability of and to minimize the effects of damage caused by hostile action without the intention of taking the initiative, *eg* digging in, constructing shelters, erecting wire etc.

Passive electronic countermeasures. Examination and/or analysis of electromagnetic radiations to determine, for the purpose of electronic countermeasures use, the existence, origin, and pertinent characteristics of those electromagnetic radiations which the enemy may be using. *See also* **Electronic countermeasures.**

Passive homing guidance. A system of homing guidance wherein the receiver in the missile utilizes radiation from the target.

Pass time (road). The time that elapses between the moment when the leading vehicle of a column passes a given point and the moment when the last vehicle passes the same point. Used particularly in movement tables (*qv*).

Password. A secret word or distinctive sound used to reply to a challenge. *See also* **Challenge; Countersign; Reply.**

Pathfinder aicraft. An aircraft with a specially trained crew carrying drop zone/landing zone marking teams, target markers, or navigational aids, which precedes the main force to the drop zone/landing zone or target.

Pathfinder team. A team dropped or air landed at an objective to establish and operate navigational aids for the purpose of guiding aircraft to drop and landing zones.

Patients. All sick, injured, or wounded personnel receiving medical care or treatment.

Patrol (ptl). A detachment of ground, sea or air forces sent out for the purpose of gathering information or carrying out a destructive, harassing, mopping-up, or security mission.

Patrol (ground). A detachment sent out by a larger unit for the purpose of gathering information or carrying out, as harassing action, a destructive, mopping-up, or security mission. The commonest forms in the Army are reconnaissance patrols which gain information without fighting; combat patrols which are prepared to fight to gain it and standing patrols which remain static and gain information by observation.

Pattern laying (land mine warfare). The laying of individual mines in a fixed relationship to each other.

Patton (US). The brand name of American battle tanks. The M.60 is the version now in use in the US Army. It is armed with the British 105 mm gun.

Payload.
1. The sum of the weight of passengers and cargo that an aircraft can carry. *See also* **Load** (air).
2. The warhead, its container, and activating devices in a military missile.
3. The satellite or research vehicle of a space probe or research missile.
4. The load (expressed in tons of cargo or equipment, gallons of liquid, or number of passengers) which the vehicle is designed to transport under specified conditions of operation, in addition to its unladen weight. *See also* **Airlift**.

Peace establishment (PE). The authorized scale of personnel, weapons, equipment and vehicles held on charge to a unit in peace-time, usually increased on mobilization (*qv*) to a War Establishment (WE) (*qv*).

Peak overpressure. The maximum value of overpressure at a given location which is generally experienced at the instant the shock (or blast) wave of an explosion reaches that location.

Pecked line (cartography). A symbol consisting of a line broken at regular intervals.

Penetration (ground forces). A form of offensive manoeuvre which seeks to break through the enemy's defensive position, widen the gap created, and destroy the continuity of his positions.

Pentagon (US). Equivalent to British Ministry of Defence (*qv*).

Performance Evaluation Report (PER). The Canadian equivalent to the Confidential Report (*qv*).

Perigee. The point at which a satellite orbit is the least distance from the centre of the gravitational field of the controlling body or bodies.

Permanent Staff Instructor (PSI). The regular element in the Territorial Army Volunteer Reserve.

Pershing. A US surface to surface battlefield support ballistic missile system.

Personal Assistant (PA). The confidential secretary of a senior officer. May be military or civilian, male or female.

Personal locator beacon. A locator beacon capable of providing homing signals to help search and rescue operations. *See also* **Crash locator beacon**.

Personal services. A branch of the A Staff (*qv*) which deals with such matters as discipline, dress, leave, morale, pay, welfare, etc., usually referred to as A (PS).

Personnel reaction time (nuclear). The time required by personnel to take prescribed protective measures after receipt of a nuclear strike warning.

Perspective grid. A network of lines drawn or superimposed on an oblique photograph representing the perspective of a grid on the ground or datum plane.

Petrol Point (PP). A designated area, usually opened at stated times, where POL (*qv*) is kept for replenishment of vehicles.

Petroleum. An oily, liquid solution of hydrocarbons which, when fractionally distilled, yields paraffin, kerosene fuel oil, gasoline, etc. *See also* **Bulk petroleum products; Packaged petroleum products;** *and* **Petroleum, oils and lubricants.**

Petroleum intersectional service. An intersectional or interzonal service in a theatre of operations that operates pipelines and related facilities for the supply of bulk petroleum products to theatre Army elements and other forces as directed.

Petroleum, oils, and lubricants (POL). A broad term which includes all petroleum and associated products used by the armed forces.

Phase line (PL). *See* **Report line.**

Phony mine (land mine warfare). An object used to simulate a mine in a phony minefield. It may be made of any available material. *See also* **Mine.**

Phony minefield (land mine warfare). An area of ground used to simulate a minefield with the object of deceiving the enemy. *See also* **Minefield** (land mine warfare).

Photoflash bomb. A bomb designed to produce a brief and intense illumination for medium altitude night photography.

Photoflash cartridge. A pyrotechnic cartridge designed to produce a brief and intense illumination for low altitude night photography.

Photogrammetric control. Control established by photogrammetric methods as distinguished from control established by ground methods. Sometimes called 'minor control'.

Photogrammetry. The science or art of obtaining reliable measurements from photographic images.

Photographic filter. A layer of glass, gelatine, or other material used to modify the spectrum of incidental light.

Photographic intelligence. The collected products of photographic interpretation, classified and evaluated for military use.

Photographic interpretation. The extraction of information from photographs or other recorded images.

Photographic reading. The simple recognition of natural or cultural features from photographs.

Photographic scale. The ratio of a distance measured on a photograph or mosaic to the corresponding distance on the ground, classified as follows: very large scale 1:6,000 and larger, large scale 1:6,000 to 1:12,000, medium scale 1:12,000 to 1:30,000, small scale 1:30,000 to 1:70,000, very small scale 1:70,000 and smaller. *See also* **Scale.**

Photographic sortie. *See* **Imagery sortie.**

Photographic strip. A series of successive overlapping photographs taken along a selected course or direction.

Photo interpretation key. *See* **Imagery interpretation key.**

Photomap. A reproduction of a photograph or photomosaic upon which the grid lines, marginal data, contours, place names, boundaries and other data may be added.

Photo nadir. The point at which a vertical line through the perspective centre of the camera lens intersects the photo plane.

'P'-Hour (Airborne). The time of drop of the first sticks of the main body.

Physical security. That part of security concerned with physical measures designed to safeguard personnel, to prevent unauthorized access to equipment, facilities, material and documents, and to safeguard them against espionage, sabotage, damage and theft.

Pick-up-scale. *See* **Scale** (logistic).

Pick up zone (PZ). A designated area where helicopters or VTOL aircraft can embark passengers or stores.

Picture. Situation, *eg* to be 'in the picture' means to be abreast of the situation. To 'paint the picture', explain the situation.

Pictorial symbolization. A method of representing prominent map details by means of stylized symbols.

Pig (slang). A Humber ten ton armoured vehicle.

Pillbox. A small, low fortification that houses machine guns, anti-tank weapons, etc. A pillbox is usually made of concrete, steel, or filled sandbags. A number, erected in World War 2 may still be seen in England.

Pilot model. The first or only pre-production model.

Pilot's trace. A rough overlay to a map made by the pilot of a photographic reconnaissance aircraft during or immediately after a sortie. It shows the location, direction, number, and order of photographic runs made, together with the camera(s) used on each run.

Pin-point.
1. A precisely identified point, especially on the ground, that locates a very small target, a reference point for rendezvous or for other purposes; the co-ordinates that define this point.
2. The ground position of aircraft determined by direct observation of the ground.

Pin-point photograph. A single photograph or a stereo pair of a specific object or target.

Pin-point target. A target which is less than 50 metres in diameter.

Pipe line. In logistics, the channel of support or a specific portion thereof by means of which *matériel* or personnel flow from sources of procurement to their point of use.

Pipeline time. The time that elapses between the time of despatch of a Demand or Issue order and the date of receipt of *matériel* by the consignee.

Pipers. Men borne on the establishment of Scottish and Irish regiments who play the bagpipes. Equivalent to the fife player in English regiments. The pipe major is equivalent to a drum major.

Pioneers.
1. Infantry soldiers especially trained in elementary engineering.
2. Members of the Royal Corps of Pioneers.

Pistol. A handheld weapon which feeds cartridges from a box magazine as opposed to a revolving chamber. *See also* **Revolver.**

Pitch. *See* **Tip.**

Plain clothes. The everyday dress of a civilian as applied to an officer when not in uniform, sometimes referred to as mufti.

Planned execution time. The time between the issue, without previous warning, of

orders to execute an operation and
the arrival of the first troops in the objective area. When applicable it includes any
warning period to start operations
required by the forces involved.

Planned load. A load that has been planned
for a specific type of aircraft sortie.
See also **Load.**

Planned resupply. The shipping of
supplies in a regular flow as envisaged by
existing preplanned schedules and
organizations, which will usually include
some form of planned procurement. *See
also* **Elements of resupply.**

Planned target. A registered target on
which artillery fire has been prearranged.

Planning factor(s) (logistics). A properly
selected multiplier, used in planning to
estimate the amount and type of effort
involved in a contemplated operation.
Planning factors are often expressed as
rates, ratios, or lengths of time.

Planning staff. *See* **Central Planning
team.**

Plan position indicator. A cathode ray
tube on which radar returns are so displayed as to bear the same relationship
to the transmitter as the objects giving
rise to them.

Plan range. In air photographic
reconnaissance, the horizontal distance
from the point below the aircraft
to an object on the ground.

Plastic range. The stress range in which
a material will not fail when subjected
to the action of a force, but will not
recover completely so that a permanent
deformation results when the force is
removed.

Plastic spray packaging. *See* **Cocooning.**

Plastic zone. The region beyond the
rupture zone associated with crater
formation resulting from an explosion in

which there is no visible rupture, but
in which the soil is permanently deform-
ed and compressed to a high density.
See also **Rupture zone.**

Plate.
1. In cartography:
    1. a printing plate of zinc,
       aluminium, or engraved copper;
    2. collective term for all 'states' of
       an engraved map reproduced from
       the same engraved printing plate;
    3. all detail to appear on a map or
       chart which will be reproduced
       from a single printing plate (*eg* the
       'blue plate' or the 'contour plate').
2. In photography, a transparent
medium, usually glass, coated with a
photographic emulsion. *See also*
Diapositive; Transparency.

Platform drop. The air drop of loaded
platforms from rear loading aircraft with
roller conveyors. *See also* **Airdrop;
Airdrop platform.**

Platoon (pl). An infantry unit of
approximately thirty men normally
commanded by a subaltern officer.

Plot. In photographic interpretation,
a portion of a map or overlay on which
are drawn the outlines of the areas
covered by one or more photographs.
See also **Master plot.**

Plunging fire. Fire brought to bear from
a height on to ground below.

Pluton. A French surface to surface
tactical nuclear missile.

Point. In movement a place designated
in orders where action may be expected.
Critical *, A point on a route to which
reference is made when describing
another point; **Start** point, the point on
a route when troops come under command
of the officer or formation in charge for
movement; **Release** point is where troops
cease to be under his command. *See also*
Ammunition * *and* **Petrol *.**

Point designation grid. A system of lines,
having no relation to the actual scale, or

orientation, drawn on a map, chart, or air photograph dividing it into squares so that points can be more readily located.

Point of no return. A point along an aircraft track beyond which its endurance will not permit return to its own or some other associated base on its own fuel supply.

Point target. A target which requires the accurate placement of bombs or fire.

Polar plot. The method of locating a target or point on the map by means of polar co-ordinates.

Pontoons. Light open boats placed side by side across a river and covered by a plank or metal roadway to form a temporary bridge.

Population Protection and Resources Management (PPRM) (US). The political, military, social and economic measures taken by government to protect the public and its resources during an insurgency situation by denying help to the enemy and strengthening support for the government.

Port committee. A joint service committee including the commander of the Rear Area or his representative formed to ensure the smooth working of a port or beach head and control the flow of supplies through it.

Portable. Denotes equipment designed to be carried by a man or men with not more than such minor dismantling and reassembling as would be within the capabilities of user units.

Port capacity. The estimated capacity of a port or an anchorage to clear cargo in 24 hours usually expressed in tons. *See also* **Beach capacity.**

Positive. In photography, an image on film, plate, or paper having approximately the same total rendition of light and shade as the 'original subject'.

Position defence. The type of defence in which the bulk of the defending force is disposed in selected tactical localities where the decisive battle is to be fought. Principal reliance is placed on the ability of the forces in the defended localities to maintain their positions and to control the terrain between them. The reserve is used to add depth, to block, or to restore the battle position by counterattack.

Post. The position taken up by a sentry or picquet.

Post design. Further development work undertaken after acceptance into service to ensure that the item of *matériel* continues to meet its approved specification or Staff requirement.

Post flight inspection. *See* **After-flight inspection.**

Post production lead time. The interval, expressed in months, between the end of Production Lead Time (*qv*) and the date that the initial quantity of an item of *matériel* is brought on charge. This includes time for despatch and transit, any inspection necessary and receipt procedures.

Postal and courier communications (PCC). Each division has one PCC unit (PCCU) RE consisting of a Forces Post Office (FPO) which provides the same service as a civilian post office and operates a Forces Courier Service (FCS). The former handles all unclassified official mail and private correspondence. The latter distributes all official mail which is classified as confidential and above between units and HQ.

Pouch. A case for carrying ammunition attached to a soldier's equipment.

Pounds per Square Inch (PSI). A measure used in calculating the weight of a vehicle in relation to the bridge, culvert or terrain which it has to cross. Also used to measure blast effects.

Practice mine (land mine warfare).
A replica of a standard mine, having
the same features and weight as the mine
it represents. It is constructed to emit
a puff of smoke or make a noise to
simulate detonation. *See also* **Mine.**

Pre-arranged fire. Fire from any weapon
or group of weapons that has been
planned in advance to be executed at
some predetermined time or phase of
the operation.

Preassault operations. Operations conducted in the objective area prior to
the assault. They include reconnaissance,
minesweeping, bombardment, bombing,
underwater demolition, and destruction
of beach obstacles.

Precedence. A designation assigned to a
message by the originator to indicate to
communication personnel the relative
order of handling and to the addressee
the order in which the message is to be
noted.

Predominant height. In air reconnaissance,
the height of 51% or more of the
structures within an area of similar surface
material.

Pre-empt. To forestall. Usually used in
conjunction with the word attack to
denote an offensive move designed to
disrupt an enemy attack.

Preflight inspection. *See* **Before-flight
inspection.**

Pre-issue inspection. An examination
carried out, where appropriate, on an
item of *matériel* immediately prior to
issue to ensure that it is fit in all
respects for the purpose required.

Preliminary demolition. A target
prepared for demolition preliminary to
a withdrawal, the demolition of which
can be executed as soon after preparation as convenient on the orders of the
officer to whom the responsibility for
such demolitions has been delegated.

Preload loading. The loading of selected
items aboard ship at one port prior to
the main loading of the ship at another.
See also **Loading.**

Preparation fire. Fire delivered on a
target preparatory to an assault.

Prepayment issue. The authorized issue
of *matériel,* payment for which is
received before issue and credited to
public funds.

Prepayment loan. A loan which is subject
to a hire or rental charge payable in
advance; a deposit may also be required.

Preplanned air support. Air support in
accordance with a programme planned
in advance of operations. *See also*
Air support.

Pre-position. To place military units,
equipment, or supplies at or near the
point of planned use or at a designated
location to reduce reaction time, and
to ensure timely support of a specific
force during initial phases of an operation.

Prescribed nuclear load. A specified
quantity of nuclear weapons to be carried
by a delivery unit. The establishment and
replenishment of this load after each
expenditure is a command decision and is
dependent upon the tactical situation,
the nuclear logistical situation, and the
capability of the unit to transport and
utilize the load. It may vary from day
to day and among similar delivery units.

Prescribed nuclear stockage. A specified
quantity of nuclear weapons, components
of nuclear weapons, and warhead test
equipment to be stocked in special
ammunition supply points or other
logistical installations. The establishment
and replenishment of this stockage is a
command decision and is dependent upon
the tactical situation, the allocation, the
capability of the logistical support unit
to store and maintain the nuclear weapons,
and the nuclear logistical situation.

The prescribed stockage may vary from time to time and among similar logistical support units.

President of the Mess Committee (PMC). The officer in charge of the general running of the Officers' Mess. He is responsible for the funds and sets the standard of living.

President of the Regimental Institutes (PRI). A senior officer in a regiment or battalion in charge of unit funds, controls the NAAFI canteen and supervises generally all amenity and welfare activities.

Pressure altitude. An atmospheric pressure, expressed in terms of altitude which corresponds to that pressure in the standard atmosphere. *See also* **Altitude.**

Pressure breathing. The technique of breathing which is required when oxygen is supplied direct to an individual at a pressure higher than the ambient barometric pressure.

Pressure front. *See* **Shock front.**

Pressure suit.
1. Partial. A skin tight suit which does not completely enclose the body but which is capable of exerting pressure on the major portion of the body in order to counteract an increased intrapulmonary oxygen pressure.
2. Full. A suit which completely encloses the body and in which a gas pressure, sufficiently above ambient pressure for maintenance of function may be sustained. *See also* **Water suit.**

Pressurized cabin. The occupied space of an aircraft in which the air pressure has been increased above that of the ambient atmosphere by compression of the ambient atmosphere into the space.

Price fixing. The process of negotiating prices.

Primary demolition belt. *See* **Demolition belt.**

Primary packaged quantity. The quantity of an item of *matériel* selected as being the most suitable for packaging for issue to the ultimate user.

Principal Administrative Officer (PAO). The commander of the Communications Zone (*qv*) who advises the Force Commander on logistic matters and co-ordinates the work of the administrative staff and services.

Principal parallel. On an oblique photograph, a line parallel to the true horizon and passing through the principal point (*qv*).

Principal plane. A vertical plane which contains the principal point (*qv*) on an oblique photograph, the perspective centre of the lens and the ground nadir.

Principal point. The foot of the perpendicular to the photo plane through the perspective centre. Generally determined by intersection of the lines joining opposite collimating or fiducial marks.

Principal scale. In cartography, the scale of a reduced or generating globe representing the sphere or spheroid, defined by the fractional relation of their respective radii. Also know as 'nominal scale'. *See also* **Scale.**

Principal vertical. On an oblique photograph, a line perpendicular to the true horizon and passing through the principal point (*qv*).

Print reference. A reference to an individual print in an air photographic sortie.

Priority. When used in a signal or letter gives precedence over other communications except those marked 'Immediate'.
* Call. A formation or unit having a supporting arm unit at 'priority call' has first call on that unit's support for a specified task or period of time. *** Suppliers.** Non-profit making

bodies to whom preference is given
in the allocation of Government orders.

Prior permission (Air). Permission
granted by the appropriate authority
prior to the commencement of a
flight or a series of flights landing in
or flying over the territory of the nation
concerned.

Prisoner of War (PW). Captured enemy
personnel who can be identified as
soldiers of a legitimate Army, and as
such have specified rights under
international conventions. * **Branch
camp.** A subsidiary camp under the
supervision and administration of the
prisoner of war camp of which it is a
branch. * **Cage.** A temporary construction, building or enclosed area, to which
prisoners of war are evacuated for
interrogation and temporary detetention
pending further evacuation. * **Camp.**
A camp of a semipermanent nature
established in the communication zone
or zone of interior (home country)
for the internment and complete
administration of prisoners of war. It
may be located on, or independent of,
other military installations. * **Collecting
point.** A designated locality in a forward
battle area where prisoners are
assembled pending local examination
for information of immediate tactical
value and subsequent evacuation.
* **Compound.** A subdivision of a prisoner
of war enclosure. * **Enclosure.** A
subdivision of a prisoner of war camp.
* **Personnel record.** A form for recording
photograph, fingerprints, and other
pertinent personal data concerning the
prisoner of war, including that required
by the Geneva Convention. * **Processing
station.** An installation established for
the processing and temporary detention
of prisoners of war pending assignment
to camps.

Private (Pte). An abbreviation of the
obsolete Private Centinel, a soldier
holding no rank in the army. In Rifle
Regiments the Private Rifleman has been
abbreviated to Rifleman (*qv*).

Probability of damage. The probability
that damage will occur to a target
expressed as a percentage or as a decimal.

Probable error. *See* **Horizontal error.**

Probably destroyed (aircraft). A damage
assessment on an enemy aircraft seen
to break-off combat in circumstances
which lead to the conclusion that it must
be a loss although it is not actually seen
to crash.

Procedure turn. An aircraft manoeuvre in
which a turn is made away from a
designated track followed by a turn in
the opposite direction, both turns being
executed so as to permit the aircraft to
intercept and proceed along the recip-
rocal of the designated track.

Processing. In photography, the operations
necessary to produce negatives, diapositives,
or prints from exposed films, plates,
or paper.

Production lead time. The interval
expressed in months, between the date
of placing an order for the purchase,
manufacture or repair of an item of
matériel and the date that the initial
quantity is ready for despatch or
collection. This includes any time necessary for inspection and/or packaging
required at this stage.

Proforma.
1. A message, the nature of the
successive elements of which is understood by prearrangement.
2. A standard form.

Progress payment. A payment made to the
contractor based on his own statement
of expenditure incurred under the contract and not necessarily related to the
attainment of a defined stage of work.

Prohibited area. A specified area within
the land areas of a state or territorial
waters adjacent thereto over which the
flight of aircraft is prohibited. *See also*
Danger area; Restricted area.

Projectile. An object, projected by an applied exterior force and continuing in motion by virtue of its own inertia, as a bullet, bomb, shell, or grenade. Also applied to rockets and to guided missiles.

Projection. In cartography, any systematic arrangement of meridians and parallels portraying the curved surface of the sphere or spheroid upon a plane.
* Print. An enlarged or reduced photographic print made by projection of the image of a negative or a transparency on to a sensitized surface.

Project study. A detailed examination of the scientific and technical problems involved in meeting a Staff requirement, leading to a plan of development, quantified in terms of money, manpower and time, and to an estimate of subsequent production costs.

Propaganda. Any information, ideas, doctrines, or special appeals disseminated to influence the opinion, emotions, attitudes, or behaviour of any specified group in order to benefit the sponsor either directly or indirectly. *Black* – Propaganda which purports to emanate from a source other than the true one. *Grey* – Propaganda which does not specifically identify any source. *White* – Propaganda disseminated and acknowledged by the sponsor or by an accredited agency thereof.

Propellant. That which provides the energy required for propelling a projectile. Specifically, an explosive charge for propelling a bullet, shell or the like; also a fuel, either solid or liquid, for propelling a rocket or missile.

Protective clothing. Clothing especially designed, fabricated, or treated to protect personnel against hazards caused by extreme changes in physical environment, dangerous working conditions, or enemy action.

Protective minefield (land mine warfare). A minefield employed to assist a unit

in its local, close-in protection. *See also* **Minefield** (land mine warfare).

Proteus. A hand-held signalling rocket.

Provisional unit. An assemblage of personnel and equipment temporarily organized for a limited period of time for the accomplishment of a specific mission.

Provost (pro). Military policemen (slang Redcaps, from the colour of the covering of their service dress hats). At their head is the * Marshal (PM); below him Deputy * Marshals (DPM), Assistant * Marshals (APM) and Deputy Assistant * Marshals (DAPM) of officer rank. The soldiers are in the Corps of Military Police and are of non commissioned and warrant rank.

Proximity fuse. A fuse designed to detonate a projectile, bomb, mine, or charge when activated by an external influence in the close vicinity of a target. The variable time fuse is one type of a proximity fuse. *See also* **Fuse**

Prudent limit of endurance. The time during which an aircraft can remain airborne and still retain a given safety margin of fuel.

Prudent limit of patrol. The time at which an aircraft must depart from its operational area in order to return to its base and arrive there with a given safety margin (usually 20%) of fuel reserve for bad weather diversions.

Psychological action. The use of psychological media and supporting activities in peace and war designed to reduce the potential or actual enemy's prestige and influence in potentially hostile or neutral countries and to increase friendly influence and attitudes in these countries.

Psychological consolidation. Actions designed to foster the establishment or maintenance of order and security in the combat zone and rear areas of friendly forces and to gain the support of a local population in a territory occupied by friendly forces, in order to advance political and military objectives.

Psychological media. The media, technical or non-technical, which establish any kind of communication with a target audience.

Psychological operations (PSYOP). Planned psychological activities in peace and war directed towards enemy, friendly and neutral audiences, in order to create attitudes and behaviour favourable to the achievement of political and military objectives. These operations include psychological action (*qv*). Psychological warfare (*qv*), and psychological consolidation (*qv*) and encompass those political, military, economic, ideological, and information activities designed for achieving a desired psychological effect.

Psychological operations approach. The technique adopted to indicate a desired reaction on the part of the target audience.

Psychological situation. The current emotional state, mental disposition, or other behavioural motivation of a target audience, basically founded on its national psychological political, social, economic, and psychological peculiarities but also subject to the influence of circumstances and events.

Psychological theme. An idea or topic on which a psychological operation is based.

Psychological warfare. The planned use of propaganda and other measures, designed to influence the opinions, emotions, attitudes, and behaviour of enemy, neutral, or friendly groups in support of current policy and aims, or of a military plan.

Public information. Information which is released or published for the primary purpose of keeping the public fully informed, thereby gaining their understanding and support.

Public married quarter hiring. Any type of building or construction appropriated by the Mod for the accommodation of an entitled family, *eg* permanent and temporary homes, furnished and unfurnished married quarter hirings, caravans, mobile homes, converted hutting, etc.

PULHEEMS. The medical assessment of a person's physique categorized under standard headings.

Pulk. A small sledge used to transport stores in Arctic conditions.

Pull-up point. The point at which an aircraft must start to climb from a low-level approach in order to gain sufficient height from which to execute the attack or retirement. *See also* **Air control team; Contact point; Turn-in point.**

Pulse repetition frequency (PRF). A characteristic of a radar transmission.

Pulsejet. A jet-propulsion engine, containing neither compressor nor turbine. Equipped with valves in the front which open and shut; it takes in air to create thrust in rapid periodic bursts rather than continuously.

Puma. An Anglo-French tactical utility helicopter.

Quadrant elevation. The angle between the level base of a gun when laid and its bore.

Quadrantal error. The error in an aircraft direction finding loop bearing caused by the reflection and re-radiation of radio frequency energy from the aircraft structure.

Quarter.
n. To give quarter is to spare the life of a prisoner. It is now the normal practice amongst civilized people.

v. To place troops under cover in any building.

Quartermaster (QM). The unit staff officer who deals with all quartering (*qv*) matters. He is assisted by Quartermaster Sergeants (QMS).

Quartermaster General (QMG). The member of the Army Board who is responsible for all quartering (*qv*) matters. Junior to him is the Deputy *, Assistant *s, and Deputy Assistant *s. Below them are Staff Captains (*qv*).

Quartering (Q). The division of the staff which deals with all supply matters, ammunition, food, clothing, houses, etc, and troop movements.

Quarters. The house or room in which an officer or soldier has his sleeping accommodation.

Queen's Bodyguard for Scotland. The Royal Company of Archers was organized in 1676 and reconstituted in 1703. It has ceremonial duties about the Sovereign in Scotland and is commanded by a Captain General.

Queen's Bodyguard of the Yeomen of the Guard. Short title Yeomen of the Guard, popularly known as Beefeaters. A body of old soldiers of impeccable character, dressed in the same style as when they were founded in 1485, who perform a number of ceremonial duties. They are commanded by a senior retired officer who is their Captain. The other officers of the bodyguard are a Lieutenant, a Clerk of the Cheque and Adjutant, an Ensign and two Exons.

Queen's Regulations (QR). The rules laid down by the Sovereign for the conduct of the army. They are supplemented by the Manual of Military Law (MML) (*qv*) and the Rules of Procedure (RP) (*qv*).

Quick search procedure (Air). A method of search done as quickly as possible by searching the entire area on the outbound leg and by using twice as many aircraft as are normally used.

Quick time. The ordinary marching pace of the infantry.

Quota post. An appointment on an international organization which a nation has accepted to fill indefinitely.

Rad. Unit of absorbed dose of radiation. It represents the absorption of 100 ergs of nuclear (or ionizing) radiation per gram of the absorbing material or tissue.

Radar. Radio detection and ranging equipment that determines the distance and usually the direction of objects by transmission and return of electromagnetic energy. *** Altimetry area.** A large and comparatively level terrain area with a defined elevation which can be used in determining the altitude of airborne equipment by the use of radar. *** Altitude.** In an automatic flight control system, a control mode in which the altitude of an aircraft is maintained by reference to signals from a radar or radio altimeter. *** Camouflage.** The use of radar absorbent or reflecting materials to change the radar echoing properties of a surface of an object. *** Clutter.** Unwanted signals, echoes, or images on the face of the display tube which interfere with observation of desired signals. *** Countermeasures.** *See* **Electronic countermeasures; Chaff. * Coverage.** The limits within which objects can be detected by one or more radar stations. *** Echo.** The signal indication of an object which has reflected energy transmitted by a primary radar. *** Fire.** Gunfire aimed at a target which is tracked by radar. *** Horizon.** The line at which direct radar rays are tangential to the surface of the earth. *** Intelligence item.** A feature which is radar significant but which cannot be identified exactly at the moment of its appearance as homogeneous. *** Netting.** The linking of several radars to a single centre to provide integrated target information. * **Netting station.** A centre which can receive data from radar tracking stations and exchange this data among other radar tracking stations, thus forming a radar netting system. * **Picket.** Any aircraft or vehicle, stationed at a distance from the force protected, for the purpose of increasing the radar detection range. * **Return.** *See* * **Echo.** * **Silence.** An imposed discipline prohibiting the transmission by radar of electro-magnetic signals on some or all frequencies.

Radarscope overlays. Transparent overlays for placing on the radarscope for comparison and identification of radar returns.

Radarscope photography. A film record of the returns shown by a radar screen.

Radiac. A term devised to designate various types of radiological measuring instruments or equipment. (This term is derived from the words radioactivity, detection, indication and computation, and is normally used as an adjective.) * **Dosimeter.** An instrument used to measure the ionizing radiation absorbed by that instrument.

Radial displacement. On vertical photographs, the apparent 'leaning out', or the apparent displacement of the top of any object having height in relation to its base.

Radiant exposure. *See* **Thermal exposure.**

Radiation dose. The total amount of ionizing radiation absorbed by material or tissue, commonly expressed in rads (qv). The * **rate** (Dosage) absorbed per unit of time.

Radiation intensity (RI). The radiation dose rate (qv) at a given time and place. It may be used, coupled with a figure, to denote the radiation intensity at a given number of hours after a nuclear burst, *eg* RI-3 is the radiation intensity 3 hours after the time of the burst.

Radiation scattering. The diversion of radiation (thermal, electromagnetic, or nuclear) from its original path as a result of interaction or collisions with atoms, molecules, or larger particles in the atmosphere or other media between the source of the radiation (*eg* a nuclear explosion) and a point at some distance away. As a result of scattering, radiation (especially gamma rays and neutrons) will be received at such a point from many directions instead of only from the direction of the source.

Radiation sickness. An illness resulting from excessive exposure to ionizing radiation. The earliest symptoms are nausea, vomiting, and diarrhoea, which may be followed by loss of hair, haemorrhage, inflammation of the mouth and throat, and general loss of energy.

Radiation situation map. A map showing the actual and/or predicted radiation situation in the area of interest.

Radioactivity concentration guide. The amount of any specified radio-isotope that is acceptable in air and water for continuous consumption.

Radio approach aids. Equipment making use of radio to determine the position of an aircraft with considerable accuracy from the time it is in the vicinity of an airfield or carrier until it reaches a position from which landing can be carried out.

Radio beacon. A radio transmitter which emits a distinctive, or characteristic, signal used for the determination of bearings, courses, or location. *See also* **Beacon.**

Radio detection. The detection of the presence of an object by radio location without precise determination of its position.

Radio direction finding. Radio-location in which only the direction of a station is determined by means of its emissions.

Radio fix.
1. The location of a friendly or enemy radio transmitter, determined by finding the direction of the radio transmitter from two or more listening stations.
2. The location of a ship or aircraft by determining the direction of radio signals coming to the ship or aircraft from two or more sending stations, the locations of which are known.

Radio navigation. Radio-location intended for the determination of position or direction or for obstruction warning in navigation.

Radio range finding. Radio-location in which the distance of an object is determined by·means of its radio emissions, whether independent, reflected, or retransmitted on the same or other wavelength.

Radio range station. A radio navigation land station in the aeronautical radio navigation service providing radio equi-signal zones. (In certain instances a radio range station may be placed on board a ship.)

Radio recognition. The determination by radio means of a friendly or enemy character, or the individuality, of a ship, aircraft or installation.

Radio recognition and identification. *See* **Identification friend or foe** (IFF).

Radio silence. A period during which all or certain radio equipment capable of radiation is kept inoperative. (In combined or Joint or Intra-Service communications the frequency bands and/or types of equipment affected are specified.)

Radio telegraphy. The transmission of telegraphic codes by means of radio.

Radio telephony. The transmission of speech by means of modulated radio waves.

Radiological defence. Defensive measures taken against the radiation hazards resulting from the employment of nuclear and radiological weapons.

Radiological monitoring. *See* **Monitoring.**

Radiological operations. Employment of radioactive materials or radiation producing devices to cause casualties or restrict the use of terrain. Includes the intentional employment of fallout from nuclear weapons.

Radiological survey. The directed effort to determine the distribution and dose rates of radiation in an area.

Radius of action. The maximum distance a ship, aircraft, or vehicle can travel away from its base along a given course with normal combat load and return without refuelling, allowing for all safety and operating factors.

Radius of safety. The horizontal distance from ground zero beyond which the weapon effects on friendly forces are acceptable.

Raid. An operation, usually small scale, involving a swift penetration of hostile territory to secure information, confuse the enemy, or destroy his installations. It ends with a planned withdrawal upon completion of the assigned mission.

Rail capacity. The maximum number of trains which can be planned to move in both directions over a specified section of track in a 24-hour period.

Railway end-loading ramp. A sloping platform situated at the end of a track and rising to the level of the floor of the rail cars (wagons).

Rainout. Radioactive material in the atmosphere brought down by precipitation.

Rakete. A German tracked guided weapon launcher.

Ramjet. A jet-propulsion engine containing neither compressor nor turbine which depends for its operation on the air compression accomplished by the forward motion of the engine.

Random minelaying. *See* **Scattered laying** (land mine warfare).

Range.
1. The distance between any given point and an object or target.
2. Extent or distance limiting the operation or action of something, such as the range of an aircraft, ship, or gun.
3. The distance which can be covered over a hard surface by a ground vehicle, with its rated payload, using the fuel in its tank and in cans normally carried as part of the ground vehicle equipment.
4. Area equipped for practice in shooting at targets. In this meaning, also called 'target range'.

Range finder. The instrument used to determine the distance between the firer and his target.

Range marker. A single calibration blip fed on to the time base of a radial display. The rotation of the time base shows the single blips as a circle on the plan position indicator scope. It may be used to measure range.

Range resolution. The ability of the radar equipment to separate two reflecting objects on a similar bearing, but at different ranges from the antenna. The ability is determined primarily by the pulse length in use.

Range spread. Where fire is spread along the line between the gun and its target.

Range warden. The civilian official in charge of firing ranges, responsible for their upkeep and maintenance.

Ranger (rgr). The equivalent in Irish regiments of the line of a private (*qv*) in other units.

Ranging. The process of establishing target distance. Types of ranging include echo, intermittent, manual, navigational, explosive echo, optical, radar, etc. *See also* **Spot**.

Ranking (US). Senior; used as an adjective, usually before 'Officer' to denote one holding high rank.

Rapier. A British low level anti-aircraft guided missile.

Rarden. An automatic cannon with a maximum range of 10,200 m mounted on or conveyed by a number of British vehicles.

Rate of fire. The number of rounds fired per weapon per minute.

Rate of march. The average number of miles or kilometres to be travelled in a given period of time, including all ordered halts. It is expressed in miles or kilometres in the hour (mih/kih).

Rates of effort. Rates of activity and ammunition expenditure on which levels of war reserves are based.
1. Quiet Rate. The average rate of wastage of equipment when units are out of contact with the enemy.
2. Sustained Rate. The sustained rate is based on the average effort and expenditure of stocks, equipment and ammunition over an extended period of some months of active operations.
3. Intensive Rate. The intensive rate represents a higher degree of effort and expenditure than the sustained rate and can be maintained only for a short specific period or operation.

Rats. Low flying enemy raids.

R Day. In logistic planning the day on which stock replenishment can be expected.

Reaction time. The time lag between the emission of a call for assistance, *eg* artillery support or an air strike, and its implementation.'

Ready position (helicopter). A designated place where a stick (*qv*) waits for the order to emplane in a helicopter.

Reallocation of resources. The provision of logistic resources by the military forces of one nation from those deemed 'made available' under the terms incorporated in appropriate NATO documents, to the military forces of another nation or nations as directed by the appropriate military authority. *See also* **Integrated logistic support; Logistic assistance; Mutual aid.**

Rear. Any thing or body placed behind some other, *eg* * rank, * guard, (*qv*) etc.

Rear area security. The measures taken prior to, during and/or after an enemy airborne attack, sabotage action, infiltration, guerilla action and/or initiation of psychological or propaganda warfare to minimize the effects thereof.

Rear echelon (air transport). Elements of a force which are not required in the objective area.

Rear guard.
1. The rearmost elements of an advancing or withdrawing force. It has the following functions.
    1. To protect the rear of a column from hostile forces.
    2. During the withdrawal, to delay the enemy.
    3. During the advance, to keep supply routes open.
2. Safety element which a moving ground force detaches to the rear to keep it informed and covered.

Rear maintenance area (RMA). The maintenance area located near an airfield in the vicinity of the port or beaches through or over which seaborne supplies are delivered and held until required. This area provides the replenishment required for the forward maintenance area (FMA) and such troops as are based on the FMA.

Rearsight. *See* **Backsight.**

Receipt inspection. An examination carried out on receipt of *matériel* to determine its identity, quantity and condition.

Receptivity. The vulnerability of a target audience to particular psychological operations media.

Recognition. The determination by any means of the friendly or enemy character or of the individuality of another, or of objects such as aircraft, ships, or tanks, or of phenomena such as communications-electronics patterns.

Recoil. The explosion of the propellant charge in a shell case forces the missile up the barrel and at the same time initiates a backward movement of the breech. This is known as 'recoil' and is now absorbed within the mechanism of the gun so that it has not got to be relaid on to its target after each shot, as was previously necessary.

Recoiless. Applied to a weapon denotes that the rear of the tube which houses the missile is open ended so that there is a backblast but no recoil.

Reconnaissance. A mission undertaken to obtain, by visual observation or other detection methods, information about the activities and resources of an enemy or potential enemy; or to secure data concerning the meteorological, hydrographic, or geographic characteristics of a particular area.
* **by fire.** A method of reconnaissance in which fire is placed on a suspected enemy position to cause the enemy to disclose his presence by movement or return of

fire. * **Group.** A group composed of a commander with his necessary advisers and assembled to reconnoitre for the purpose of making a plan. The basic composition of this group is normally prescribed in the standing orders of the unit or function concerned. * **Patrol** (ground). A small patrol used to gain information of the enemy, preferably without his knowledge. *See also* **Patrol; Combat air patrol; Fighting patrol.**

Recovery. The process of extricating a vehicle or equipment casualty from the place where it has become disabled or defective and moving it to the first place where repairs can be effected, or from which it can be backloaded. In its broader sense the term not only covers this process but also backloading and evacuation. * **and repair** is carried out by the Royal Electrical and Mechanical Engineers. For the former duty the Corps finds recovery companies and platoons which are allotted to formations, and for the latter Workshops. Their function is usually discernible from their title *eg* Army recovery company, electronic workshop, etc. * **Control.** The arrangements set up to execute a recovery plan, to provide continuous control of recovery resources, and to collect and pass back recovery information. * **Post.** A small recovery detachment mounted at a specific point, for duty at a defile, in a certain area or between certain limits on a route.

Recruit. A newly joined soldier. He ceases to be a recruit when he has completed individual training.

Rectification. In photogrammetry, the process of projecting a tilted or oblique photograph on a horizontal reference plane.

Rectified airspeed. *See* **Calibrated airspeed.**

Recuperator. In conjunction with the buffer absorbs the recoil of a gun thereby reducing strain on the mounting and returning the gun to its firing position.

Red Caps (slang). *See* **Provost.**

Redeployment airfield. An airfield not occupied in its entirety in peacetime, but available immediately upon outbreak of war for use and occupation by units redeployed from their peace-time locations. It must have substantially the same standard of operational facilities as a main airfield. *See also* **Alternative airfield; Departure airfield; Main airfield.**

Redeye. A US manportable shoulder fired surface to air guided missile.

Reduced execution time. The execution time that may be possible when some preparatory warning has been given. Reduced execution time will always state the main factor on which it depends.

Reduced to arisings. To break down items of *matériel* for the purpose of recovering assemblies, sub-assemblies, detail parts or scrap.

Re-engage. A soldier who completes his term of service may be allowed under certain conditions to re-engage for a further period.

Re-entry vehicle. That part of a space vehicle designed to re-enter the earth's atmosphere in the terminal portion of its trajectory.

Reference box. *See* **Information box.**

Reference datum. As used in the loading of aircraft, an imaginary vertical plane 139 at or near the nose of the aircraft from which all horizontal distances are measured for balance purposes. Diagrams of each aircraft show this reference datum as 'balance station zero'.

Refugee. A civilian who by reason of real or imagined danger has left his home to seek safety elsewhere. *See also* **Displaced person; Evacuees.**

Refused flank. When the right (or left) of a linear defensive position is protected by a formation facing at right angles to the main position that flank is said to be refused.

Regiment.
1. In the British Army the Regiment is an organization which may vary in size from many units, eg Royal Regiment of Artillery to a single unit eg Queens Own Own Hussars or battalion eg Duke of Edinburghs Royal Regiment. It has no tactical significance as such but is the military home of its members and enshrines their loyalty and traditions.
2. In many other armies it is the tactical formation equivalent to the British Brigade (*qv*).

Regimental Aid Post (RAP). The place where casualties are brought by regimental stretcher bearers. After immediate and basic treatment, *eg* application of first field dressing and morphia injection, they are evacuated by a Field Ambulance RAMC.

Regimental Combat Team (RCT). A composite force above battalion size organized for a specific task.

Regimental Medical Officer (RMO). The doctor, an officer of the RAMC, attached to a regiment or battalion. In battle is in charge of the RAP (*qv*).

Regimental Quartermaster Sergeant (RQMS). The senior administrative warrant officer in a major unit. Second in command to the Quartermaster (*qv*).

Regimental Sergeant Major (RSM). The senior combatant warrant officer in a major unit.

Register. In cartography, the fit of the components of a map, together or one with another, at each stage of production.

Register glass. In photography, a glass plate at the focal plane against which the film is pressed during exposure.

Register marks. In cartography, designated marks, such as small crosses, circles, or other patterns applied to original copy prior to reproduction to facilitate registration of plates and to indicate the relative positions of successive impressions.

Registered matter. Any classified matter registered, usually by number, and accounted for periodically.

Registration point. Terrain feature or other designated point on which fire is adjusted for the purpose of obtaining corrections to firing data.

Registered publication. A classified publication bearing a register number as well as a long and short title, and for which periodic accounting is required.

Registration fire. Fire delivered to obtain accurate data for subsequent effective engagement of targets.

Regular. Used (incorrectly) as a noun to denote a Regular Officer or Soldier (US Officer equivalent is career officer) as distinct from a Territorial, Short Service Officer etc. who does not hold a regular commission.

Regulated item. Any item over which proper authority exercises close supervision of distribution to individual units or commands because the item is scarce, costly, or of a highly technical or hazardous nature. *See also* **Critical supplies and materials.**

Regulatory sign. Signs used by competent authority to regulate and control traffic.

Rehabilitation.
1. The processing, usually in a relatively quiet area, of units or individuals recently withdrawn from combat or arduous duty, during which units recondition their equipment and are rested, furnished with special recreation facilities, filled up with replacements,

issued replacement supplies and equipment, given training, and generally made ready for employment in future operations. Known to soldiers as 'fattening up'.
2. The action taken to prepare immobilized individuals, such as military prisoners and hospital patients, for their return to military duty or useful civilian employment.
3. The action performed in restoring an installation to authorized design standards.

Reinforced Theatre Plan (RTP).
A contingency plan for intervention in counterinsurgency situations or for limited war involving the participation of units of the strategic reserve (*qv*).

Reinforcements. Units or individuals added to the order of battle to replace casualties or to increase its effectiveness.

Relative aperture. The ratio of the equivalent focal length to the diameter of the entrance pupil of photographic lens expressed f:4.5, etc. Also called 'f-number', 'stop', 'aperture stop', or 'diaphragm stop'. *See also* **Aperture.**

Relative biological effectiveness. The ratio of the number of rads of gamma (or X) radiation of a certain energy which will produce a specified biological effect to the number of rads of another radiation required to produce the same effect is the relative biological effectiveness of the latter radiation.

Relative Index of Combat Effectiveness (RICE) (US). A formula for use in War Games (*qv*), to indicate the battle worthiness of a formation or unit.

Released. In air defence, weapons and crews which have been released from commitments and states of readiness. When so released they are given a time at which a state of readiness will be resumed.

Release point.
1. In road movements, a well-defined

point on a route at which the elements composing a column return under the authority of their respective commanders, each one of these elements continuing its movement towards its own appropriate destination.
2. In air transport, a point on the ground directly above which the first paratroop or cargo item is air dropped. *See also* **Computed air release point.**

Releasing commander (nuclear weapons). A commander who has been delegated authority to approve the use of nuclear weapons within prescribed limits. *See also* **Commander(s).**

Reliability diagram. In cartography, a diagram showing the dates and quality of the source material from which a map or chart has been compiled. *See also* **Information box.**

Reliability of source (intelligence). *See* **Evaluation** (intelligence).

Relief.
1. (Cartography) Inequalities of elevation and the configuration of land features on the surface of the earh which may be represented on maps or charts by contours, hypsometric tints, shading, or spot elevations.
2. A unit/individual taking over the role or duties of another similar unit/individual is known as his relief.
* in place. An operation in which, by direction of higher authority, all or part of a unit is replaced in an area by the incoming unit. The responsibilities of the replaced elements for the mission and the assigned zone of operations are transferred to the incoming unit. The incoming unit continues the operation as ordered.

Render safe procedures. The portion of the explosive ordnance disposal procedure involving the application of special explosive ordnance disposal methods and tools to provide for the interruption of functions or separation of essential components of unexploded explosive ordnance to prevent an unacceptable detonation.

Reorganization Objective Army Division (ROAD) (US). A concept whereby the former division of three brigades with integral battalions is replaced by one in which its 16 to 20 individual units can be allotted to any brigade for a specific mission.

Rep. A suffix abbreviation for report, *eg* **Shell** * (*qv*), in which all appropriate details are given. In common use in IS situations are **Ammo** * for an exchange of fire; **Arrest** *, insurgents arrested; **Bang** * for explosions; **Baton** * for use of rubber etc; bullets **Car** * for suspected vehicles; **Cas** * for casualties; **Crowd** * for hostile mobs; **Explo** * for explosions; **Find** * for discovery of arms, ammunition etc; **Inc** * for any incident; **Int** * intelligence report; **Shot** * when fire is opened by insurgents; **Tug** * for a vehicle breakdown.

Repair. Repairs to vehicles and equipment are divided into four categories according to the work entailed. **Unit** * refers to minor work carried out by LADs. **Field** * can usually be carried out in Divisional or Corps Workshops. **Intermediate** * is work requiring greater skill and more sophisticated equipment than can be found in the field. **Base** * involves complete overhaul or rebuild.

Repayment issue. The authorized issue of *matériel*, payment for which is made after delivery and credited to public funds.

Repayment loan. A loan which is subject to a hire or rental charge payable in arrears; a deposit may be required before the item of *matériel* is supplied.

Repeater jammer. A receiver transmitter device which amplifies, multiplies and retransmits the signals received, for purposes of deception or jamming.

Replacement factor. The estimated percentage of equipments or repair parts in use that will require replacement during a given period due to wearing out beyond repair, enemy action, abandonment, pilferage, and other causes except catastrophes.

Replenishment Park (RP). Located within the Corps area near enough to the division it supports to allow daily replenishment by divisional transport; a Replenishment Park holds limited stocks of ammunition, POL (*qv*), rations and medical stores. It is controlled by the DDOS (*qv*) at Corps HQ.

Reply. An answer to a challenge. *See also* **Challenge: Countersign; Password.**

Report line. The line utilized for control and co-ordination of military operations, usually a terrain feature extending across the zone of action.

Reporting post (air defence). An element of the control and reporting system used to extend radar coverage of the control and reporting centre. It does not undertake the control of aircraft.

Representative fraction. The scale of a map, chart, or photograph expressed as a fraction or ratio. *See also* **Scale.**

Reprimand. A rebuke which is included in the army under the heading of punishments but carries no penalty either financial or in regard to seniority.

Required military force. The armed forces necessary to carry out a military mission over a specified period of time.

Required supply rate (ammunition). The amount of ammunition expressed in terms of rounds per weapon per day for ammunition items fired by weapons, and in terms of other units of measure per day for bulk allotment and other items, estimated to be required to sustain operations of any designated force without restriction for a specified period.

Requisition.
1. To request the initiation of procurement action for the supply or repair of *matériel* or the performance of a service.
2. To acquire *matériel* or property under statutory powers.
3. The document by which such actions are requested.

Research Analysis Corporation (RAC) (US). A commercial firm of McLean Virginia which has invented the Theater Combat Model.

Research and Development (R & D). The process or organization dealing with the introduction of new weapons or equipment from the drawing board stage until issued for service.

Reserve Officers Training Corps (ROTC) (US). A scheme whereby a number of universities and colleges offer a course in military studies to men between the ages of 17 and 25 years. Students are paid subsistence money in exchange for an undertaking that they will serve for six years in the active or reserve army.

Reserved demolition target. A target for demolition, the destruction of which must be specifically controlled at whatever level of command, either because it plays a vital part in the tactical or strategical plan, because of the importance of the structure itself or because the demolition may be executed in the face of the enemy.

Reserved route. A route, the use of which is:
1. allocated exclusively to a particular authority or formation, or
2. intended to meet a particular requirement.
See also **Route.**

Reserves.
1. The quantities of stocks required to be held against emergency, unforeseen fluctuations and expenditure, delays in production and transit, misfortune etc. In peace they include provision for requirements from the outbreak of war

until adequate supplies become available from production.
2. Personnel, units or formations earmarked for future use on mobilization or against an operational requirement, or withheld from action at the beginning of an engagement.

Residual contamination. Contamination which remains after steps have been taken to remove it. These steps may consist of nothing more than allowing the contamination to decay normally.

Residual radiation. Nuclear radiation caused by fallout, radio-active material dispersed artificially, or irradiation as a result of a nuclear explosion. *See also* **Contamination.**

Resolution. The measure of the ability of a lens, a photographic material, or a photographic system to distinguish detail under certain specific conditions. The measure of this ability is normally expressed in lines per millimetre or angular resolution.

Restitution. The process of determining the true planimetric position of objects whose images appear on photographs.

Restitution factor. *See* **Correlation factor.**

Restraint factor. A factor, normally expressed in multiples of the force of gravity, which determines the required strength of lashings and tie-downs to secure a particular load.

Restraint of loads. The process of binding, lashing, and wedging items into one unit on to or into its transporter in a manner that will ensure immobility during transit.

Restricted air cargo. Cargo which is not highly dangerous under normal conditions, but which possesses certain qualities which require extra precaution in packing and handling.

Restricted area. An air space of defined dimensions above the land areas or territorial waters of the state within which the flight of aircraft is restricted in accordance with certain specified conditions. May also refer to land areas to which access is restricted. *See also* **Danger area; Prohibited area.**

Resupply. Resupply is the act of replenishing stocks in order to maintain required levels of supply. *** of Europe.** The shipping of supplies to Europe during the period from the outbreak of war until the end of such a requirement. These supplies exclude any material already located upon land in Europe, but include other items irrespective of their origin or location. *See also* **Elements of resupply.**

Retail messing rate. The amount per person, authorized for messes provided with facilities for preparing, cooking and serving meals, but without access to Service supplies and drawing from retail (which may include NAAFI) sources.

Retractory Handle (US). *See* **Cocking handle.**

Retread. Slang. A retired officer re-employed by the army.

Retreat. A bugle or trumpet call traditionally sounded at sunset to signify the end of the day's work. To beat retreat is the ceremonial sounding of the call accompanied by the band, drums and, in Scottish and Irish Regiments, pipes who give a display of music and drill.

Return. n. A statement rendered by a unit to its superior formation giving factual information on its state *eg* casualty *, ration *, etc., *** Load.** Personnel and/or cargo to be transported by a returning carrier. *** to Unit** (RTU). An officer or soldier, attending a course of instruction who fails to make the grade is sent back to his parent unit.

Reveille. The morning bugle or trumpet call sounded to notify the start of the

day. Also sounded at military funerals after the Last Post (*qv*) to signify the end of mourning for the deceased. A shorter form is the Rouse.

Reverse slope. Any slope which descends away from the enemy.

Revolver. A hand held gun with a revolving chamber from which rounds are fed into the breech.

Rhumb line. A line on the surface of the earth transecting all meridians at the same angle.

Ricochet. A bullet which has hit an obstacle in its path and continues its flight at an angle.

Rifle. A shoulder mounted, hand held gun with a rifled barrel. It is the personal weapon of most infantrymen.

Rifleman (Rfn). The equivalent in Rifle Regiments of a private (*qv*) in other units.

Rifling. A barrel is rifled when it has grooves (*qv*) cut into it. The effect is to give spin and therefore stability to the projectile.

Rig. v. To prepare a load for air drop.

Right (or Left). See **Left (*or* Right).**

Riot control agent. A chemical that produces temporary irritating or disabling effects when in contact with the eyes or when inhaled.

Road block. A barrier or obstacle (usually covered by fire) used to block, or limit the movement of, hostile vehicles along a route.

Road clearance time. The total time a column requires to travel over and clear a section of the road.

Road space. The length of roadway allocated to, and/or actually occupied by, a column on a route, expressed in miles or kilometres.

Roamer. A series of grids constructed to common map scales and marked out on a sheet of transparent material. It is used to assist in determining map references.

Rocket.
1. A form of recoilless artillery operated by the reaction effect of high velocity gas.
2. (Slang). A resounding reproof.

Roentgen. A unit of exposure of gamma (or X-) radiation.

Roger. A word of acknowledgement used over the radio or telephone to confirm that instructions have been received and are understood.

Roland. A Franco-German land mobile surface to air weapon system using tube launched guided missiles.

Roll.
1. The list of names of men in a unit is a nominal roll. When all are paraded for checking their presence the parade is known as roll call or muster.
2. On a drum, a continuous and uniform beat.
3. *See* **Tilt.**

Roller conveyor. A materials handling aid containing rollers over which cargo is moved.

Rollers. Unsprung wheels which are part of the suspension of tracked vehicles.

Rookie. (Slang). A recruit.

Rope. An element of chaff consisting of a long roll of metallic foil or wire which is designed for broad, low-frequency responses. *See also* **Chaff.**

Rotational post. An appointment filled by persons of different nations/services on an international/joint Headquarters according to an agreed rota.

Rotor governing mode. A control mode. in which helicopter rotor speed is maintained automatically.

Round. A cartridge comprising bullet, propellant and detonator contained in one case.

Rouse. A short form of the Reveille (*qv*).

Route. The prescribed course to be travelled from a specific point of origin to a specific destination. *See also* **Axial *; Controlled *; Despatch *; Lateral *; Reserved *; Signed *; Supervised *.**

Route classification. Classification assigned to a route using factors of minimum width, worst route type, least bridge, raft or culvert military load classification, and obstructions to traffic flow. *See also* **Military load classification.**

Rover group. A small group of vehicles which accompanies the commander when he is away from his headquarters and by means of which he can maintain contact with his own and other headquarters. The commander is normally accompanied by a staff officer and/or a liaison officer.

Row marker (land mine warfare). A marker, natural, artificial, or specially installed, located at the start and finish of a mine row where mines are laid by individual rows. *See also* **Marker** (land mine warfare).

Royal Armoured Corps (RAC). Comprises all the mechanized cavalry regiments and all units of the Royal Tank Regiment.

Royal Corps of Transport (RCT). The Corps responsible for movement of personnel and stores which have not got own unit transport for the purpose.

Royal Military Academy Sandhurst (RMAS). The training college in Berkshire where all potential officers receive military training before joining their units.

Royal Military College of Science (RMCS). A military college of higher education at Shrivenham to which selected officers are sent to study technical military subjects and gain the appropriate scientific degrees.

Royal Ulster Constabulary (RUC). The Police Force of Northern Ireland.

Royal United Services Institute (RUSI). An independent institute for studying the defence of Great Britain in all its aspects. Several other countries have modelled their own institutes upon it.

Rules of engagement. Directives issued by competent military authority which specify the circumstances and limitations under which forces will initiate and/or continue combat engagement with other forces encountered.

Rules of Procedure (RP). Contain the regulations made from time to time by the Secretary of State for Defence and his predecessor the Secretary of State for War, to implement the provisions of the Army Act contained in the Manual of Military Law (*qv*).

Run. That part of flight of one photographic reconnaissance aircraft during which photographs are taken.

Running contract. An agreeement for the supply of *matériel* or provision of a service or demand over a period of time.

Running fix. The intersection of two or more position lines, not obtained simultaneously adjusted to a common time.

Running time. The total distance of a route divided by the average speed of the vehicles.

Run-up area. A zone within the manoeuvring area reserved for testing aircraft engines prior to take-off.

Rupture zone. The region immediately adjacent to the crater boundary in which the stresses produced by an explosion have exceeded the ultimate strength of the medium. It is characterized by the appearance of numerous radial cracks of various sizes. *See also* **Plastic zone.**

Sabot. Light weight carrier in which a subcalibre projectile is centred to permit firing the projectile in the larger calibre weapon. The carrier fills the bore of the weapon from which the projectile is fired; it is normally discarded a short distance from the muzzle.

Sabotage. An act with an intent to damage, interfere with, or obstruct by wilfully damaging or destroying or attempting to damage or destroy material, premises, or utilities in the interests of a foreign power or subversive political organization.

Saboteur. A saboteur is a supporter of a dissident faction who damages property, equipment or plant for political ends; *ie* commits an act of sabotage.

Saddler. NATO codename for USSR ICBM (*qv*).

Safe burst height. The height of burst at or above which the level of fallout, or damage to ground installations is at a predetermined level acceptable to the military commander.

Safeguard. A US anti ballistic missile programme for the protection of bases and command centres.

Safety angle. *See* **Angle of safety.**

Safety catch. The mechanism which, when applied, prevents unintentional discharge of a weapon.

Safety distance (road). The distance between vehicles travelling in column specified by the command in light of safety requirements.

Safety height. *See* **Altitude; Minimum safe altitude.**

Safety line. Delimitation line for trip wire or wire-actuated mines in a minefield. It serves to protect the laying personnel. It is not marked or measured after the minefield has been completed.

Safety zone. An area (land, sea, or air) reserved for noncombat operations of friendly aircraft, surface ships, or ground forces.

Sagger. NATO codename for a small USSR wire-guided anti-tank missile.

Saladin. The standard wheeled armoured car of the British Army mounting one 76 mm and two 0.30 inch machine guns.

Salted weapon. A nuclear weapon which has, in addition to its normal components, certain elements or isotopes which capture neutrons at the time of the explosion and produce radioactive products over and above the usual radioactive weapon debris.

Salute. The military form of greeting given by a junior to his superior officer and returned by the latter. It acknowledges the authority of an officer, derived from his commission from the Crown, and has no connotation of servility. A gun salute is paid to Royalty and its representatives on certain ceremonial occasions, *eg* Queen's Birthday. The number of blank rounds fired varies according to the rank of the recipient.

Salvage procedure. The recovery, evacuation, and reclamation of damaged, discarded, condemned, or abandoned allied or enemy *matériel,* ships, craft, and floating equipment for re-use, repair, refabrication or scrapping.

Salvo. A number of rounds of artillery fired at the same moment cf **Volley.**

Sam Browne. The leather belt with cross strap(s) worn by officers. Invented by a one armed cavalry officer of that name of the old Indian Army to facilitate drawing his sword. Now used by many armies.

Samaritan. A British armoured ambulance, based on the Scorpion (*qv*), designed to evacuate casualties under fire.

Samson. A British armoured recovery vehicle, based on the Scorpion (*qv*), with an internal winch driven by the main engine.

Sandal. NATO codename for USSR MRBM (*qv*).

Sandhurst. The Royal Military Academy at Sandhurst (*qv*).

Sandtable. A large, shallow, lidless box containing sand and symbols which can be modelled to represent terrain; used for indoor instruction.

Sangar. A defensive post built up above ground level where the soil is unsuitable for excavation.

Sap. An extension to a trench normally undertaken to facilitate offensive action.

Sapper (spr). The equivalent in the Royal Engineers of a private in other units.

Saracen. Similar to the Saladin, and designed as an armoured troop carrier, but adaptable to other roles.

SARPAC. A French portable anti-tank rocket launcher.

Sasin. NATO codename for USSR ICBM.

Savage. NATO codename for USSR ICBM.

Scabbard. The sheath containing a sword or bayonet.

Scale.
1. (Cartographic). The ratio between

the distance on a map, chart, or photograph and the corresponding distance on the ground. *See* **Representative fraction.** *See also* **Bar *; Conversion *; Graphic *; Linear *; Nominal *; Numerical *; Photographic *; Principal *.**
2. (Logistic). The type and quantity of equipment *ie* ammunition, vehicles, warlike stores etc. allocated to a unit. **Assault *.** Equipment required for an actual operation. **Fly-in-*.** Airportable equipment necessary to enable it to operate effectively for a short period as soon as it lands; **Follow up *.** The balance of a unit's G 1098 scale (*qv*) after it has received its Fly-in-scale and Pick-up scale. **Pick-up *,** (Equipment within a unit's G 1098 scale which is held in the mounting base (*qv*) and is required to supplement the fly-in-scale to make it operational until the arrival of the follow-up scale).
3. v. To climb.

Scaleboard. NATO codename for a USSR medium range ballistic missile.

Scaling law. A mathematical relationship which permits the effects of a nuclear explosion of given energy yield to be determined as a function of distance from the explosion (or from ground zero), provided the corresponding effect is known as a function of distance for a reference explosion, *eg* of 1-kiloton energy yield.

Scamp. NATO codename for USSR weapon system comprising a Scapegoat (*qv*) missile and its erector/launcher.

Scan. In electro-magnetic or acoustic search one complete rotation of the antenna. It may determine a time base.

Scapegoat. NATO codename for USSR IRBM.

Scarp. NATO codename for USSR ICBM.

Scattered laying (land mine warfare). The laying of mines without regard to pattern.

Scheduled fire. Fire pre-arranged to be brought to bear at a pre-determined time.

Scheduled service (air transport). A routine air transport service operated in accordance with a time-table.

Scheduled target. A target to be engaged by artillery fire at a specific time.

Scheduled wave. *See* **Wave.**

Schnorkel. A tube which enables a tank to breathe when fording in deep water.

Schutzenpanzer Gruppe. The West German family of AFVs, similar to the British Saracen in the APC role.

Scimitar. A British light tank, a variant of Scorpion (*qv*), but mounting a Rarden cannon instead of a 76 mm gun.

Scorpion.
1. A British light tank mounting a 76 mm gun.
2. A target illuminating radar used with Bloodhound (*qv*).

Scrag. NATO codename for USSR ICBM.

Scrambler. A security device built into a telephone which garbles the speech in transit but does not affect its reception by the hearer to whom it is addressed. *See also* **Go Green.**

Screen.
1. In cartography, a sheet of transparent film, glass or plastic carrying a regularly repeated pattern which may be used in conjunction with a mask, either photographically or photomechanically to produce areas of the pattern. *See also* **Half-tone screen.**
2. In camouflage and concealment any material which is opaque to surveillance sensors interposed between them and the object to be camouflaged or concealed.

Scribing. In cartography, a method of preparing a map or chart by cutting the lines into a prepared coating.

Scrooge. NATO codename for USSR IRBM.

Scud. NATO codename for the USSR family of heavy artillery battlefield rockets.

Sea echelon. A portion of the assault shipping which withdraws from, or remains out of, the transport area during an amphibious landing and operates in designated areas to seaward in an on-call or unscheduled status.

Sea tail. Equipment which does not accompany the unit but is subsequently transported by sea.

Sealed cabin. The occupied space of an aircraft characterized by walls which do not allow any gaseous exchange between the ambient atmosphere and the inside atmosphere and containing its own ways of regenerating the inside atmosphere.

Sear. The part of the trigger mechanism which locks into the bolt (*qv*) of a small arm when the safety catch (*qv*) is applied.

Search and rescue. The use of aircraft, surface craft, submarines, specialized rescue teams and equipment to search for and rescue personnel in distress on land or at sea. * **Area.** An area in which the co-ordination of search and rescue is integrated by a single rescue co-ordination centre.

Searching fire. Fire distributed in depth by successive changes in the elevation of the gun.

Search jammer. *See* **Automatic search jammer.**

Search mission (air). An air reconnaissance by one or more aircraft despatched to locate an object or objects known or suspected to be in a specific area.

Second. v. Applied to officers or soldiers lent to another Government *eg* Muscat and Oman.

Second strike capability. The ability to survive a first strike with sufficient

resources to deliver an effective counter-blow (generally associated with nuclear weapons).

Secondary radar. Radar using automatic retransmission on the same or on a different radio frequency.

Section (sect). The smallest tactical subunit in a battery, troop or platoon. US equivalent squad.

Sector.
1. A defence area designated by boundaries within which a unit operates, and for which it is responsible.
2. One of the subdivisions of a coastal frontier. *See also* **Area of influence; Zone of action.** * **Commander.** The local air defence commander of a fighter sector * **Controller.** An officer appointed to act on behalf of a sector commander in a sector operations centre. He is responsible for operational control of all active air defences in the sector area in co-ordination with those of adjacent sector. In these tasks he is subject to overall direction by the group or command controller. * **Fire.** An area which is required to be covered by fire by an individual, a weapon, or a unit. * **Operations centre.** The headquarters from which the sector commander exercises operational control over the air defences including AA guns, within his sector. * **Scan.** Scan in which the antenna oscillates through a selected angle.

Secure (operations). To gain possession of a position or terrain feature, with or without force, and to make such disposition as will prevent, as far as possible, its destruction or loss by enemy action.

Security. A condition which results from the establishment of measures which protect designated information, personnel, systems, components and equipment against hostile persons, acts, or influences. *See also* **Physical ***.

Security classification. A category or grade assigned to defence information or material to indicate the degree of danger to NATO/national security that

would result from its unauthorized disclosure and the standard of protection it requires. The order of importance is:
Top Secret (TOPSEC)
Secret
Confidential (CONFD)
Restricted (RESTD)
Unclassified (UNCLAS)

Security clearance. A certification issued by National Authority to indicate that a person has been investigated and is eligible for access to classified matter to the extent stated in the classification.

Security countermeasures. Measures designed to impair the effectiveness of an unfriendly or hostile attack upon security.

Security forces. All indigenous and allied police, military and para military forces used by a government to maintain law and order.

Selection. The process of choosing and physically removing by manual or mechanical means a quantity of *matériel* from its storage location.

Selective identification feature. Airborne pulse-type transponder which provides automatic selective identification of aircraft in which it is installed — to friend-or-foe identification installations, whether ground, shipboard, or airborne.

Selective loading. The arrangement and stowage of equipment and supplies aboard ship in a manner designed to facilitate issues to units. *See also* **Loading.**

Self accounting unit. A unit equipped to function financially on its own when divorced from its parent body.

Self-destroying fuse. A fuse designed to burst a projectile before the end of its flight. *See also* **Fuse.**

Self-propelled (SP). Normally used of artillery to denote that the weapon is

part of the vehicle which moves it and not towed behind it.

Semi-active homing device. A system of homing guidance wherein the receiver in the missile utilizes radiations from the target which has been illuminated by an outside source.

Semi-automatic Command to Line of Sight (SACLOS). A guided weapon system which requires the operator to maintain his line of sight on the target whilst a missile tracker and computer measure flight error and apply adjustment through a command link and missile control system. Both Rapier and Hot use this method.

Semi-controlled mosaic. A mosaic which is composed of photographs of approximately the same scale laid so that major ground features match their geographical co-ordinates. *See also* **Mosaic.**

Semi-fixed ammunition. Ammunition in which the cartridge case is not permanently attached to the projectile. *See also* **Ammunition.**

Semi-flush fitting. A fitting having its periphery level with the surrounding paved surface and those parts of the fitting which project above the surface not exceeding certain specified heights.

Semi-trailer. A trailer, the front end of which is fitted with a coupling, which when coupled to a tractor, forms an articulated vehicle.

Sensor. A technical means to extend man's natural senses; an equipment which detects and indicates terrain configuration, the presence of military targets, and other natural and man-made objects and activities by means of energy emitted or reflected by such targets or objects. The energy may be nuclear, electromagnetic, including the visible and invisible portions of the spectrum, chemical, biological, thermal, or mechanical, including sound, blast and earth vibration.

Sentry. A soldier placed in a selected position, which he must not quit, for protective duties.

Separate loading ammunition. Ammunition in which the projectile and charge are loaded into a gun separately. *See also* **Ammunition.**

Sergeant.
1. (sgt). A senior non commissioned officer.
2. A US battlefield support ballistic missile.

Serial. An element or a group of elements within a series which is given a numerical or alphabetical designation for convenience in planning, scheduling, and control.

Seriously ill. A patient is seriously ill when his illness is of such severity that there is cause for immediate concern but there is no imminent danger to life. *See also* **Very seriously ill.**

Service and Repair. Damage or wear in a vehicle or aircraft is categorized as first, second, third or fourth line, the first line being minor, usually carried out within the unit holding it on charge and the fourth, the most extensive, requiring attention at base.

Services. In staff parlance the technical advisers, *eg* ordnance, medical, who give the staff advice on matters affecting their own service.

Shaded relief. A cartographic technique that provides an apparent three-dimensional configuration of the terrain on maps and charts by the use of graded shadows that would be cast by high ground if light were shining from the northwest. Usually used in combination with contours. *See also* **Hill shading.**

Shadow factor. A multiplication factor derived from the sun's declination, the latitude of the target and the time of photography, used in determining the heights of objects from shadow length. It is also known as 'tan alt'.

Shako. An old fashioned military headdress resembling an inverted flower pot.

Shallow fording. The ability of a self-propelled gun or ground vehicle equipped with built-in waterproofing, with its wheels or tracks in contact with the ground, to negotiate a water obstacle without the use of a special waterproofing kit.

Sheetlines. *See* **Neatlines.**

Shelf life. The period of time during which an item of *matériel*, having a limited storage life, is considered to remain serviceable while stored.

Shelling report (SHELREP). Any report of enemy shelling containing information on calibre, direction, item, density and area shelled. *See also* **Rep.**

Sheridan. A US light tank used primarily in the reconnaissance role.

Sherman. A US medium tank.

Shielding.
1. Material of suitable thickness and physical characteristics used to protect personnel from radiation during the manufacture, handling and transportation of fissionable and radioactive materials.
2. Obstructions which tend to protect personnel or materials from the effects of a nuclear explosion.

Shift (radar). The ability to move the origin of a radial display away from the centre of the cathode ray tube.

Shillelagh. A US light close-support anti-tank missile which can be operated from an armoured vehicle, a gun or a helicopter.

Ship's commandant. The army or air force officer appointed in command of all army and/or air force personnel embarked in a troop transport.

Ship-to-shore movement. That portion of the assault phase of an amphibious operation which includes the deployment of the landing force from the assault shipping to designated landing areas.

Shmell. A USSR surface to surface guided anti-tank missile known to NATO as Snapper.

Shock front. The boundary between the pressure disturbance created by an explosion (in air, water, or earth) and the ambient atmosphere, water, or earth.

Shock wave. The continuously propagated pressure pulse formed by the blast from an explosion in air by the air blast, underwater by the water blast, and underground by the earth blast.

Shore bombardment lines. Ground lines established to delimit bombardment by friendly surface ships.

Shore party. A task organization of the landing force, formed for the purpose of facilitating the landing and movement off the beaches of troops, equipment, and supplies; for the evacuation from the beaches of casualties and prisoners of war; and for facilitating the beaching, retraction and salvaging of landing ships and craft. It comprises elements of both the naval and landing forces. *See also* **Naval beach group.**

Shoreland. A light British Armoured car, based on the Land Rover, mounting a machine gun in its turret.

Short (Artillery). A round which bursts or impacts in front of the target. The opposite to **Over** (*qv*).

Short distance navigational aid. An equipment or system which provides navigational assistance to a range not exceeding 200 statute miles/320 kilometres.

Short take-off and landing (STOL). The ability of an aircraft to clear a 50-foot obstacle within 1,500 feet of commencing take-off or, in landing, to stop within 1,500 feet after passing over a 50-foot obstacle.

Short title. A short, identifying combination of letters, and/or numbers assigned to a document or device for purposes of brevity and/or security.

Shuttered fuse. A fuse in which inadvertent initiation of the detonator will not initiate either the booster or the burst charge. *See also* **Fuse.**

Shyster. NATO codename for USSR MRBM.

Side arms. A bayonet.

Side lap. *See* **Overlap.**

Side looking airborne radar. An airborne radar, viewing at right angles to the axis of the vehicle, which produces a presentation of terrain or moving targets.

Sight. The device attached to a weapon which enables the firer to take a correct aim. A rifle has a back sight and a fore sight and may be issued with a telescopic sight or a night sight. Different sorts of guns and mortars have their own sights.

Signal.
1. As applied to electronics, any transmitted electrical impulse.
2. Operationally, a type of message, the text of which consists of one or more letters, words, characters, signal flags, visual displays, or special sounds, with prearranged meaning and which is conveyed or transmitted by visual, accoustical or electrical means. * **Area.** An area on an airfield used for the display of ground signals. * **Centre.** *See* **Communication centre.** * **Letters.** *See* **International call sign.**

Signals intelligence (SIGINT). Information about the enemy or friendly signals operation or organization.

Signal support. The provision of personnel and equipment from other forces for the establishment of a special or supplementary communications system.

Signature (target). The characteristic pattern of the target displayed by detection and identification equipment.

Signed route. A route along which a unit has placed directional signs bearing its unit identification symbol. The signs are for the unit's use only and must comply with movement regulations.

Significant obstruction. *See* **Obstruction.**

Significant tracks (air defence). Tracks of aircraft or missiles which behave in an unusual manner which warrants attention and could pose a threat to a defended area.

Silence. v. In artillery parlance to silence an enemy's guns is to obtain such superiority of fire as to prevent him from replying.

Simfire. A weapon effects simulator for tanks and vehicles operated by a laser beam.

Simray. A gun used by umpires on training exercises to 'kill' tanks at up to 3,000 metres.

Simulator. A training device, the use of which enables instruction and practice to be given without the expenditure of costly ammunition or material.

Single Integrated Operational Plan (SIOP) (US). The co-ordination of strategic weapon systems.

Situation map. A map showing the tactical or the administrative situation at a particular time.

Situation report (SITREP). A report giving the situation in the area of a reporting unit or formation.

Skean. NATO codename for USSR IRBM.

Ski-jor. v. to tow ski borne soldiers behind a vehicle.

Skirmishers. (Obsolescent). Soldiers infiltrating an enemy position in front of the main attack.

Skive (Slang) *see* **Malinger.**

Skot. Czechoslovakian armoured personnel carrier.

Skycrane. A US helicopter specially designed to raise heavy loads.

Skyshout. A helicopter borne amplifier used to control crowds in an internal security situation or similar circumstances where speech security is unnecessary.

Slant range. The line of sight distance between two points not at the same elevation.

Sling. The web cord attached to a weapon which enables it to be carried over the shoulder.

Slow time. A pace of 13 inches at 75 paces to the minute used at funerals and on certain other ceremonial occasions.

Slug. (slang). Bullet.

Small arms (SA). Light weapons which are carried and fired by one man, *eg* pistols, revolvers, rifles, submachine guns.

Small circle. A circle on the surface of the earth, the plane of which does not pass through the earth's centre.

Smoke screen. Cloud of smoke used to mask either friendly or enemy installations or manoeuvres.

Snake mode. A control mode in which the pursuing aircraft flies a programmed weaving flight to allow time to accomplish identification functions.

Snapper. NATO codename for the USSR wire-guided anti-tank missile Shmell (Bumblebee).

Snobs. (slang). The regimental boot mender.

Soft missile base. A launching base that is not protected against a nuclear explosion.

Soil shear strength. The maximum resistance of a soil to shearing stresses.

Sol-Sol-Balistique-Strategique (SSBS). A French medium-range two-stage solid-propellant missile with a nuclear warhead.

Soldiers Sailors and Airmen's Family Association (SSAFA). A voluntary organization which deals with all problems connected with a service man's family, including widows whose husbands have died in the service.

Sonar. A sonic device used primarily for the detection and location of underwater objects. (This term is derived from the words: sound navigation and ranging.)

Sonic. Of or pertaining to sound or the speed of sound. *See also* **Speed of sound.**

Sortie (air). An operational flight by one aircraft. * **Number.** A reference used to identify the images taken by all the sensors during one air reconnaissance sortie.

South East Asia Treaty Organization (SEATO). A loose organization for the defence of South East Asia, the original members (1954) being Australia, France, New Zealand, Pakistan, Phillipines, Thailand, United Kingdom and USA.

Spartan.
1. A British Armoured Personnel Carrier, a variant of Scorpion.
2. A US missile with a range of several hundred miles designed to intercept hostile missiles in the stratosphere.

Special flight. An air transport flight, other than a scheduled service, set up to move a specific load.

Special job cover map. A small-scale map used to record progress on photographic reconnaissance tasks covering a very large area. As each portion of the task is completed, the area covered is outlined on the map.

Special messing allowance. A cash allowance authorized as necessary by Ministry of Defence (DGST (N)) for payment to individuals who incur extra costs through having to purchase meals, *eg* in foreign messes, at prices that exceed the normal Service charges.

Special Warfare Armoured Transporter (SWAT). An amphibious vehicle designed primarily as an APC (*qv*).

Specialist intelligence report. A category of specialized, technical reports used in dissemination of intelligence. *See also* **Intelligence reporting.**

Specialist Teams Royal Engineers (STRE). A controlling staff of specialist clerks of works and construction engineers formed to supervise some technical project.

Speed of sound. The speed at which sound travels in a given medium under specified conditions. The speed of sound at sea level in the International Standard Atmosphere is 1,108 ft/second, 658 knots, 1,215 km/hour. *See also* **Hypersonic; Sonic; Subsonic; Supersonic; Transonic.**

Sperry. An automatic navigating device.

Spigot. *See* **Sprag.**

Split cameras. An assembly of two cameras disposed at a fixed overlapping angle relative to each other.

Split pair. *See* **Split vertical photography.**

Split vertical photography. Photographs taken simultaneously by two cameras mounted at an angle from the vertical, one tilted to the left and one to the right, to obtain a small sidelap (*qv*).

Spoking (radar). Periodic flashes of the rotating time base on a radial display. Sometimes caused by mutual interference.

Sponson. A gun mount attached to a tank's side. Such a weapon has only limited traverse.

Sponsor (exercise). The commander who conceives a particular exercise and orders that it be planned and executed either by his staff or by a subordinate headquarters.

Spot. v.
1. To determine by observation, deviations of gunfire from the target for the purpose of supplying necessary information for the adjustment of fire.
2. To place in a proper location. *See also* **Adjustment of fire.**

Spot elevation. A point on a map or chart whose elevation is known.

Spot jamming. The jamming of a specific channel or frequency. *See also* **Barrage jamming; Electronic jamming.**

Spot size. The size of the electron spot on the face of the cathode ray tube.

Sprag. A projection preventing the movement of platforms or pallets in the side guidance rails in an aircraft cabin.

Squad. US equivalent of section (*qv*). In British usage any small body of men formed from different parent units or subunits assembled and paraded for a common purpose.

Squadron. A subunit in an armoured regiment composed of three or more troops, equivalent to the infantry company and artillery battery.

Stability augmentation. In a flight control system, an automatic device which operates to augment the short term stability characteristics of an aircraft.

Stable base film. A particular type of film having a high stability in regard to shrinkage and stretching.

Staff. The officers and soldiers at a Headquarters who assist a commander to formulate a plan and do the paper work which translates it into orders. They are distinct from the Services (*qv*) who provide technical advice and information. *See also* **Combined staff; Integrated *; Joint *; Parallel *.**
* Captain (SC). The most junior appointment on the Quartermaster General's (*qv*) staff. *** College.** Situated in Camberley, Surrey, it trains selected officers for higher command. **Directing *.** The body of officers and soldiers employed on an exercise (*qv*) to control the proceedings. *** Duties** (SD). The senior branch of the General Staff (*qv*) is concerned particularly with establishments (*qv*) and co-ordination. *** Message control** (SMC). A collection and distribution point at a large HQ where all incoming signal traffic is routed to the appropriate recipient.

Stage.
1. v. To process, in a specified area, troops which are in transit from one locality to another. *See also* **Marshalling; Staging area.**
2. n. An element of the missile or propulsion system that separates from the missile at burnout or cut-off. Stages are numbered chronologically in order of burning.
3. n. The part of an air route from one air staging unit to the next.

Staging area.
1. Amphibious or airborne – A general locality between the mounting area and the objective of an amphibious or airborne expedition, through which the

expedition or parts thereof pass after mounting, for refuelling, regrouping of ships, and/or exercise, inspection, and redistribution of troops.
2. Other movements. A general locality, containing accommodation for troops, established for the concentration of troop units and transient personnel between moves along the lines of communication.

Stand To. The period during which all ranks adopt a defensive posture in anticipation of attack. Frequently ordered at dawn and dusk.

Standard.
1. An exact value, a physical entity, or an abstract concept, established and defined by authority, custom, or common consent to serve as a reference, model, or rule in measuring quantities or qualities, establishing practices or procedures, or evaluating results. A fixed quantity or quality.
2. From the earliest days all regiments of cavalry and infantry have carried flags, known as standards on which the unit could rally. Originally square or oblong their size and design was varied over the years. The Household Cavalry, Dragoon Guards and Royal Tank Regiment retain this shape whereas the Light Cavalry, Dragoons, Lancers and Hussars carry a swallow tailed Guidon. Infantry of the line carry square Colours; the Queen's Colour is the union flag and bears the battle honours of the two World Wars, the Regimental Colour is the same as the Regiment's facings and bears pre-Great War battle honours. In the Foot Guards the Queen's colours are crimson and the Regimental Colours are the Union. Rifle regiments have no colours as they would have been an encumbrance in their original role as skirmishers.

Standard load. A load which has been pre-planned as to dimensions, weight, and balance, and designated by a number or some other classification.

Standard parallel. A parallel on a map or chart along which the scale is as stated for that map or chart.

Standard pattern (land mine warfare). The agreed pattern to which mines are normally laid.

Standardization. The process by which member nations achieve the closest practicable co-operation among forces, the most efficient use of research, development and production resources, and agree to adopt on the broadest possible basis the use of:
1. Common or compatible operational, administrative and logistic procedures.
2. Common or compatible technical procedures and criteria.
3. Common, compatible or interchangeable supplies, components, weapons, or equipment.
4. Common or compatible tactical doctrine with corresponding organizational compatibility.

Standardization agreement (NATO). The record of an agreement among several or all of the member nations to adopt like or similar military equipment, ammunition, supplies, and stores; and operational, logistic and administrative procedures. National acceptance of a NATO Allied publication issued by the Military Agency for Standardization may be recorded as a Standardization Agreement (STANAG).

Standardized product. A product that conforms to specifications resulting from the same technical requirements.

Standby. In a flight control system, the condition in which all elements of the system are energized and the system is ready for engagement.

Standing operating procedure (SOP). A set of instructions covering those features of operations which lend themselves to a definite or standardized procedure without loss of effectiveness. The procedure is applicable unless prescribed otherwise in a particular case.

Thus, the flexibility necessary in special situations is retained.

Standing order. Promulgated orders which remain in force until amended or cancelled.

Standing patrol. A patrol which will be of a strength decided by the commander allotting the task. Its task may be recce, listening, fighting, or a combination of these. It differs from a recce, fighting or listening patrol in that, having taken up its allotted position it is not free to manoeuvre in the performance of its task without permission. *See also* **Patrol.**

Star rank. Officers above the rank of Colonel who carry stars on their official motor cars: Brigadiers one, Major Generals two, Lieutenant Generals three, Generals four and Field Marshals five, are said to be of star rank.

Start line. *See* **Line of departure.**

Start point (SP). A well-defined point on a route at which a movement of vehicles begins to be under the control of the commander of this movement. It is at this point that the column is formed by the successive passing, at an appointed time, of each of the elements composing the column. In addition to the principal start point of a column there may be secondary start points for its different elements.

State of readiness – armed (demolition). Demolition is ready for immediate firing.

State of readiness – safe (demolition). A demolition target upon or within which the demolition agent has been placed and secured. The firing or initiating circuits have been installed, but not connected to the demolition agent. Detonators or initiators have neither been connected nor installed.

Stateless person. A person who is without citizenship.

Static line (air transport). A webbing line attached to a parachute pack and hooked to a strop hanging from a cable in an aircraft so that after the exit of man or load the static line breaks open the pack and part of the pack is left hanging from the aircraft on the end of the static line. The canopy is thus said to have deployed 'automatically' having been inflated by the wind currents.

Static line cable. *See* **Static line** (air transport). The cable which runs the length of the interior of the aircraft and is positioned below the ceiling of the fuselage.

Station time (air transport). Time at which crews, passengers, and cargo are to be on board and ready for the flight.

Stereogram. A stereoscopic set of photographs or drawings correctly oriented and mounted for stereoscopic viewing.

Stereoscope. A binocular optical instrument for helping an observer to view photographs or diagrams in order to obtain a three-dimensional mental impression.

Stereoscopic cover. Photographs taken with sufficient overlap to permit complete stereoscopic examination.

Stereoscopic model. The mental impression of an area or object seen as being in three dimensions when viewed stereoscopically on photographs.

Stereoscopic pair. Two photographs with sufficient overlap of detail to make possible stereoscopic examination of an object or an area common to both.

Stereoscopic vision. The ability to perceive three-dimensional images.

Stereoscopy. The science which deals with three-dimensional effects and the methods by which they are produced.

Sterling. A light, shoulder fired, sub machine gun.

Sterling Patchett. A silent version of the Sterling (*qv*).

Stick (air transport). A number of paratroopers who jump from one aperture or door of an aircraft during one run over a dropping zone. In clandestine operations stick may also refer to the individual groups or patrols on the ground. *** Commander.** A designated individual, not necessarily the most senior, who acts as No. 1 and controls parachutists from the time they enter the aircraft until their exits. *** Length.** The distance on the ground between the first and last man to touch down.

Stinger. A development of the US man-portable shoulder fired surface to air guided missile Redeye.

Stock. A generic term covering the quantities of items of *matériel* held on charge in store as opposed to *matériel* in use. *** Control.** Process of maintaining inventory data on the quantity, location, and condition of supplies and equipment due-in, on-hand and due-out, to determine quantities of material and equipment available and/or required for issue and to facilitate distribution and management of *matériel*. *See also* **Inventory control. * Location record.** A record or index of the storage location of stock items.

Stockpile to target sequence. The order and permutations of events involved in removing a nuclear weapon from storage and assembling, testing, transporting, and delivering it on target.

Stocktaking. The physical counting, measuring or weighing of *matériel* held for comparison with appropriate accounting records.

Stocktaking reconciliation. The comparison of the quantity of stock found at stocktaking with the account balance, allowing for any factors which affect the balance, and any subsequent adjustment made to *matériel* accounting records.

Stores. Except for some technical engineer and medical stores and joint common user items (*qv*) supplied by another Service, the RAOC is responsible for all the requirements of the Army. These stores are categorized as:
1. Combat supplies (*qv*).
2. Ordnance stores which include vehicle and aircraft assemblies and their spare parts, personal clothing and equipment.
3. General stores such as camp equipment.
4. Technical and war-like stores *ie* armaments, including guns, guided weapons and small arms; radio and electrical equipment; and assemblies and spares for them.
5. Vehicles (*qv*).

Strategic aeromedical evacuation. That phase of aeromedical evacuation which provides airlift for patients from overseas areas or from theatres of active operations, to NATO countries, or to a temporary safe area.

Strategic air transport operations. The carriage of passengers and cargo between theatres by means of:
1. scheduled services;
2. special flights;
3. air logistic support;
4. aeromedical evacuation.

Strategic air warfare. Air operations designed to effect the progressive destruction and disintegration of the enemy's war-making capacity.

Strategic concentration. The assembly of designated forces in areas from which it is intended that operations of the assembled forces shall begin so that they are best disposed to initiate the plan of campaign.

Strategic concept. The course of action accepted as a result of the estimate of the strategic situation. It is a statement of what is to be done expressed in broad terms sufficiently flexible to permit its use in framing the basic undertakings which stem from it. *See also* **Basic undertakings.**

Strategic intelligence. Intelligence which is required for the formation of policy and military plans at national and international levels.

Strategic psychological warfare. Actions which pursue long-term and mainly political objectives, in a declared emergency or in war, and which are designed to undermine the enemy's will to fight and to reduce his capacity for waging war. It can be directed against the enemy (the dominating political group, the government and its executive agencies) and/or towards the population as a whole or particular elements of it. The policy governing it is laid down by the highest authority.

Strategic reserve. That part of United Kingdom Land Forces (*qv*) which is nominated for use in future operations.

Strategic Surface to Surface Guided Weapon Systems (SSGW). Usually taken to mean those with a range bracket in excess of 500 miles.

Strategic transport aircraft. Aircraft designed primarily for the carriage of personnel and/or cargo over long distances

Strategy. The plans for conducting a war in the widest sense including diplomatic, political and economic considerations as well as those of a purely military nature.

Stratosphere. The layer of the atmosphere above the troposphere in which the change of temperature with height is relatively small. *See also* **Atmosphere.**

Stream take-off. Aircraft taking off in trail/column formation.

Strela. A heat seeking missile used in Viet Nam.

Strength. *See* **Economic potential; Unit strength.**

Stressed platform. Stores, equipment, and vehicles which are to be airdropped are fixed to a stressed platform. There are three types, Stores (SSP) for dropping light loads; medium (MSP) for heavier equipment and vehicles and Heavy (HSP) for engineer plant and the like.

Stretcher. *See* **Litter.**

Stretcher patient. *See* **Litter patient.**

Strike. An attack which is intended to inflict damage on, seize, or destroy an objective.

Strike photography. Air photography taken during an air strike.

Striker. A British anti-tank guided weapon vehicle based on the Scorpion but mounting a Swingfire guided weapon system.

Strip marker (land mine warfare). A marker, natural, artificial, or specially installed, located at the start and finish of a mine strip. *See also* **Marker** (land mine warfare).

Strip plot. A portion of a map or overlay on which a number of photographs taken along a flight line is delineated without defining the outlines of individual prints.

Stripe. Slang for the chevrons on the uniform of a non commissioned officer. Getting ones first strope denotes appointment to lance corporal. Also wound stripe, good conduct stripe.

Strongpoint (land warfare). A key point in a defensive position, usually strongly fortified and heavily armed with automatic weapons, around which other positions are grouped for its protection.

Strongpoint (aircraft). Attachment points supporting the anchor cable in an aircraft especially strengthened to resist the pull of the strops and static lines when dropping personnel or ejecting cargo, and so breaking the ties on the parachute packs. The term is also used for a point in the fuselage of the aircraft to which cargo is lashed for security in flight

Strop (air transport). A length of webbing connecting the static line to the anchor cable.

Strv 103. The Swedish battle tank which is unique in having no turret. The gun is mounted in a fixed position in the hull and targets are engaged by traversing the whole vehicle, and altering the pitch of the hull: a revolutionary design which has attracted world wide attention

Subaltern. A second lieutenant or a lieutenant.

Sub-collection centres. *See* **Nuclear, Biological, Chemical collection centre.**

Subgravity. A condition in which the resultant ambient acceleration is between O and one G.

Sub-kiloton weapon. A nuclear weapon producing a yield below one kiloton. *See also* **Kiloton weapon; Nominal weapon.**

Sub machine gun (SMG). A light automatic weapon with a limited range which continues firing on automatic as long as the trigger is pressed.

Subsidiary demolition belt. *See* **Demolition belt.**

Subsonic. Of or pertaining to speed less than the speed of sound. *See also* **Speed of sound.**

Subversion. Action designed to undermine:
1. The military, economic, psychological morale, or political strength of a nation.
2. The loyalty of the subjects.

Sultan. A British armoured command vehicle, a variant of the Scorpion, from which a commander can control the battle.

Sunray. The code name for the commander of a unit or formation.

Superimposed fire. Fire which augments that originally planned for a given target.

Supernumary. An officer supernumary to the establishment is one detached for some other duty whose place on the establishment may be filled by someone else. * **Rank.** The line of non commissioned officers standing behind the rear rank when a unit is formed up in line.

Supersonic. Of or pertaining to speed in excess of the speed of sound. *See also* **Speed of sound.**

Supervised route. A roadway over which control is exercised by a traffic control authority by means of traffic control posts, traffic patrols, or both. *See also* **Route.**

Supplement. A separate publication, related to a basic publication and prepared for purposes of promulgating additional information or summaries, and may include extracts from the basic publication.

Supply management. *See* **Inventory control.**

Supply point. Any point where supplies are issued in detail.

Support (Sp). The action of a force, or portion thereof, which aids, protects, complements, or sustains any other force. * **Area.** Those areas which contain concentration of manpower, industrial potential, and sources of food and raw materials. Support areas, which are of such importance that they are essential to our war effort are prefixed by the word 'main'. Others may be prefixed by the word 'minor'.

Supporting arms co-ordination centre. *See* **Fire support co-ordination centre.**

Supporting fire. Fire delivered by supporting units to assist or protect a unit in combat. *See also* **Close ***; **Deep ***; **Direct ***.

Supreme Headquarters Allied Powers in Europe (SHAPE). Responsible for the defence of all territory of NATO (*qv*) members in Europe except Great Britain and Portuguese coastal waters. Its operational command organization is ACE (*qv*).

Surface code. *See* **Panel code.**

Surface to Air missile (SAM). Missile fired from the ground to destroy enemy aircraft or missiles. Equally applicable to large or small systems.

Surface to Surface Guided Weapon Systems (SSGW). Those in which guided missiles (*qv*) are launched from the ground to targets on the ground. They may be Tactical (*qv*) or Strategic (*qv*).

Surface to Surface Missile (SSM). Missile fired from the ground or a vehicle against a ground target *eg* AFV (*qv*).

Surface zero. *See* **Ground zero.**

Surgeon. The ranks of * Captain, * Major, * Lieutenant Colonel and * Colonel are now peculiar to the Household Cavalry whose medical officers are members of those regiments and not seconded from the Royal Army Medical Corps.

Surplus. A quantity disclosed by physical check as being in excess of the quantity indicated on the appropriate records. * **Stock.** Stock held in excess of estimated requirements or authorized holdings.

Surround. To encircle an enemy by physical presence on the ground.

Surveillance. The systematic observation of aerospace, surface or subsurface areas, places, persons, or things, by visual, aural, electronic, photographic, or other means.

Survey photography. *See* **Air cartographic photography.**

Susceptibility. The vulnerability of a target audience to particular forms of psychological operations approach.

Suspension. The connection between a tank's track and its hull which provides a means of support for the track.

Suspension strop. A length of webbing or wire rope between the helicopter and cargo sling.

Swatter. NATO codename for a USSR wire guided anti-tank missile.

Sweep jamming. A narrow band of jamming that is swept back and forth over a relatively wide operating band of frequencies.

Swingfire. A British long range, wire-guided, command-controlled, anti-tank weapon system. Also used by Belgian forces.

Table of organization, and equipment. *See* **Establishment.**

Tacan. An ultra high frequency electronic rho-theta air navigation system which provides a continuous indication of bearing and distance to the Tacan station, common components being used in distance and bearing determination. The term is derived from tactical air navigation.

Tacfire (US). An automated system for the direction of artillery fire.

Tactics. The method employed by a commander to implement his strategic plan.

Tactical aeromedical evacuation. That phase of evacuation which provides airlift for patients from the combat zone to points outside the combat zone, and between points within the communications zone.

Tactical air commander. The officer who commands the **Tactical air force** (*qv*).

Tactical air control centre. The principal air operations installation (land or ship based) from which all aircraft and air warning functions of tactical air operations are controlled.

Tactical air controller. The officer in charge of all operations of the tactical air control centre (*qv*). He is responsible to the tactical air commander for the control of all aircraft and air warning facilities within his area of responsibility. *See also* **Air controller.**

Tactical air force. An air force charged with carrying out tactical air operations in co-ordination with ground or naval forces.

Tactical air operation. An air operation involving the employment of air power in co-ordination with ground or naval forces to:
1. gain and maintain air superiority;
2. prevent movement of enemy forces into and within the objective area and to seek out and destroy these forces and their supporting installations; and
3. join with ground or naval forces in operations within the objective area in order to assist directly in attainment of their immediate objective.

Tactical air supply. The transportation and delivery by air of maintenance requirements direct to formations in the battle area forward of L. of C. terminals, *ie* corps, divisions and brigades.

Tactical air support. Air operations carried out in co-ordination with surface forces which directly assist the land or naval battle. *See also* **Air support.**

Tactical air transport operations. The carriage of passengers and cargo within a theatre by means of:

1. Airborne operations:
   a. parachute assault,
   b. helicopter borne assault,
   c. air landing;
2. Air logistic support;
3. Special mission;
4. Aeromedical evacuation missions.

Tactical call sign. A call sign which identifies a tactical commander or tactical communication facility. *See also* **Call sign.**

Tactical control. The detailed and, usually, local direction and control of movements and manoeuvres necessary to accomplish missions or tasks assigned.
* **Radar.** A ground radar used for air surveillance and target selection.

Tactical Exercise without Troops (TEWT). A device for training commanders on the ground as opposed to in a lecture hall. The Directing Staff (*qv*) paints the picture (*qv*) and the Officers/Warrant Officers/NCOs state what action they would take, or orders they would give under the circumstances.

Tactical group (air). A part of a tactical air force designed to operate in conjunction with an army.

Tactical loading. *See* **Unit loading.**

Tactical locality. An area of terrain which, because of its location or features, possesses a tactical significance in the particular circumstances existing at a particular time.

Tactical psychological warfare. Actions designed to bring psychological pressure to bear on enemy forces and civilians in support of tactical military ground, air, or sea operations and in areas where these operations are planned or conducted. It must conform to the overall strategic psychological warfare policy but will be conducted as an integral part of combat operations.

Tactical reserve. A part of a battalion, regiment, or similar force, held initially under the control of the commander as a manoeuvring force to influence future action.

Tactical Surface to Surface Guided Weapon Systems (SSGW). Usually taken to mean systems with a range bracket up to 500 miles.

Tactical transport aircraft (TACT). Aircraft designed primarily for the carriage of personnel and/or cargo over short or medium distances.

Tail. The tail of an army comprises all those supply services and installations without which the teeth arms (*qv*) could not function.

Take off charge. Enter an item as an issue on a *matériel* accounting record.

Tan alt. *See* **Shadow factor.**

Tank. An armoured fighting vehicle. It has assumed the roles which used to belong to cavalry.

Tank destroyer. An armoured fighting vehicle specifically designed to engage enemy armour; now only in use in the Soviet and West German Armies.

Tanky (US slang). An officer or soldier of an armoured regiment.

Tape (slang). n. The chevrons worn on the sleeve to denote non-commissioned rank.

Taps. US equivalent of Lights Out (*qv*).

Target
1. The screen or figure target at which troops shoot on the range.
2. The desired place of impact for shell, bomb, bullet or missile. Area target is one where no exact target can be located *eg* a wood as opposed to a Point target such as a house.

Target acquisition. The detection, identification, and location of a target in sufficient detail to permit the effective employment of weapons. *See also* **Target analysis.**

Target analysis. An examination of potential targets to determine military importance, priority of attack, and weapons required to obtain a desired level of damage or casualties. *See also* **Target acquisition.**

Target approach point. In air transport operations, a navigational check point over which the final turn into the drop zone/landing zone is made.

Target area survey base. A base line used for the locating of targets or other points by the intersection of observations from two stations located at opposite ends of the line.

Target audience. An individual or group selected for influence or attack by means of psychological operations.

Target complex. A geographically integrated series of target concentrations.

Target date. The date on which it is desired that an action be accomplished or initiated.

Target director post (air). A special control element of the tactical air control system. It performs no air warning service but is used to position friendly aircraft over pre-determined target co-ordinates, or other geographical locations, under all weather conditions.

Target discrimination. The ability of a surveillance or guidance system to identify or engage any one target when multiple targets are present.

Target dossiers. Files of assembled target intelligence about a specific geographic area.

Target folders. The folders containing target intelligence and related materials prepared for planning and executing action against a specific target.

Target grid. Device for converting the observer's target locations and corrections with respect to the observer target line to target locations and corrections with respect to the gun target line.

Target illustration print. A single contact print or enlarged portion of a selected area from a single print, providing the best available illustration of a specific installation or pin-point target.

Target illustration sheet. Brief description of the target, completing the 'descriptive target data'. It should include technical and physical characteristics, details on exact location, disposition, importance, and possible obstacles for an aircraft flying at low altitudes.

Target intelligence. Intelligence which portrays and locates the components of a target or target complex and indicates its vulnerability and relative importance.

Target number. The reference number given to the target by the fire control unit.

Target of opportunity. A target which appears during combat and which can be reached by ground fire, naval fire, or aircraft fire, and against which fire has not been scheduled.

Target range. *See* **Range.**

Target response (nuclear). The effect on men, materials, and equipment of blast, heat, light and nuclear radiation resulting from the explosion of a nuclear weapon.

Target status board. A wall chart maintained by the air intelligence division of the joint operations centre. It includes target lists, locations, priority and status of action taken. It may also include recommended armament and fusing for destruction.

Target system. All the targets situated in a particular geographic area and functionally related.

Task force (TF).
1. A temporary grouping of units, under one commander, formed for the purpose of carrying out a specific operation or mission.
2. Semi-permanent organization of units, under one commander, formed for the purpose of carrying out a continuing specific task.

Tattoo.
1. The beat of drum or bugle call sounded at 2200 hours. Originally 'tap to', it was the signal for soldiers to leave the alehouses and return to billets. Now a purely ceremonial call.
2. A military display of which, currently, the Tidworth Tattoo is the best known.

Taxiway. A specially prepared or designated path on an airfield for the use of taxiing aircraft.

Technical intelligence. Intelligence concerning foreign technological developments, performances and operational capabilities of foreign *matériel*, which now or may eventually, have a practical application for military purposes. It is the end product resulting from the processing and collation of technical information.

Technical specifications. A detailed description of technical requirements stated in terms suitable to form the basis for the actual design, development and production processes of an item having the qualities specified in the operational characteristics. *See also* **Operational characteristics.**

Teeth arms. Those arms whose function is actually to engage the enemy, *eg* armour and infantry.

Telebrief. Direct telephone communications between an air controller and pilots in their aircraft on the ground.

Telecommunication. Any transmission, emission, or reception of signs, signals, writing, images, and sounds or information of any nature by wire, radio, visual, or other electro-magnetic systems.

Telecon. A conversation over the telephone.

Teleconference. A conference between persons remote from one another but linked by a telecommunications system.

Temporary cemetery. A cemetery for the purpose of:
1. the initial burial of the remains if the circumstances permit or
2. the re-burial of remains exhumed from an emergency burial.

Tentacle. A detachment of signals with its own radio and transport.

Terminal control area. A control area or a portion thereof normally situated at the confluence of air traffic service routes in the vicinity of one or more major airfields. *See also* **Airway; Controlled airspace; Control area; Control zone.**

Terminal guidance. The guidance applied to a missile between midcourse guidance and its arrival in the vicinity of the target.

Terminal velocity.
1. Hypothetical maximum speed a body could attain along a specified flight path under given conditions of weight and thrust if diving through an unlimited distance in air of specified uniform density.
2. Remaining speed of a projectile at the point in its downward path where it is level with the muzzle of the weapon.

Terrain avoidance. A system which provides the pilot or navigator of an aircraft with a situation display of the ground or obstacles which project above either a horizontal plane parallel to the aircraft or a plane con-

taining the aircraft pitch and roll axis, so that the pilot can manoeuvre the aircraft in a lateral direction to avoid the obstruction.

Terrain clearance. A system which provides the pilot, or auto-pilot, of an aircraft with climb or dive signals such that the aircraft will maintain a selected height over flat ground and clear the peaks of undulating ground within the selected height in a vertical plane through the flight vector. This system differs from Terrain following (*qv*) in that the aircraft need not descend into a valley to follow the ground contour.

Terrain following. A system which provides the pilot, or auto-pilot of an aicraft with climb or dive signals such that the aircraft will maintain, as closely as possible, a selected height above a ground contour, in a vertical plane through the flight vector.

Territorial Army and Volunteer Reserve (TAVR). Units composed of civilians who voluntarily undergo military training in their spare time and can be mobilized for war to reinforce the regular army. Regular instructors are attached to each unit.

Territorial command. Denotes that all units within a defined area *eg* District (*qv*) in the UK are the responsibility, to a greater or lesser degree, of the Headquarters concerned, according to the role of the unit. Thus a school may be administered by its District Headquarters but be responsible to the Ministry of Defence for training. *See also* **Functional command.**

Terrorist. A terrorist is a supporter of a dissident faction who resorts to violence in order to intimidate and coerce people for political ends.

Theater Combat Model (TCM) (US). A model of terrain on which combat can be simulated to assist the staff in evaluating the effectiveness of alternative compositions of Brigades and Divisions in any given theatre of war.

Thermal exposure. The total normal component of thermal radiation striking a given surface throughout the course of a detonation; expressed in the units; calories per square centimetre.

Thermal imagery (infrared). Imagery produced by measuring and recording electronically the thermal radiation (*qv*) of objects.

Thermal radiation. The heat and light produced by a nuclear explosion.

Thermal X-rays. The electro-magnetic radiation, mainly in the soft (low-energy) X-ray region, emitted by the extremely hot weapon debris by virtue of its extremely high temperature.

Thermonuclear. An adjective referring to the process (or processes) in which very high temperatures are used to bring about the fusion of light nuclei, with the accompanying liberation of energy. * **Weapon.** A weapon in which very high temperatures are used to bring about the fusion of light nuclei such as those of hydrogen isotopes (*eg* deuterium and tritium) with the accompanying release of energy. The high temperatures required are obtained by means of fission.

Through running. In transport terminology denotes that the same driver takes his vehicle from the start to the end of the journey. *See also* **Continuous running.**

Thunderbird. A British medium to high-level anti-aircraft guided missile.

Tie down. *See* **Lashing.** * **Diagram.** A drawing indicating the prescribed method of securing a particular item of cargo within a specific type of vehicle or aircraft. * **Point.** An attachment point provided on or within a vehicle or aircraft for securing cargo. * **Point pattern.** The pattern of tie down points within a vehicle or aircraft.

Tigercat. A British ground to air close range guided missile.

Tilt. In air photography, the camera rotation about the longitudinal axis of the aircraft. Also known as 'Roll'. * **Angle.** The angle between the axis of an air camera and the vertical relative to the longitudinal axis of the aircraft. The angle at the perspective centre between the photograph perpendicular and the plumb line. *See also* **Angle of depression.**

Time fuse. A fuse which contains a graduated time element to regulate the time interval after which the fuse will function. *See also* **Fuse.**

Time of flight. The time expressed in seconds from the firing of a weapon until the missile bursts or impacts.

Time on target.
1. The method of firing on a target in which various artillery units and naval gunfire support ships so time their fire as to assure all projectiles reaching the target simultaneously.
2. Time at which aircraft are scheduled to attack/photograph a target.

Tip. In air photography, the camera rotation about the transverse axis of the aircraft. Also known as 'pitch'.

Titan. A US ICBM (*qv*).

Title block. *See* **Information box.**

Titling strip. The information added to negatives and/or positives, in accordance with regulations to identify and provide reference information.

TNT equivalent. A measure of the energy released from the detonation of a nuclear weapon, or from the explosion of a given quantity of fissionable material, in terns of TNT (Trinitrotoluene) which would release the same amount of energy when exploded.

Toggle rope. A piece of rope with a small piece of wood fastened to the ends and used in rescue operations.

Tommy Atkins (slang). A British soldier.

Tone. Each distinguishable shade variation from black to white on photographs.

Topographic base. *See* **Chart base.**

Torsion bar. A flexible rod anchored to the tracked vehicle's hull, the opposite end carrying a sprung crank, at the end of which is a suspension bogie or wheel. Movement of the wheel and crank twists the rod.

Total lead time. The interval, expressed in months, between a date a requirement for an item of *matériel* is determined by the authority responsible for overall provisioning and the date that the initial quantity is brought on charge. Total lead time comprises 'Administrative lead time', 'Production lead time', and 'Post production lead time'.

Tote (air). A wall display showing detailed minute-to-minute information such as fighter sorties, squadron and airfield states, and anti-aircraft states.

Touch-down. The contact, or moment of contact, of an aircraft or spacecraft, with the landing surface.

Tow. An Anti-tank Guided Weapon System (ATGW) in use in the US Army.

Toxic Report (TOXREP). A report rendered by troops who are being, or suspect they are being, attacked by biological or chemical agents.

Toxic biological, chemical or radiological attack. An attack directed at man, animals, or crops using injurious agents of radiological, biological or chemical origin.

Track.
1. v. To display or record the successive positions of a moving object; also to lock on to a point of radiation and obtain guidance therefrom.
2. v. To keep a gun properly aimed, or to point continuously a target-locating instrument, at a moving target.
3. n. The projection on the surface of the earth of the path of an aircraft, the direction of which path at any point is usually expressed in degrees from North (true, magnetic, or grid).
4. n. One of two endless belts on which a full-track or half-track vehicle runs.
5. n. A metal part forming a path for a moving object.

Track handover. In air defence, the process of transferring the responsibility for production of a track from one track production area to another.

Track links. The basic element of a tank track, usually linked together by pins.

Track mode. In a flight control system, a control mode in which the ground track of an aircraft is maintained automatically.

Track production area.
1. An area in which tracks are produced by one radar station.
2. (air defence). The area of responsibility of a control and reporting centre, or equivalent unit, for the production of a clear and comprehensive picture of the air situation.

Track symbology. Symbols used to display tracks on a data display console or other display device.

Track telling. The process of communicating air surveillance and tactical data information between command control systems and facilities within the systems. Telling may be classified into the following areas:
1. Back tell – The transfer of information from a higher to a lower echelon of command.

2. Cross tell – The transfer of information between facilities at the same operational level.
3. Forward tell – The transfer of information to a higher level of command.
4. Lateral tell – *See* Cross tell.
5. Overlap tell – The transfer of information to an adjacent facility concerning tracks detected in the adjacent facilities' area of responsibility.
6. Relateral tell – The relay of information between facilities through the use of a third facility. This type of telling is appropriate between automated facilities in a degraded communications environment.

Tracked vehicle. Any vehicle which uses tracks as opposed to wheels to move. *See also* **Half track.**

Tracking. Precise and continuous position-finding of targets by radar, optical or other means.

Traffic Account Analysis System (TAAS). A system of investigation of the circumstances and causes of traffic accidents amongst army drivers designed to reduce the overall rate.

Traffic control police (road transport). Any persons ordered by a military commander and/or by national authorities to facilitate the movement of traffic and to prevent and/or report any breach of road traffic regulations.

Traffic density. The average number of vehicles that occupy one mile or one kilometre of road space, expressed in vehicles per mile or per kilometre.

Traffic flow. The total number of vehicles passing a given point in a given time. Traffic flow is expressed as vehicles per hour.

Traffic post. A small RMP detachment established along a route to be used for troop or stores convoys to regulate traffic.

Trafficability. Capability of terrain to bear traffic. It refers to the extent to which the terrain will permit continued movement of any and/or all types of traffic.

Train headway. The interval of time between two trains boarded by the same unit at the same point.

Training (Trg). Any form of instruction or practice undergone by a unit or individual to fit it/him for war.
Adventure *. A non military activity, approved by the Ministry of Defence, involving officers and soldiers, designed to develop their courage, initiative and self reliance, *eg* mountaineering. *** Aids.** Any device, *eg* vufoil, rifle rest, used for instructional purposes which has no function in action. *See also* **Collective *; Continuation *; Individual *.**

Trainpath. The opportunity offered to a train to move along a given route. This opportunity is reflected in timings. The whole of the train paths on any given route constitutes a time-table.

Transfer loader. A wheeled or tracked vehicle with a platform capable of vertical and horizontal adjustment used in the loading and unloading of aircraft, ships, or other vehicles.

Transient. An individual awaiting orders, transport, etc., at a post or station to which he is not attached or assigned.

Transit area. *See* **Staging area.**

Transition altitude. The altitude at or below which the vertical position of an aircraft is controlled by reference to true altitude. *See also* **Altitude; Transition level.**

Transition layer. The airspace between the transition altitude and the transition level.

Transition level. The lowest flight level available for use above the transition altitude. *See also* **Altitude; Transition altitude.**

Transmission factor (nuclear). The ratio of the dose inside the shielding material to the outside (ambient) dose. It is used to calculate the dose received through the shielding material. *See also* **Half thickness; Shielding.**

Transonic. Of or pertaining to the speed of a body in a surrounding fluid when the relating speed of the fluid is subsonic in some places and supersonic in others. This is encountered when passing from subsonic to supersonic speeds and vice versa. *See also* **Speed of sound.**

Transparency. A photographic print on a clear base, especially adaptable for viewing by transmitted light. *See also* **Diapositive.**

Transponder. A transmitter-receiver capable of accepting the electronic challenge of an interrogator and automatically transmitting an appropriate reply.

Transport capacity. The capacity of a vehicle as defined by the number of persons, the tonnage (or volume) of equipment which can be carried by this vehicle under given conditions.

Transport control centre (air transport). The operations centre through which the air transport force commander exercises control over the air transport system.

Transport group (amphibious). A subdivision of an amphibious task force, composed primarily of transports.

Transport network. The complete system of the routes pertaining to all means of transport available in a particular area. It is made up of the network particular to each means of transport.

Transport stream. Transport vehicles proceeding in trail formation.

Transportable. Equipment which can be moved from place to place by mechanical means, but not on its own wheels, tracks or skids, or by self-propulsion.

Transportation. A generic term covering the physical movement of personnel and *matériel.*

Traverse.
1. v. To turn a weapon to the right or left on its mount.
2. n. In surveying, a series of straight lines running from point to point. the distances and angles being accurately measured.
3. n. In trench warfare, the passage way between fire trenches set back from them as a protection from enfilade fire.

Trench. An excavation in the ground to give protection to a defensive position. Maybe a **Fire ***, **Communication ***, **Slit *** *ie* one without Parapet (*qv*) or Parados (*qv*); as opposed to Sangar (*qv*). *** Burial.** A method of burial resorted to when casualties are heavy whereby a trench is prepared and the individual remains are laid in it side by side, thus obviating the necessity of digging and filling individual graves.

Trews. Tartan trousers worn in Scottish Regiments.

Triangulation station. A point on the earth, the position of which is determined by triangulation. Also known as 'trig point'.

Tri-camera photography. Photography obtained by simultaneous exposure of three cameras systematically disposed in the air vehicle at fixed overlapping angles relative to each other in order to cover a wide field. *See also* **Fan camera photography.**

Trimetrogon photography. *See* **Fan camera photography.**

Trim for take-off. A flight control system in which the control surfaces of an aircraft are automatically trimmed to a predetermined take-off position.

Trim size. The size of a map or chart sheet when the excess paper outside the margin has been trimmed off after printing.

Tripwire. A weak military defensive force confronting a much stronger one whose presence, it is hoped, will deter the aggressor from inviting massive, probably nuclear, retaliation.

Troop (tp). In mounted units the equivalent of a platoon of infantry. An artillery battery is also divided into troops. * **Ship** (obsolete), one designed or converted for the purpose of moving units by sea.

Trooper (tpr). A private soldier in a cavalry regiment. Equivalent to private in infantry.

Tropopause. The transition zone between the stratosphere and the troposphere. The tropopause normally occurs at an altitude of about 25,000 to 45,000 feet in polar and temperate zones, and at 55,000 feet in the tropics. *See also* **Atmosphere.**

Troposphere. The lower layers of atmosphere, in which the change of temperature with height is relatively large. It is the region where clouds form, convection is active, and mixing is continuous and more or less complete. *See also* **Atmosphere.**

Tropospheric scatter. An over-the-horizon ground-to-ground radio system which utilizes the reflective properties of the troposphere to provide a multi-channel communication system.

True airspeed. Equivalent airspeed corrected for error due to air density (altitude and temperature).

True altitude. The height of an aircraft as measured from sea level.

True bearing. The direction to an object from a point, expressed as a horizontal angle measured clockwise from true North.

True convergence. The angle at which one meridian is inclined to another on the surface of the earth. *See also* **Convergence.**

True horizon. The boundary of a horizontal plane passing through a point of vision, or, in photogrammetry, the perspective centre of a lens system.

True north. The direction from an observer's position to the geographic North pole. The North direction of any geographic meridian.

Trumpet. A wind instrument used in the cavalry instead of a bugle.

Trunk air route. An established air route along which strategic moves of military forces can take place.

Tube-launched, optically-tracked wire-guided (TOW). A surface to surface or air to surface anti-tank guided weapon system.

Tunic. A uniform coat extending below the waist as opposed to a jacket (*qv*).

Turbulence. An unsettled state within a unit induced by frequent cross-posting of personnel. It does not indicate, but if carried to excess may induce, a lowering of morale.

Turnaround. The length of time between arriving at a point and departing from that point. It is used in this sense for the turnaround of shipping in ports, and for aircraft refuelling and rearming * **Cycle.** This term is used in conjunction with vehicles and aircraft, and comprises the following: loading time at home, time to and from destination, unloading and loading time at destination; unloading time at home, planned maintenance time and, where applicable, time awaiting facilities.

Turn-in point. The point at which an aircraft starts to turn from the approach direction to the line of attack. *See also* **Air control team; Contact point; Pull-up point.**

Turning point (land mine warfare). A point of the centreline of a mine strip or row where strips or rows change direction.

Turret. A rotating armoured structure resting on ball bearings running in a traverse ring. It may be powered by hand cranking or by electric or hydraulic motors.

Turret down. A tactical position in which the tank commander alone can see the target thereby shielding the entire tank from a view relative to the target. From this position only indirect fire can be brought to bear on the target.

Twilight. The periods of incomplete darkness following sunset and preceding sunrise. Twilight is designated as civil, nautical or astronomical, as the darker limit occurs when the centre of the sun is 6°, 12°, or 18° respectively below the celestial horizon.

Two-up. A formation with two elements of a formation, *eg* Brigade, disposed abreast; the remaining element(s) in rear.

Type I married quarter. A Service officer's married quarter built or purchased to the standard laid down in JSP 315 Scale 21 or previously authorized synopsis scales, or constructed or acquired to satisfy these requirements. Also **Types II, III, IV and V.**

Type VI married quarter. An Army Department Service officer's obsolescent two bedroom married quarter provided within an area of 780 square feet.

Type load. *See* **Standard load.**

Types of burst. *See* **Airburst; High altitude burst; Nuclear airburst; Nuclear surface burst; Nuclear underground burst; Nuclear underwater burst.**

Ubique. (Latin: everywhere). The motto of the Royal Regiment of Artillery and of the Corps of Royal Engineers, whose individual units are not awarded Battle Honours (*qv*) as is the case in Armoured and Infantry Regiments.

Ullage. The difference between the rated capacity of a receptable for liquid and its contents.

Umpire. Officer who acts as a judge on an exercise.

Uncharged demolition target. A demolition target which has been prepared to receive the demolition agent, the necessary quantities of which have been calculated, packaged, and stored in a safe place. Installation instructions have been prepared. *See also* **Demolition.**

Unclassified matter. Official matter which does not require the application of security safeguards but the disclosure of which may be subject to control for other reasons. *See also* **Classified matter.**

Uncontrolled mosaic. A mosaic composed of uncorrected photographs, the details of which have been matched from print to print without ground control or other orientation. Accurate measurement and direction cannot be accomplished. *See also* **Mosaic.**

Unconventional warfare. General term used to describe operations conducted for military, political, or economic purposes within an area occupied by the enemy and making use of the local inhabitants and resources.

Under command. A formation, unit or detachment under command receives orders from the formation or unit under whose command it has been placed covering tactical matters, including movement but not necessarily administration.

Underwater demolition. The destruction or neutralization of underwater obstacles; this is normally accomplished by specialist teams.

Unfurnished married quarter hiring.
A house or flat, normally abroad, taken on individual short term lease, of usually not more than three years, to accommodate an entitled family. It is furnished to scale by the Mod and the rent paid from the Defence Lands Vote.

Unified command.
1. The command organization in which a unified force composed of two or more Services operates under an officer specifically assigned to be the commander thereof by the Joint Chiefs of Staff.
2. A joint force under a single commander which is composed of significant assigned or attached components of two or more Services, and which is constituted and so designated by the Joint Chiefs of Staff or by the commander of an existing unified command which was established by the Joint Chiefs of Staff.

Uniform. The distinctive clothing worn by any formed and organized body of men which is a prerequisite for recognition as a legitimate combatant under the Geneva Convention of 1949.

Uniform Code of Military Justice (UCMJ). The US code of rules which govern the treatment of officers and men under suspicion of having committed a crime.

Unit.
1. Any military element whose structure is prescribed by competent authority, such as a table of organization and equipment; specifically, part of an organization. A major unit is of battalion (*qv*) strength and a minor unit will not much exceed company (*qv*) strength. *See also* **Self accounting ***.
2. An organization title of a subdivision of a group in a task force.
3. A standard or basic quantity into which an item of supply is divided, issued or used. In this meaning, also called 'unit of issue'.

Unit emplaning officer (UEO). In air transport, a representative of the transported unit responsible for organizing the movment of that unit. He is responsible in collaboration with the ATLO (*qv*) for the emplanement of personnel and stores.

Unit families officer (UFO). Responsible to the Commanding Officer for all matters in connection with the administration, welfare and housing of all the unit's families.

Unit guides. A group of representatives of various elements of the unit sent ahead to facilitate the reception of a unit in an area, whether tactical or administrative.

Unit helicopter tasking officer. A unit officer responsible for tasking and allocation of troops for a helicopter operational move.

Unit landing officer (amphibious). An officer of an assault battalion detailed to land with an early wave of the assault to reconnoitre beach exits for his battalion, and to establish a rendezvous inland of these exits where his battalion HQ will subsequently be set up. Unit landing officers may also be detailed for RAC, RA, RE, etc., units taking part in the assault.

Unit load. One item, or a number of items suitably put together to form one load, capable of being lifted by the appropriate handling equipment.

Unit loading. The loading of troop units with their equipment and supplies in the same vessels, ships, aircraft, or land vehicles. *See also* **Loading.**

Unit of choice (US). The system whereby a volunteer for the US army is allowed to select the regiment in which he wishes to serve.

Unit of issue. *See* **Unit.**

Unit strength. As applied to a friendly or enemy unit, relates to the number of personnel, amount of supplies, armament equipment and vehicles and the total logistic capabilities.

United Kingdom Land Forces (UKLF), with its HQ at Wilton comprises the formations of the Strategic Reserve and units in the old geographical commands in the United Kingdom.

United Nations Peace Keeping Force in Cyprus (UNFICYP). An international Force, including a British element, stationed in Cyprus to keep the peace between the Muslim (Turkish) and Christian (Greek) population. It provides military backing for the United Nations Civilian Police Force (UNCIVPOL).

Universal transverse mercator grid (UTM). A grid co-ordinate system based on the transverse mercator projection, applied to maps of the earth's surface extending to 84°N and 80°S latitudes.

Unobserved fire. Fire for which points of impact or burst are not observed.

Unsurveyed area. Areas on a map or chart where both relief and planimetric data are unavailable. These areas are usually labelled 'unsurveyed'. Or an area on a map or chart which shows little or no chartered data because accurate information is limited or not available.

Unserviceable (us). Equipment or weapons condemned by a Board as having no further capability for the purpose for which it was designed. It can then be put to other use, *eg* an unserviceable tank can be used as a target.

Unwarned exposed. The vulnerability of friendly forces to nuclear weapon effects. In this condition, personnel are assumed to be standing in the open at burst time, but to have dropped to a prone position by the time the blast wave arrives. They are expected to have areas of bare skin exposed to direct thermal radiation, and some personnel may suffer dazzle. *See also* **Warned exposed; Warned protected.**

Uzi. An Israeli designed and manufactured personal weapon with a range of about 100 m. One of the best of its type in the world.

Valise.
1. A sleeping bag.
2. A light container made of felt or canvas and used particularly in connection with parachute descents.

Valuable supply/cargo. A commodity which may be of value during a later stage of the war. This will comprise such things as basic raw materials and manufactured goods. *See also* **Cargoes.**

Vanguard. The foremost part of an advanced guard. The remainder is known as the mainguard.

Vapour trail. *See* **Condensation trail.**

Variability. The manner in which the probability of damage to a specific target decreases with the distance from ground zero; or, in damage assessment, a mathematical factor introduced to average the effects of orientation, minor shielding and uncertainty of target response to the effects considered.

Variable time fuse. A fuse designed to detonate a projectile, bomb, mine, or charge when activitated by external influence other than contact in the close vicinity of a target. *See also* **Fuse.**

Variation of price. The adjustments to take account of movements of specified elements in a fixed price.

Vectored attacks. Attacks in which a weapon carrier (air, surface, or subsurface) not holding contact on the target, is vectored to the weapon delivery point by a unit (air, surface, or subsurface) which holds contact on the target.

Vehicle (veh). A self-propelled, boosted, or towed conveyance for transporting a burden on land, sea or through air or space. **Army land** * are categorized as **A** * which includes all types of vehicles which are armoured and armed. **B** * are all unarmoured or soft skinned. **C** * are sepcialist RE plant vehicles, such as bulldozers, etc. * **Borne.** An item of equipment designed for use on the ground but which is normally moved on/in a vehicle. * **Commander** (ground). The leader of a vehicle crew appointed for each mission. He is responsible for crew discipline and the execution of the mission. * **Mounted.** An item of equipment which is designed solely for use on/in a vehicle.

Verify. To ensure that the meaning and phraseology of the transmitted message conveys the exact intention of the originator.

Vertical air photograph. An air photograph taken with the optical axis of the camera perpendicular to the surface of the earth.

Vertical circle. A great circle on the celestial sphere joining the observer's zenith and nadir.

Vertical loading. A type of loading whereby items of like character are vertically tiered throughout the holds of a ship, so that selected items are available at any stage of the unloading. *See also* **Loading.**

Vertical replenishment. The use of helicopters for the transfer of stores and/ or ammunition from ship-to-ship or ship-to-shore.

Vertical separation. A specified vertical distance measured in terms of space between aircraft in flight at different altitudes or flight levels.

Vertical take-off and landing. (VTOL). The capability of an aircraft to take-off and land vertically and to transfer to or from forward motion at heights required to clear surrounding obstacles.

Very seriously ill. A patient is very seriously ill when his illness is of such severity that life is imminently endangered. *See also* **Seriously ill.**

Veterinary. All such work in the army is carried out by the Royal Army Veterinary Corps. It falls generally into two categories, the supply and care of working animals *eg* war dogs and the inspection of animals *eg* cattle purchased by the RAOC for food. Its most important function today is the training of war dogs and their handlers in the different skills demanded of them *eg* guard dogs, tracker dogs and those trained to smell out ammunition or arms dumps.

Vigilant. A British man portable anti-tank wire guided missile.

Vignetting. In cartography, a technique of graduated shading to emphasize the outline of a feature.

Vijayanta. The Indian main battle tank (MBT) which has been developed by the British from the Chieftain and the Centurion. It is superior to the Chinese and (American) Pakistani MBTs.

Visibility range. The horizontal distance (in kilometres or miles) at which a large dark object can just be seen against the horizon sky in daylight.

Visual Aids. Any device, *eg* overhead projector, which supplements the spoken word in teaching.

Visual call sign. A call sign provided primarily for visual signalling. *See also* **Call sign.**

Visual fire (air defence). Fire which is continuously aimed at the future position of an aircraft, the aim being derived from visual sources.

Visual identification. In a flight control system, a control mode in which the aircraft follows a radar target and is automatically positioned to allow visual identification.

Visual inspection. An examination limited to the assessment of *matériel* condition based on the external appearance of an item or its package.

Vital ground. *See* **Key terrain.**

Voice call sign. A call sign provided primarily for voice communication. *See also* **Call sign.**

Volley. A number of rounds of small arms fire discharged at the same time.

Vulcan.
1. Code name for a new US ICBM project.
2. A US 20 mm six barrel gun.

Wad
1. The material packing which separates the charge from the projectile in a missile.
2. (Slang.) A bun, cake or biscuit.

Wading crossing. *See* **Deep fording; Shallow fording.**

Waiting position (fast coastal forces). Any geographical position in which fast patrol boats can be kept ready for operations at immediate notice.

Walking patient. A patient not requiring a litter while in transit.

War. 'The strife of communities, expressed through conflict, of organized bands of armed men' (Fortescue).

War Establishment (WE). The scale of personnel, weapons and equipment authorized to be held on charge to a unit when it is placed on a war footing.

War dogs. *See* **Veterinary.**

War game. A simulation, by whatever means, of a military operation involving two or more opposing forces, using rules, data, and procedures designed to depict an actual or assumed real life situation.

War gas. *See* **Chemical agent.**

War Office. Until lately the civilian department of state, situated in Whitehall, responsible for the Army, in which the Secretary of State for War, the Permanent Under Secretary, the Chief of the (Imperial) General Staff and other officers, both civil and military, worked. It has now been absorbed by the Ministry of Defence, but its memory is perpetuated in the Old War Office Building which houses a part of the staff.

War reserves. Stocks of materials amassed in peace-time to meet the increase in military requirement consequent upon an outbreak of war. They are intended to provide the interim support essential to sustain operations until resupply can be effected.
There are three categories:
1. War Maintenance Reserves (WMR).
Stocks comprising:
    a. Equipment, vehicles and stores to make good war wastage and usage.
    b. Combat supplies, *ie* ammunition, fuel and rations.
War maintenance reserves are based on an anticipated wastage in foreseen circumstances, and are normally expressed as a number of days requirements for a specified force.
2. Pre-Stocked Unit Equipment (PUE).
Unit equipment, vehicles and stores including first line ammunition and initial stocks for storeholding units, to bring units up to the scale required for a particular contingency. This includes the initial equipment of a newly raised unit, and applies to both regular and reserve army. Stocks may be located in UK or overseas.
3. Special Task Stores (STS). Stores and equipment required for an operational or administrative contingency, not provided for from other authorized holdings and reserves.

Warhead. That part of a missile, projectile, torpedo, rocket, or other munition which contains either the nuclear or thermonuclear system, high explosive system, chemical or biological agents or inert materials intended to inflict damage. * Section. A completely assembled warhead including appropriate skin sections and related components.

Warlike Stores. *See* **Stores.**

Warned exposed. The vulnerability of friendly forces to nuclear weapon effects. In this condition, personnel are assumed to be prone with all skin covered and with thermal protection of at least that provided by a two-layer summer uniform. *See also* **Unwarned exposed; Warned protected.**

Warned protected. The vulnerability of friendly forces to nuclear weapon effects In this condition, personnel are assumed to have some protection against heat, blast and radiation such as that afforded in closed armoured vehicles or crouched in fox holes with improvised overhead shielding. *See also* **Unwarned exposed; Warned exposed.**

Warning area. *See* **Danger area.**

Warning order. A preliminary notice of an order or action which is to follow. It is designed to give subordinates time to make necessary plans and preparations.

Warrant. A writ of authority.

Warrant Officer (WO). The rank between commissioned (*qv*) and non commissioned officer (*qv*), approximately equivalent to junior managerial status in civil life.

Water suit. A G-suit in which water is used in the interlining thereby automatically approximating the required hydrostatic pressure-gradient under G forces. *See also* **Pressure suit.**

Wave. A formation of forces, landing ships, craft, amphibious vehicles or aircraft, required to beach or land about the same time. Can be classified as to type, function or order as shown:
1. assault wave;

2. boat wave;
3. helicopter wave;
4. numbered wave;
5. on-call wave;
6. scheduled wave.

Weapon. Any device which can inflict damage or casualties on an enemy.
* **Debris (nuclear).** The residue of a nuclear weapon after it has exploded; that is, materials used for the casing, and other components of the weapon, plus unexpended plutonium or uranium, together with fission products.

Weapons free (air defence). The situation when targets other than those recognized as friendly or designated as friendly by an air situation report or by the Air Defence Commander may be engaged. This order is cancelled by 'weapons tight' or 'hold fire.

Weapons recommendation sheet. A sheet or chart which defines the intention of the attack, and recommends the nature of weapons, and resulting damage expected, tonnage, fusing, spacing, desired mean points of impact, and intervals of reattack.

Weapons selector. A circular scale used to relate assessed nuclear damage radii to a target on a map.

Weapons system. A weapon and those components required for its operation. The term is not precise unless specific parameters are established.

Weapons tight (air defence). The situation when friendly aircraft are in the area. Targets must not be engaged unless they are recognized positively as hostile, or are acting in a hostile manner as defined in the appropriate rules of engagement. This order is cancelled by 'hold fire' or 'weapons free'.

Weather factor. The average number of whole days (or nights) fit for flying, expressed as a fraction of the total period.

Weight and balance sheet. A sheet which records the distribution of weight in an aircraft and shows the centre of gravity of an aircraft at take-off and landing.

West Point. The United States equivalent to the Royal Military Academy Sandhurst. Situated in Orange County, New York, on the West bank of the Hudson River.

Wheelbase. The distance between the centres of two consecutive wheels. In the case of vehicles with more than two axles or equivalent systems, the successive wheelbases are all given in the order front to rear of the vehicle.

Whiteout. Loss of orientation with respect to the horizon caused by sun reflecting on snow or overcast sky.

Wilco. A word of acknowledgement given over the radio or telephone to mean that instructions or orders have been understood and will be carried out.

Window. Strips of frequency-cut metal foil, wire, or bars usually dropped from aircraft or expelled from shells or rockets as a radar countermeasure. *See also* **Chaff.**

Wind velocity. The horizontal direction and speed of air motion.

Withdrawal action. A manoeuvre whereby a force disengages from an enemy force in accordance with the will of the commander.

Wombat. A 120mm anti-armour weapon issued to infantry battalions.

Women's Voluntary Service (WVS). Assists the army by providing services, such as canteens, in the UK.

Wounded in action (WIA). A battle casualty other than 'killed in action' who has incurred an injury due to an external agent or cause. The term encompasses all kinds of wounds and other injuries incurred in action, whether there is piercing of the body, as in a penetrating or perforated wound, or none, as in the contused wound; all fractures, burns, blast concussions, all effects of biological and chemical warfare agents, the effects of exposure to ionizing radiation or any other destructive weapon or agent.

Wrap up. (Slang). v. To complete all details pertaining to a project so that it may be launched without delay.

X-roads. Cross roads.

X-scale. On an oblique photograph, the scale along a line parallel to the true horizon.

Yaw. The rotation of an aircraft about its vertical axis so as to cause the longitudinal axis of the aircraft to deviate from the flight line.

Yeomanry. Previously volunteer part-time cavalry who were part of the Territorial Army. Most units were disbanded after the Second World War but some have survived as armoured or artillery regiments.

Yeomen of the Guard. *See* **Queens Bodyguard of the Yeomen of the Guard.**

Y-scale. On an oblique photograph, the scale along the line of the principal vertical, or any other line inherent or plotted which, on the ground, is parallel to the principal vertical.

Zeroing. In small arms the process of ensuring that the flight of the bullet is in accordance with the sights. When the necessary adjustments have been made laterally or for height the weapon is said to be zeroed.

Zero-length launching. A technique in which the first motion of the missile or aircraft removes it from the launcher.

Z marker beacon. Equipment identical with the fan marker except that it is installed as part of a four-course radio range at the intersection of the four range legs, and radiates vertically to indicate to aircraft when they pass directly over the range station. It is usually not keyed for identification. Also known as 'cone of silence marker'. *See also* **Beacon.**

Zone. *See* **Air defence identification zone; Combat zone; Communication zone; Control zone (air); Dead zone; Demilitarized zone; Dropping zone; Landing zone; Rupture zone; Safety zone;** *See also* **Area.**

Zone of action. A tactical subdivision of a larger area, the responsibility for which is assigned to a tactical unit; generally applied to offensive action.

Zone time system. A system whereby the world is divided into 24 zones for time-keeping purposes, and where the time in one zone differs from that used in the adjacent zone by one hour, thereby effecting an exact number of hours difference between zone and Greenwich mean time (GMT).

Z-scale. On an oblique photograph, the scale used in calculating the height of an object. Also the name given to this method of height determination.

Zulu time. Greenwich mean time (GMT).

Appendix 1

Abbreviations

The army relies heavily on acronyms and abbreviations. Some are offical, listed and defined in military publications. Others given below are, or were recently, in common use. Many have been adopted by the civilian community. This appendix gives most of the more common ones. It is not comprehensive because new ones are always being added and old ones fall into desuetude.

A Phonetic alphabet: Alfa.

A
1. Before rank or appointment denotes acting or assistant.
2. *See* **A Staff.**

AA Anti-Aircraft.

AA and QMG Assistant Adjutant and Quartermaster General (*qv*).

AAC Army Air Corps (*qv*).

AACC Administrative Area Control Centre. *See* **Administrative.**

AAM Air to air missile.

AAvn Army Aviation.

AB Airborne.

ABM *See* **Anti Ballistic Missile System.**

AC Armoured Car.

ac Aircraft.

ACC
1. Army Catering Corps
2. Artillery Control Console (*qv*).

accn Accommodation.

ACE Allied Command Europe (*qv*).

ACF Army Cadet Force. *See under* **Force.**

ACG Assistant Chaplain General, C of E and UB.

ack Acknowledge, acknowledged or acknowledgement.

ACLOS Automatic Command to Line of Sight (*qv*).

ACO Air Contact Officer.

ACRA An acronym for Anti-Char Rapide Autopropulse, a French anti-tank weapon system.

ACV Armoured Command Vehicle (*qv*).

AD Air Defence.

ADA Air Defence Area.

ADAC Air Defence Artillery Commander.

ADAH Assistant Director of Army Health.

ADC Aide-de-camp (*qv*).

adjt. Adjutant (*qv*).

ADLOG Advanced Logistic Command. *See under* **Logistic Command.**

admin Administer, administration or administrative.

admin O Administrative Order.

ADMS Assistant Director of Medical Services. *See under* **Medical.**

ADOS Assistant Director of Ordnance Services. *See under* **Ordnance.**

ADPS Automatic Data Processing System.

ADS Advanced Dressing Station (*qv*).

adv Advance or advanced.

AFCENT Allied Forces Central Europe (*qv*).

AFNORTH Allied Forces Northern Europe.

AFS Army Fire Service (*qv*).

AFSOUTH Allied Forces Southern Europe (*qv*).

AFV Armoured Fighting Vehicle (*qv*).

AG Adjutant General (*qv*).

AIDA Automatic Intruder Detector Alarm (*qv*).

AK Automat Kalashnikov (*qv*).

ALO Air Liaison Officer.

altn Alternate or alternative.

AMA Airhead Maintenance Area (*qv*).

amb Ambulance.

amdt Amendment.

AMETS Artillery Meteorological System (*qv*).

AMF(L) Allied Command Europe Mobile Force (Land) (*qv*).

AML Auto-mitrailleuse Légère. A French Armoured Car.

ammo Ammunition.

amph Amphibious.

AMX A French tracked vehicle. The type is denoted by figures or letters following AMX. *eg* AMX30 is the main battle tank. AMXVTT (vehicle transport de troupe) is the APC (*qv*).

AO Air Observer (*qv*).

AP
1. Armour Piercing (*qv*).
2. Ammunition Point (*qv*).

APC Armoured Personnel Carrier (*qv*).

APDS Armour Piercing Discarding Sabot (*qv*).

APIS Army photographic interpretation section (*qv*).

APM Assistant Provost Marshal (*qv*).

APO Army Post Office.

approx Approximate, approximately or approximation.

APTC Army Physical Training Corps (*qv*).

AQMS Artificer, Armourer or Artisan Quarter Master Sergeant.

ARAAV Armoured Reconnaissance Airborne Assault Vehicle.

armd Armoured.

armt Armament.

ARPAC A French manportable anti-tank weapon effective up to 50 m.

art Artificer.

arty Artillery.

ARV Armoured Recovery Vehicle (*qv*).

asg Assign or assigned.

aslt Assault.

ASM
1. Air to Surface Missile (*qv*).
2. Artificer or Armament Sergeant Major.

ASOC Air Support Operations Centre (*qv*).

asst Assistant.

Assy Assembly.

ATC Air Traffic Control (*qv*).

ATGW Anti Tank Guided Weapon Systems (*qv*).

ATL Air Transport Liaison.

ATLAS Anti Tank Laser Assisted System (*qv*).

ATLO Air Transport Liaison Officer (*qv*).

ATMCC Air Transport Movement Control Centre (*qv*).

ATOC Air Transport Operations Centre (*qv*).

att Attach, attached or attachment.

attn Attention.

aut Authority or authorized.

aval Available.

AVGAS Aviation gasoline.

avn Aviation.

AVR Army Veterinary and Remount Services. *See under* **Veterinary.**

AVRE Assault Vehicle Royal Engineers.

AVTUR Aviation Turbine Fuel

AWOL Absent without leave.

AYT Army Youth Team (*qv*).

az Azimuth.

B Phonetic alphabet: Bravo.

BAA Brigade Administrative Area (*qv*).

BAD Base Ammunition Depot (*qv*).

BAIO Brigade Artillery Intelligence Officer.

BALOG Base Logistic Command. *See under* **Logistic Command.**

BAR The British Army Review (*qv*).

BARV Beach armoured recovery vehicle (*qv*).

BASO Brigade Air Support Officer.

BASOC Brigade Air Support Operations Centre. *See* **ASOC.**

BBP Bulk breaking point (*qv*).

BC Battery Commander. *See* **Battery.**

BCP Battery Command Post. *See* **CP.**

BD Bomb Disposal.

BDA Bomb damage assessment.

BDU Battery Display Unit (*qv*).

bde Brigade (*qv*).

bdr Bombadier (*qv*).

bdry Boundary (*qv*).

bdsm Bandsman.

BEME Brigade Electrical and Mechanical Engineer.

BER Beyond economic repair (*qv*).

BGS Brigadier, General Staff.

Bhd Beach head (*qv*).

BL Bomb line (*qv*).

BLP Back loading point. *See* **Backloading.**

BLR Beyond local repair (*qv*).

BM Brigade major (*qv*).

BMEWS Ballistic Missile Early Warning System (*qv*).

BMRA Brigade Major Royal Artillery. *See* **Brigade Major.**

bn Battalion (*qv*).

BOMREP Bombing Report. *See* **Rep.**

BOO Brigade Ordnance Officer.

BOWO Brigade Ordnance Warrant Officer.

BQMS Battery Quartermaster Sergeant.

br Bridge or bridging.

BRA Brigadier Royal Artillery.

brig Brigadier (*qv*).

BSM Battery Sergeant Major.

BSU Blood supply unit.

BTO Brigade Transport Officer.

BTR Bronje Transporter, a Russian APC (*qv*).

bty Battery.

BUIC Backup Interceptor Control (*qv*).

BW Biological warfare (*qv*).

BZ (US) A chemical agent which temporarily incapacitates the mental faculties of a person who breathes it, making him irresolute and confused. It is not lethal and the effects quickly wear off after inhalation ceases.

C Phonetic alphabet: Charlie.

CA Civil affairs.

CA Avn Commander Army Aviation.

CAIO Corps Artillery Intelligence Officer.

cal Calibrate, calibration or calibre (*qv*).

cam Camouflage or camouflaged.

capt Captain.

carr Carrier.

cas Casualty or casualties.

cav Cavalry.

CB Counter battery fire (*qv*).

CBGLO Carrier Borne Ground Liaison Officer (*qv*).

CBGL sect Carrier Borne Ground Liaison Section (*qv*).

CCF Combined Cadet Force. *See under* **Force.**

CCM Counter counter measures.

CCP Casualty Collecting Post (*qv*).

CCRA Commander, Corps Royal Artillery.

CCRCT Commander, Corps Royal Corps of Transport.

CCRE Commander, Corps Royal Engineers.

CCS Casualty Clearing Station (*qv*).

CCT Command Cadet Team. *See under* **Command.**

cdo Commando.

CDS Chief of the Defence Staff.

CENTAG Central Army Group (*qv*).

CENTO Central Treaty Organization (*qv*).

CETME The standard rifle of the West German army firing the 7.62 mm round.

CF Chaplain to the Forces.

CFC Central Fire control.

cfm Confirm or confirmed.

cfn Craftsman.

CGS Chief of the General Staff.

Ch Chaplain to the Forces.

CI Counter intelligence.

C in C Commander in Chief.

civ Civil or civilian.

CL Centre Line.

cl Class or classification.

CLCU Civil Labour Control Unit.

CLOS Command to line of sight (*qv*).

CM Counter measures.

CMA Corps Maintenance Area. *See under* Maintenance (area).

CMG Composite Maintenance Group. *See under* Maintenance (area).

CO
1. Commanding Officer.
2. Conscientious Objector.

C of S Chief of Staff.

col Colonel (*qv*).

colm Column.

COLOS Command off the Line of sight (*qv*).

comd Command, commanding or commander.

comdt Commandant.

comint Communications intelligence (*qv*).

comm Communication.

COMMCEN Communication centre (*qv*).

comm Z Communications zone.

comp Composite.

con Control or controlled.

conc Concentrate, concentrated or concentration.

CONFD Confidential. *See under* Security Classification.

const Construct, constructed or construction.

cont Continue, continued or continuation.

conv Convalescent.

coord Coordinate, coordinated, co-ordinating or coordination.

coy Company.

CP Command Post (*qv*).

cpl Corporal (*qv*).

CPU Central Processing Unit.

CPX Command Post Exercise (*qv*).

CQMS Company Quartermaster Sergeant.

CRA Commander Royal Artillery.

CRAOC Commander Royal Army Ordnance Corps.

CRC Control and Reporting Centre (*qv*).

CRCT Commander Royal Corps of Transport.

CRE Commander Royal Engineers.

CREME Commander Royal Electrical and Mechanical Engineers.

CR Sig Commander Royal Signals.

CS
1. A nonlethal incapacitating gas used for riot control in IS (*qv*) operations.
2. Close support.

CSM Company Sergeant Major.

C sups Combat supplies (*qv*).

CV Command vehicle.

CVHQ Central Volunteer Headquarters.

CW Chemical Warfare.

CZ Combat zone.

D Phonetic alphabet: Delta.

D In appointments:
1. Director *eg* DAT: Director of Army Training
2. Deputy *eg* DDSD: Deputy Director of Staff Duties.

DAA Divisional Administrative Area.

DADAH Deputy Assistant Director of Army Health.

DADMS Deputy Assistant Director of Medical Services. *See under* **Medical.**

DADOS Deputy Assistant Director of Ordnance Services. *See under* **Ordnance.**

DAIO Divisional Artillery Intelligence Officer.

DALS Director of Army Legal Services (*qv*).

DCRE Deputy Commander Royal Engineers.

DDME Deputy Director of Electrical and Mechanical Engineering.

DDMS Deputy Director of Medical Services. *See under* **Medical.**

DDOS Deputy Director of Ordnance Services. *See under* **Ordnance.**

decon Decontamination.

def Defend, defended, defence or defensive.

DEL Directly employed labour.

del Delivery.

DEME Director of Electrical and Mechanical Engineering.

dep Depot.

dept Department, departmental.

det Detach, detached or detachment.

DF
1. Defensive fire.
2. Direction finding.

DG In appointments: Director General.

DGMS Director General of Medical Services. *See under* **Medical.**

DGZ Desired ground zero (*qv*).

DIESO Diesel fuel.

dir Direct, directed or direction.

dist District.

distr Distribution.

div Division or divisional.

DJAG Deputy Judge Advocate General. *See under* **Judge Advocate General.**

DMA Divisional Maintenance Area (*qv*).

dml Demolition

dmr Drummer (*qv*).

DO Demi official.

docu Document.

DOS Director of Ordnance Services. *See under* **Ordnance.**

DP Distribution Point (*qv*).

DPM
1. Deputy Provost Marshal. *See under*
Provost.
2. Digital plotter map (*qv*).

DR Despatch rider.

DS
1. Direct support (*qv*).
2. Directing staff (*qv*).

DTU Data Terminal Unit.

dvr Driver (*qv*).

DZ Dropping zone (*qv*).

E Phonetic alphabet: Echo

EBR Engin blundé de reconnaissance (*qv*).

ECAB Executive Committee of the
Army Board.

ECCM Electronic counter counter
measure (*qv*).

ech Echelon.

ECM Electronic counter measures (*qv*).

ECP Equipment collecting point (*qv*).

edn Education.

EEI Essential elements of information
(*qv*).

eff Effective.

EFI Expeditionary Force Institutes (*qv*).

E in C Engineer in Chief. *See under*
Corps of Royal Engineers.

elm Element.

emb Embark, embarked or embarkation.

EME Electrical and Mechanical Engineering.

empl
1. Emplacement.
2. Emplane or emplaned.

en Enemy.

encl Enclosure.

engr Engineer.

ENTAC Engin Teleguidé Antichar (*qv*).

eqpt Equipment.

ERE Extra regimental employment (*qv*).

ES Engineer stores.

est Estimate, estimated or estimation.

estb Establish, established or establishment.

ETA Estimated time of arrival.

ETC Estimated time of completion.

ETD
1. Estimated time of departure.
2. Electronic tactical display (*qv*).

ETR Estimated time of return.

evac Evacuate, evacuated or evacuation.

EW Electronic Warfare (*qv*).

ex Exercise (*qv*).

excl Exclude, excluded, excluding or
exclusive.

ext Extension.

F Phonetic alphabet: Foxtrot.

FAC Forward Air Controller (*qv*).

FACE Field Artillery Computer
Equipment (*qv*).

FAMA Forward airhead maintenance area (*qv*).

FAMTO First aid mechanical transport outfit. A vehicle standard pack for immediate repairs.

FASCOM Field Army Support Command (*qv*).

FASO Forward airfield supply organization.

FATSO First aid technical stores outfit.

FBZ Forward battle zone (*qv*).

FCP Forward Control Post.

FCS Forces Courier Service. *See under* **PCC**.

fd Field.

FDL Forward defence line.

FDS Forward Dressing Station (*qv*).

FEBA Forward edge of battle area (*qv*).

FFR
1. Free flight rocket. *See* **Free rocket**.
2. Fitted for radio.
3. Fit for Role.

flt Flight.

FM
1. Field Marshal.
2. Frequency modulated.

FMA Forward maintenance area. *See under* **Airhead Maintenance area** and **Maintenance** (area).

FMED Forward Medical Equipment Depot.

fmn Formation.

FN (Belgian) A prefix used to denote that a weapon has been designed or manufactured by the Fabrique Nationale d'Armes de Guerre.

F of F Field of Fire (*qv*).

F of S Foreman of Signals.

fol Follow, followed or following.

FOO Forward Observation Officer.

FPF Final protective fire.

FPO Forces Post Office. *See under* **PCC**.

FPS Forces Postal Service. *See under* **PCC**.

fre Frequency.

FRT Forward Repair Team (*qv*).

FSCL Fire support coordination line (*qv*).

FST Field Surgical Team.

FTU Field Transfusion Unit.

FUP Forming up place (*qv*).

fus Fusilier (*qv*).

fwd Forward or forwarded.

Fwd BAA Forward Brigade Administrative Area (*qv*).

G Phonetic alphabet: Golf.

G General Staff (*qv*).

GA Ground attack (*qv*).

gal Gallon.

gas Gasoline.

GCI Ground controlled interceptor.

GD General duties.

gdsm Guardsman (*qv*).

gen
1. General.
2. (Slang) information.

GFA Gun fire area.

GHQ General Headquarters.

GLO Ground Liaison Officer (*qv*).

GL sect. Ground Liaison Section (*qv*).

GM Guided missile (*qv*).

gnr Gunner (*qv*).

GOC General Officer Commanding.

GOC in C General Officer Commanding in Chief.

GOR Gurkha other rank.

govt Government.

gp Group.

GPMG General Purpose Machine Gun (*qv*).

GPO Gun Position Officer (*qv*).

GS
1. General Staff (*qv*).
2. General Service (*qv*).

GSO General Staff Officer. May be first, second or third grade: GSO1, GSO2, or GSO3.

GT General Transport.

GW Guided weapon (*qv*).

GZ Ground zero (*qv*).

H Phonetic alphabet: Hotel.

har Harbour.

HAW Heavy anti armour weapon.

HE High explosive (*qv*).

HEAT High explosive anti tank (*qv*).

hel Helicopter (*qv*).

HESH High explosive squash head (*qv*).

HF
1. High frequency.
2. Harassing fire.

HJ Honest John (*qv*).

HLAD High Level air defence.

HMG
1. Her Majesty's Government.
2. Heavy Machine Gun. *See under* Machine Gun.

hosp Hospital.

Hov Hovercraft (*qv*).

How Howitzer (*qv*).

HP
1. Horse power.
2. High power.

HQ Headquarters.

hr Hour.

HSP Heavy, stressed platform. *See under* Stressed platform.

HT High Tension.

Hy Heavy.

Hyg Hygiene.

I Phonetic alphabet: India.

IA Immediate Action.

IC
1. Internal combustion.
2. In charge command of. (2/IC: 2nd in cmd.)

ICBM Intercontinental ballistic missile (*qv*).

ident Identify, identified or identification.

IDF Israeli Defence Force.

IFF Identification friend or foe (*qv*).

IG Instructor in Gunnery (Royal Artillery).

incl Include, included, including or inclusive.

indep Independent.

inf Infantry.

INFANT Iroquois night fighter and night tracker (*qv*).

info Inform, informed, information or for the information of.

inst Installation.

instr Instruct, inctructed, instruction or instructor.

int Intelligence (*qv*).

Int Corps Intelligence Corps.

intercomm Intercommunication.

intg Interrogation.

intmed Intermediate.

INTREP Intelligence Report.

INTSUM Intelligence summary.

IO Intelligence Officer.

IRBM Intermediate range ballistic missile (*qv*).

IRIS Infra red intruder system (*qv*).

IS Internal security (*qv*).

IWM Imperial War Museum.

J Phonetic alphabet: Juliett.

JAG Judge Advocate General (*qv*).

JAMREP Jamming Report (*qv*).

JFACTSU Joint Forward Air Controllers Training and Standards Unit (*qv*).

JMCC Joint Movements Co-ordinating Committee (*qv*).

JMS Joint Movement Staff. *See* JMCC

JOC Joint Operations Centre (*qv*).

JSSM Joint Services Staff Manual (*qv*).

JSTPS Joint strategic target planning staff.

K Phonetic alphabet: Kilo.

KERO Kerosine.

KIA Killed in Action (*qv*).

Kih Kilometres in the hour. *See* **Rate of March.**

Kt Kiloton (*qv*).

L Phonetic alphabet: Lima.

lab
1. Labour.
2. Laboratory.

LAD Light Aid Detachment (*qv*).

LAW Light anti-armour weapon

L bdr Lance bombardier. *See under* **Lance.**

LCA Landing craft assault. *See under* **Landing Craft.**

L cpl Lance corporal. *See under* **Lance.**

LCL Landing craft logistics. *See under* **Landing craft.**

LCM Landing craft mechanized. *See under* **Landing craft.**

LCT Landing craft tank. *See under* **Landing craft.**

LCVP Landing craft vehicle and personnel. *See under* **Landing craft.**

ldr Leader.

LG Landing ground. *See under* **Landing.**

Lieut Lieutenant.

LL Light line (*qv*).

LLAD Low level air defence.

LMG Light machine gun (*qv*).

LO Liaison Officer. *See under* **Liaison.**

LOB Left out of battle (*qv*).

loc Locate, located, locating, location or locality.

L of C Lines of communication.

log Logistics or logistical.

LPD Landing Platform Dock. *See under* **Landing Platform.**

LP Low Power.

LPH Landing platform helicopter. *See under* **Landing platform.**

LPV Landing platform vehicles. *See under* **Landing platform.**

LRT Long range transport.

LSA Landing ship assault. *See under* **Landing ship.**

LSL Landing ship logistic. *See under* **Landing ship.**

LST Landing ship tank. *See under* **Landing ship.**

LT
1. Line telegraphy.
2. Low tension.

lt lieutenant.

ltr letter.

LVT Landing vehicle tracked.

LVT (A) Landing vehicle tracked (armoured).

LZ Landing zone (*qv*).

M Phonetic alphabet: Mike.

MA
1. Maintenance area (*qv*).
2. Military assistant (*qv*).
3. Military attaché.

MACC Military aid to the civil community (*qv*).

mag
1. Magazine (*qv*).
2. Magnetic.

maint Maintain, maintained or maintenance.

maj Major.

MARS Marconi automatic relay system.

MAW Medium anti-armour weapon.

Max Maximum.

MBT Main battle tank.

MC
1. Motor cycle.
2. Movement control.

MCLOS Manual control to line of sight (*qv*).

MCO Movement Control Officer.

mech Mechanical.

med
1. Medical (*qv*).
2. Medium.

memo Memorandum.

MES Military Engineer Services (*qv*).

met Meteorological or meteorology.

MFC Mortar Fire Controller.

MG Maching gun (*qv*).

MGO Master General of the Ordnance. *See under* **Ordnance.**

MIA Missing in Action.

MICV Mechanized Infantry Combat Vehicle.

mih Miles in the hour. *See* **Rate of March.**

mil Military.

min.
1. Minimum.
2. Minute.

MIRV Multiple independently targeted reentry vehicle (*qv*).

misc Miscellaneous.

mk Mark.

MLU Memory Loading Unit.

MMG Medium machine gun. *See under* **Machine gun.**

MML Manual of Military Law (*qv*).

MO Medical officer.

mob
1. Mobile.
2. Mobilization (*qv*).

MoD Ministry of Defence.

mor Mortar.

MORTREP Mortar bombing report. *See under* **Rep.**

mov Movement.

MP
1. Military Police. *See under* **Provost.**
2. Military Secretary.

MPA Manpower and Personnel Administration (*qv*).

MPSC Military Provost Staff Corps (*qv*).

MR Medium range.

MRBM Medium range ballistic missile (*qv*).

MRS Medical reception station.

MRV Multiple reentry vehicle (*qv*).

MS
1. Medical services.
2. Military secretary.

msg Message.

msl Missile.

msn Mission.

MSP Medium stressed platform. *See under* **Stressed platform.**

MSR Main supply route.

MSRD Mobile Servicing and Repair Detachment (*qv*).

MT Motor or Mechanical Transport.

mtd Mounted.

MTGAS Mechanical transport gasoline.

MTO Mechanical Transport Officer.

mv Muzzle velocity (*qv*).

MVA Modern Volunteer Army program (*qv*).

N Phonetic alphabet: November.

NAAFI Navy Army and Air Force Institutes (*qv*).

NADGE NATO (*qv*) Air defence ground environment (*qv*).

NAG Northern Army Group (*qv*).

NARAT NATO request for air transport support (*qv*).

NATO North Atlantic Treaty Organization (*qv*).

NBC Nuclear, biological and chemical (*qv*).

NCO Non Commissioned Officer (*qv*).

NDAC Nuclear Defence Affairs Committee.

nec Necessary.

NGSFO Naval Gunfire Support Forward Observer (*qv*).

ni Night.

NOK Next of Kin.

NORAD North American Air Defence Commander (*qv*).

NORTHAG Northern army group (*qv*).

NOTAM Notice to Airmen (*qv*).

NPG Nuclear Planning Group (*qv*).

NSTL (US) National Strategic Target List (*qv*).

NTR Nothing to Report.

O Phonetic alphabet: Oscar.

obj Objective (*qv*).

obs Obstacle.

obsn Observation.

OC Officer Commanding.

OCTU Officer Cadet Training Unit (*qv*).

OER Officer Evaluation Report (*qv*).

offr Officer (*qv*).

OFP Ordnance Field Park (*qv*).

OIC Officer in Charge.

OP Observation post.

op Operate, operated, operation, operational or operator.

Ops Operations staff.

OR Other rank(s) (*qv*).

ORBAT Order of battle (*qv*).

ord Ordnance.

org Organize, organized or organization.

OS Ordnance services.

OTAN French for NATO (*qv*).

P Phonetic alphabet: Papa.

PA Personal Assistant (*qv*).

P and L Pioneer and Labour.

PAO Principal Administrative Officer (*qv*).

para.
1. Parachute.
2. Paragraph.

PCC Postal and Courier Communications (*qv*).

PCLU Pioneer Civil Labour Unit.

PE Peace establishment (*qv*).

PER Performance Evaluation Report (*qv*).

pers Personnel.

PES PULHEEMS (*qv*) employment standard.

PJI Parachute Jumping Instructor.

PL
1. Phase line. *See under* **Report line.**
2. Pipe line.

pl Platoon (*qv*).

PM
1. Provost Marshal. *See under* **Provost.**
2. (US) Project Manager.

PMC President of the Mess Committee (*qv*).

pmr Paymaster.

pnr Pioneer.

PO Post Office.

POL Petrol oil and lubricants.

POM Priority of Movement. *See under* **JMCC.**

posn Position.

POW (US) Prisoner of War (*qv*).

PP Petroleum point (*qv*).

PPH Petroleum pipehead.

PPRM Population protection and resources management (*qv*).

PR
1. Photographic reconnaissance.
2. Plotting and radar.
3. Plublic relations.

pr Pounder, used of shells and bombs *eg* 25 pr.

prep Prepare, prepared, preparation or preparatory.

PRF Pulse repetition frequency (*qv*).

PRI President of the Regimental Institutes (*qv*).

pri Priority.

pro Provost (*qv*).

proj Projectile.

PS Personal Services (*qv*).

psc Passed Staff Course.

PSI Permanent Staff Instructor (*qv*).

psy Psychological.

PSYOP Psychological operation (*qv*).

pt Point.

ptbl Portable.

pte Private (*qv*).

PTF Port task force.

PTI Physical Training Instructor.

ptl Patrol (*qv*).

PUS Permanent Under Secretary.

PW Prisoner of War (*qv*).

PX (US) *See* **NAAFI.**

PZ Pick up zone.

Q Phonetic alphabet: Quebec.

Q Quartering (*qv*).

QARANC Queen Alexandra's Royal Army Nursing Corps (*qv*).

QGO Queen's Gurkha Officer.

QM Quartermaster (*qv*).

QMG Quartermaster General (*qv*).

QMS Quarter master sergeant. *See under* **Quartermaster.**

QR Queens Regulations (*qv*).

R Phonetic alphabet: Romeo.

RA Royal Regiment of Artillery (*qv*).

RAC
1. Royal Armoured Corps (*qv*).
2. (US) Research Analysis Corporation.

RACLD Royal Army Chaplains' Department.

radA Radio active.

R and D Research and Development (*qv*).

R and R (US) Rest and Recreation.

RACD Royal Army Chaplains' Department.

RAEC Royal Army Educational Corps (*qv*).

RAMC Royal Army Medical Corps (*qv*).

RAOC Royal Army Ordnance Corps (*qv*).

RAP Regimental Aid Post (*qv*).

RAPC Royal Army Pay Corps (*qv*).

rat Ration or rations.

rat P Ration Point.

RAVC Royal Army Veterinary Corps (*qv*).

RCP Regimental Command Post.

RCT
1. Royal Corps of Transport (*qv*).
2. Regimental Combat Team (*qv*).

rd Road.

RDD Rapid demolition device.

RDF Radio direction finder or finding.

RE Corps of Royal Engineers (*qv*).

rec Recover, recovered or recovery.

recce Reconnaissance (*qv*) or reconnoitre.

ref Reference or referred.

reg Regular, regulate, regulated, regulating or regulation.

regt Regiment.

rel Relief, relieved or release.

REME Corps of Royal Electrical and Mechanical Engineers (*qv*).

rep Represent, represented or representative.

req Request.

res Reserve.

RESTD Restricted. *See under* **Security Classification.**

RFA Royal Field Artillery.

rfn Rifleman (*qv*).

rft Reinforcement.

rgr Ranger (*qv*).

RHA Royal Horse Artillery.

Rhd Railhead.

RHQ Regimental Headquarters.

RI Radiation Intensity (*qv*)

RICE Relative Index of Combat effectiveness (*qv*).

rkt Rocket.

RL Rocket launcher.

RMA Rear Maintenance Area (*qv*).

RMAS Royal Military Academy Sandhurst (*qv*).

RMCS Royal Military College of Science (*qv*).

RMO Regimental Medical Officer (*qv*).

RMMU Removable media memory units.

RMP Corps of Royal Military Police (*qv*).

ROAD Reorganization Objective Army Division (*qv*).

RO
1. Retired Officer.
2. Routine order.

ROTC Reserve Officers Training Corps (*qv*).

RP
1. Regimental Police.
2. Replenishment Park (*qv*).
3. Rules of Procedure (*qv*).

RPC Royal Pioneer Corps (*qv*).

rpg Rounds per gun.

rpgpm Rounds per gun per minute.

rpmor Rounds per mortar.

rpmorpm Rounds per mortar per minute.

RQMS Regimental Quartermaster Sergeant (*qv*).

rqn Requisition.

RR Radio relay.

RSM Regimental Sergeant Major (*qv*).

RTO
1. Rail Traffic Officer or Rail Transportation Officer.
2. (incorrectly) Regimental Transport Officer.

RTP Reinforced theatre plan (*qv*).

RTU Return(ed) to unit (*qv*).

RUC Royal Ulster Constabulary (*qv*).

RUSI Royal United Services Institute (*qv*).

RV Rendezvous.

S Phonetic alphabet: Sierra.

SA Small arms (*qv*).

SAA Small arms (*qv*) ammunition.

SACLOS Semi automatic command to line of sight (*qv*).

SAGW Surface to air guided weapon. *See under* **Guided Weapons.**

SAM Surface to air missile (*qv*).

SAS Special Air Service Regiment.

SB Stretcher Bearer.

SC Staff Captain (*qv*).

SCF Senior Chaplain to the Forces.

SD Staff duties (*qv*).

SDR Special Despatch Rider.

SDS Signal despatch service.

SEATO South East Asia Treaty Organization (*qv*).

sec Secretary or secretariat.

sect Section (*qv*).

SHAPE Supreme Headquarters Allied Powers in Europe (*qv*).

SHELRER Shelling Report (*qv*).

SHF Super high frequency.

sgt Sergeant (*qv*).

SI Sergeant Instructor.

sig Signal, signaller or signalman.

SIGINT Signals Intelligence (*qv*).

sigs Signals (arm, branch or staff).

SIOP Single integrated operation plan (*qv*).

sit Situation.

SITREP Situation Report (*qv*).

SL Start line (*qv*).

SLA Supply loading airfield.

sldr Soldier.

SM Sergeant Major.

SMC Staff message control.

SMG Submachine gun (*qv*).

SMO Senior medical officer.

SO Staff Officer. *See under* **Staff.**

SOI Signal operation instructions.

SOP Standing operating procedure (*qv*).

SP
1. Self propelled (*qv*).
2. Start point (*qv*).

sp Support or supported.

spr Sapper (*qv*).

SQMS Squadron or Staff Quartermaster Sergeant. *See under* **Quartermaster.**

sqn Squadron.

SR
1. Station radio.
2. Short range (aircraft).

srg Sound ranging.

SSAFA Soldiers Sailors and Airmens Family Association (*qv*).

SSBS Sol-sol-balistique-stratégique (*qv*).

Ssgt Staff Sergeant.

SSGW Surface to surface guided weapon (system) (*qv*).

SSI
1. Staff Sergeant Instructor.
2. Standing signal instructions.

SSM
1. Squadron or Staff Sergeant Major.
2. Surface to surface missile (*qv*).

SSP Stores stressed platform. *See under* **Stressed platform.**

ST Strategic Transport (aircraft).

sta Station.

STANAG Standardization agreement (*qv*).

S-Tank. *See* **Strv 103.**

stereo Stereoscope or stereoscopic.

STOL Short take off and landing (aircraft).

str Strength.

strat Strategic.

STRE Specialist Teams Royal Engineers (*qv*).

subj Subject.

sup Supply.

SUPINTREP Supplementary intelligence report.

supt Superintendent.

surv Surveillance.

svc Service, serviced or servicing.

svy Survey.

SWAT Special Warfare Armoured Transporter (*qv*).

swbd Switchboard.

sy Security.

T Phonetic alphabet: Tango.

TAAS Traffic accident analysis system.

tac Tactic, tactics or tactical.

tac T Tactical transport (aircraft) (*qv*).

tac T (MR) Tactical transport (*qv*) (aircraft) medium range.

tac T (SR) Tactical transport (*qv*) (aircraft) short range.

TAF Tactical Air Force.

TALOG Theatre Army Logistic Command. *See under* **Logistic Command.**

T and AVR Territorial Army and Volunteer Reserve (*qv*).

TC Traffic control.

TCM (US) Theater combat model (*qv*).

TCV Troop carrying vehicle.

tech Technical or technician.

temp Temporary.

TEWT Tactical exercise without troops.

TF Task force.

tfc Traffic.

tg Telegraph or telegram.

tgt Target.

THQ Theatre Headquarters.

TIR Target illuminating radar.

tk Tank.

tlr Trailer.

tn Transportation.

TOE Table of organization and equipment. *See under* **Establishment.**

TsOET Tests of Elementary Training.

topo Topographic or topography.

TOPSEC Top secret. *See under* **Security Classification.**

TOT
1. Time on target (artillery).
2. Time over target (air).

TOXREP Toxic Report (*qv*).

TP Traffic post.

tp Troop (*qv*).

tpr Trooper (*qv*).

tpt Transport.

tptd Transported.

tptr Transporter.

TQMS Technical Quartermaster Sergeant. *See under* **Quartermaster.**

trg Training.

trig Trigonometry or trigonometrical.

TSO Technical Staff Officer.

U Phonetic alphabet: Uniform.

UC Under construction.

UCMJ (US) Uniform code of military justice (*qv*).

UEO Unit emplaning officer (*qv*).

UFO Unit Families Officer (*qv*).

UHF Ultra high frequency.

UKLF United Kingdom Land Forces (*qv*).

UNCIVPOL United Nations Civilian Police. *See under* United Nations Peace-keeping Force in Cyprus.

UNCLAS Unclassified (*qv*).

UNFICYP United Nations Peacekeeping Force in Cyprus (*qv*).

unsvc Unserviceable.

USACGSC United States Army Command and General Staff College.

USMA United States Military Academy.

UTM Universal transverse mercator grid (*qv*).

UXB Unexploded bomb.

V Phonetic alphabet: Victor.

V In title:
1. Vice *eg* VAG Vice Adjutant General
2. Volunteer *eg* T and AVR (*qv*).

VAPO Vapourizing oil.

VCP Vehicle Collecting Point.

veh Vehicle (*qv*).

vet Veterinary.

VHF Very high frequency.

VIP Very important person.

vis Visibility or visual

VO Verbal Order.

VOR Vehicle off the road.

VP Vulnerable point.

vpm Vehicles per mile.

VR Veterinary and Remount (services).

VTOL Vertical take off and landing (aircraft).

W Phonetic alphabet: Whiskey.

WD War Department or Army.

wdr Withdrawal.

WE War establishment (*qv*).

WIA Wounded in Action (*qv*).

Wks Works (service).

wksp Workshop.

wng Warning.

WO Warrant Officer.

WP Water point.

wpn Weapon (*qv*).

WRAC Women's Royal Army Corps (*qv*).

WVS Women's Voluntary Service (*qv*).

X Phonetic alphabet: Xray

xpd Expedite.

xrds Cross roads.

APPENDIX 1

Y Phonetic alphabet: Yankee.

Y of S Yeoman of Signals.

Z Phonetic alphabet: Zulu.

Z zone.

Appendix 2

National Distinguishing Letters

The following National Distinguishing Letters are used whenever it is necessary to identify any part of a NATO or SEATO Force.

AS	Australia
BE	Belgium
CA	Canada
DA	Denmark
FR	France
GE	German Federal Republic
GR	Greece
IC	Iceland
IT	Italy
LU	Luxembourg
NL	Netherlands
NO	Norway
NZ	New Zealand
PI	Philippines
PK	Pakistan
PO	Portugal
TH	Thailand
TU	Turkey
UK	United Kingdom
US	United States

Appendix 3

The Order of Precedence of Corps and Regiments of the Regular Army

1. The Household Cavalry
   The Life Guards and the Blues and Royals are armoured regiments with a mounted squadron for ceremonial duties.

2. Royal Horse Artillery (RHA)
   But on parade with their guns take the right of the line and move at the head of the Household Cavalry.

3. The Royal Armoured Corps (RAC)
   1st The Queen's Dragoon Guards
   The Royal Scots Dragoon Guards (Carabiniers and Greys)
   4th/7th Royal Dragoon Guards
   5th Royal Inniskilling Dragoon Guards
   The Queen's Own Hussars
   The Queen's Royal Irish Hussars
   9th/12th Royal Lancers (Prince of Wales's)
   The Royal Hussars (Prince of Wales's Own)
   13th/18th Royal Hussars (Queen Mary's Own)
   14th/20th King's Hussars
   15th/19th The King's Royal Hussars
   16th/5th The Queen's Royal Lancers
   17th/21st Lancers
   Royal Tank Regiment

4. Royal Regiment of Artillery (RA)
   less RHA above

5. Corps of Royal Engineers (RE)

6. Royal Corps of Signals (R. Signals)

7. Regiments of Foot Guards
   Grenadier Guards
   Coldstream Guards
   Scots Guards
   Irish Guards
   Welsh Guards

8. Regiments of Infantry
   The Royal Scots (The Royal Regiment)
   The Queen's Regiment
   The King's Own Royal Border Regiment
   The Royal Regiment of Fusiliers
   The King's Regiment
   The Royal Anglian Regiment
   The Devonshire and Dorset Regiment
   The Light Infantry
   The Prince of Wales's Own Regiment of Yorkshire
   The Green Howards (Alexandra, Princess of Wales's Own Yorkshire Regiment)
   The Royal Highland Fusiliers (Princess Margaret's Own Glasgow and Ayrshire Regiment)
   The Cheshire Regiment
   The Royal Welsh Fusiliers
   The Royal Regiment of Wales (24th/41st Foot)
   The King's Own Scottish Borderers
   The Cameronians (Scottish Rifles)
   The Royal Irish Rangers (27th (Inniskilling) 83rd and 87th)
   The Gloucestershire Regiment
   The Worcestershire and Sherwood Foresters Regiment (29th/45th Foot)
   The Queen's Lancashire Regiment
   The Duke of Wellington's Regiment (West Riding)
   The Royal Hampshire Regiment
   The Staffordshire Regiment (The Prince of Wales's)
   The Black Watch (Royal Highland Regiment)
   The Duke of Edinburgh's Royal Regiment (Berkshire and Wiltshire)
   The York and Lancaster Regiment
   Queen's Own Highlanders (Seaforth and Camerons)
   The Gordon Highlanders
   The Argyll and Sutherland Highlanders (Princess Louise's)

The Parachute Regiment
The Brigade of Gurkhas
The Royal Green Jackets.

9. Special Air Service Regiment (SAS)

10. Army Air Corps (AAC)

11. Royal Army Chaplain's Department (RAChD)

12. Royal Corps of Transport (RCT)

13. Royal Army Medical Corps (RAMC)

14. Royal Army Ordnance Corps (RAOC)

15. Corps of Royal Electrical and Mechanical Engineers

16. Corps of Royal Military Police (RMP)

17. Royal Army Pay Corps (RAPC)

18. Royal Army Veterinary Corps (RAVC)

19. Royal Military Academy Band Corps

20. Small Arms School Corps (SASC)

21. Military Provost Staff Corps (MPSC)

22. Royal Army Educational Corps (RAEC)

23. Royal Army Dental Corps (RADC)

24. Royal Pioneer Corps (RPC)

25. Intelligence Corps (Int Corps)

26. Army Physical Training Corps (APTC)

27. Army Catering Corps (ACC)

28. General Service Corps (GSC)

29. Queen Alexandra's Royal Army Nursing Corps (QARANC)

30. Women's Royal Army Corps (WRAC)

ce

this room